GALLERY

BY THE SAME AUTHOR

non-fiction
JACK THE RIPPER
MARIE LLOYD AND MUSIC HALL
OUT OF STEP
THE MAN WHO WROTE DRACULA
IN PRAISE OF DOGS
A WINDOW ON THE SEA
HENRY: AN APPRECIATION OF HENRY WILLIAMSON
A TRAVELLER IN TURKEY
SOHO IN THE FIFTIES
SACRED MONSTERS
ESCAPADES

fiction
THE DOG WHO KNEW TOO MUCH
SWANSDOWNE

GALLERY

A Personal Guide
to British Galleries
and Their Unexpected
Treasures

DANIEL FARSON

IT'S AN OBJET, BUT IS IT D'ART?

BLOOMSBURY

ACKNOWLEDGEMENTS

Making no claim to be an expert myself, I am grateful to acknowledge the help I have received from the expertise of others. The books are too numerous to mention here, except for a chosen few: *The Story of Art* by E.H. Gombrich; *British Art* by Simon Wilson; *A Concise History of English Painting* by William Gaunt; *The Penguin Dictionary of Art & Artists* by Peter and Linda Murray.

I am particularly indebted to Joan Abse for her *Art Galleries of Britain and Ireland*, which is more comprehensive than I have tried to be. Also, to Frank Whitford, the art historian and teacher at the Royal College of Art, and a regular on *Gallery*, who has been kind enough to check the typescript for errors.

Throughout, I have been helped by the goodwill of directors, keepers and curators of art galleries in Britain. I might have managed to write this book without their assistance, but it would have been an arid undertaking instead of the joy it has proved to be. My special appreciation to Joanna Banham at Leighton House; Nicholas Serota at the Tate Gallery; Giles Waterfield at Dulwich; Julian Treuherz, Keeper of the National Museums and Galleries on Merseyside; and Timothy Clifford, Director of the National Galleries of Scotland.

First published 1990
Copyright © 1990 by Daniel Farson

Bloomsbury Publishing Ltd, 2 Soho Square, London W1V 5DE

A CIP catalogue record for this book is available from the British Library

Cartoon on title page reprinted courtesy *Spectator* Magazine
All photographs taken by the author.

ISBN 0 7475 06051

10 9 8 7 6 5 4 3 2 1

Designed by Mark Foster
Typeset by Bookworm Typesetting, Manchester
Printed in Great Britain by
Butler & Tanner Ltd, Frome and London

For the Gallery team:

My old friend George Melly, and my new friends, Maggi
Hambling and Frank Whitford.

For the executives at HTV, Ron Evans and Derek Clark; and
Naomi Sargent and Gwyn Pritchard at Channel 4, who
have given us constant encouragement.

And particularly for our director, Ken Price, whose patience
and hard work has held *Gallery* together over four series.
We have never had a cross word.

Also, for Sophia Waugh, who will understand my
indebtedness and gratitude.

Front row, left to right: Frank Whitford, George Melly and Maggi Hambling
Back row: Ken Price and Daniel Farson

Contents

The Fitzwilliam Museum, Cambridge

According to Richard Luce, Minister for the Arts, the number of people attending museums in 1989 was the highest in our history — about 100 million compared to 65 million four years ago.

Introduction

> Without opening a book, or listening to music, or sitting at the play, or meditating at a picture gallery, you can lead a blameless, prosperous and even energetic life. But it will be a very dry, narrow and barren life, cut off from some of the world's greatest treasures. It will be a life of defective growth on the imaginative side.
>
> Sir Henry Irving at the Royal Hotel, Bristol,
> during his grand farewell tour of England in 1904

Let me stress at once that I am not an art expert, and that could prove a blessing, for otherwise I might be bogged down in minutiae. However, I am an enthusiast and hope to share my enthusiasm with you.

Although I had the luck to know such painters as Francis Bacon, Graham Sutherland and Lucian Freud, I knew lamentably little about painting until I conceived the idea for the television programme *Gallery*. This has the advantage of simplicity: two teams are shown a detail of a painting which they have to identify with the name of the painter. Then the picture opens up in its entirety and they discuss it. As simple as that. The element of a quiz was intended to make it livelier and avoid the usual pretentiousness of art programmes which are all too Arty. The idea of a visual quiz for television seemed so obvious that I was surprised that no one had thought of it before. They had. Simultaneously to the pilot prepared by HTV for Channel 4, a rival pilot hosted by Bamber Gascoigne was submitted by Granada. Fortunately, as Gallery discussed the paintings in greater detail, we won.

This opened a new chapter in my life. From the outset, *Gallery* has been blessed with luck. Above all, the friendly and gifted people I have worked with to whom this book is dedicated. George Melly had long been one of my closest friends and I knew of his wide knowledge of art apart from his special interest in the surrealists, so I was determined that he should be the host.

When George reached the age of sixty, he told me he wanted life to become a series of 'treats' and this is what he has done for *Gallery*, making it a treat to look forward to during the strange fortnight in Bristol (where HTV produce the programmes) cloistered in the Holiday Inn, meeting up at ten in the morning as we emerge for a gulp of fresh air before we are driven to the studio where we are incarcerated for the rest of the day, returning to 'unwind' at the hotel bar around midnight.

After rehearsals, two programmes are filmed each evening, directed with saintly patience by Ken Price. It is all surprisingly exhausting, yet we have never exchanged an angry word. Throughout it all, George remains unperturbed, unfailingly professional, and the source of constant fun.

That this is the happiest production I have worked on is due to the constant surprise of the paintings themselves. In order to choose them, I also travel all over Britain and find to my delight that I have an 'eye'. If this sounds boastful, it is a boast of infinite relief.

Going to galleries has given me a new incentive, yet I was shocked that this has come so belatedly. Until then I had gone to sensational exhibitions like the Picasso retrospective at the Tate, or to private views of friends, but rarely had the urge to visit a gallery just for the joy of it. I fear I was all too typical of those who never set foot in their local galleries because they find the prospect too daunting, associating art with sepulchral mausoleums where people talk in whispers. Because they do not find out for themselves they believe the fallacy.

Sadly, they have a point. Some galleries do exude a snobbery which suggests that art is the privilege of the élite – for *them*, but not for *us*. Yet our galleries have seldom been needed more. At a time of constant din, they provide oases of relaxation. Disconcertingly, I find that many are half empty after the tourists have gone, and a few are unwelcoming. Though it houses one of the finest collections in Britain, the Barber Institute at Birmingham University had limited access when it was opened by Queen Mary in 1939 and when I went there a pink slip of paper informed me begrudgingly: 'Whilst not a public gallery, the Barber Institute is normally open to individual members of the public during normal opening hours' presumably with a sharp look-out to ensure that the visitors are acceptable and spruce. In fairness, the attendants *inside* could not have been kinder and of course the paintings compensate, as always.

I witnessed a distressing incident in the Manchester City Art Gallery, which has been restored to its original Victorian splendour by Timothy Clifford before he moved to Edinburgh. After paying my respects to Duccio's *Crucifixion* which he saved for the nation by raising £1.8 million – 'dirt cheap at the price' – I was studying the *Cheetah and Stag with Two Indians* by Stubbs when a group of cheerful young men marched into the gallery apparently straight off a building site, covered with dust and grime. They stood out like a Beryl Cook slipped into the solemnity of the Rothko Room in the Tate and their high spirits were so pleasing that I was tempted to ask whether they had come here on a whim or whether this was the realisation of an old ambition? Either way, it was refreshing to see them there, but my good-will was forestalled when the woman behind the desk, who stared at them with chilly dislike, seized her opportunity when one of the men lit a cigarette. 'Smoking's forbidden!' she pounced. Although she was in the right, her hostile tone implied that these were not the sort of people who should have been here in the first place. The man ground out his cigarette on the polished parquet floor with disgust, the pictures cringed in sympathy, and the gallery lost its lustre as the men left without a painting seen, let alone appreciated.

'What a bloody shame!' Timothy Clifford exclaimed when I told him of the incident afterwards. He agreed that these were the very, if unlikely gallery goers to be encouraged: 'Carrot and stick, that's what we need to get them in. That's what it's all about. Not to turn them away.'

All credit therefore to Clifford Stevens at the Walker in Liverpool whom I met the following day, for his exhibitions of 'Beatles' Art' and children's paintings which attract the doting parents who might glance at the other pictures too.

After my visit to Port Sunlight a few miles away, I spoke to two men in the Central pub in Liverpool and asked if they had been to any of the local galleries.

'The only people who go to such places,' I was told, 'are art students, old age pensioners and those on the dole.' Three deserving categories, with the irony that Lord Leverhulme built his art gallery as a place where his workmen could relax.

'I wouldn't go myself,' one of the men explained, 'because I don't understand any of it. My mam has pictures on the walls, reproductions like, which mean the world to her, as much as those sold for thousands of pounds, so what's the difference?' Unanswerable, in such circumstances where the thought of a Van Gogh or a Picasso changing hands for £20 million seemed suddenly obscene, but I persevered; 'It's a very friendly gallery,' I assured them, 'you'll feel better for going there.'

'You mean,' one responded sarcastically, 'if I've got a problem it will go away.'

'It might.' With desperation I added that the collection included a large number of female nudes, and at this they perked up: 'All right then,' said one with a beatific smile, 'I'll give it a try.' I hope he did, though I doubt it.

For me, going to galleries in Britain has been a voyage of discovery, rousing my latent interest in painting, finding lesser known treasures on our doorstep in galleries we neglect, like Pollok House, within walking distance of the popular Burrell outside Glasgow, where I 'found' two small, magnificent Goyas of *Children Playing at Soldiers* which were unknown to the teams on Gallery.

Treasures on our doorstep – what a cliché that sounds! Yet this is what they prove to be with the thrill of the unexpected: Van Gogh in Walsall; Bacon in Huddersfield; Warhol in Wolverhampton; El Greco at Pollok; a Bruegel grisaille at Banbury . . . the treasure-trove is limitless and it is the purpose of this book to reveal the extraordinary range at our disposal. This is not a comprehensive guide, but one that is unashamedly personal, quirky and opinionated. I am drawn to the eccentricities which abound in British galleries – the collection of Tiffany glass (as well as the pictures) in the Howarth at Accrington, and such rare collectors as the Misses Davies, the spinster sisters who compensated for the ravages inflicted on the Welsh countryside by their father's coal mines, with the bequest of their French Impressionists to Cardiff.

In the same vein I describe the more eccentric British artists: Benjamin Robert Haydon, his own worst enemy; Richard Dadd who went mad, murdered his dad, and painted fairies; Alfred Wallis, the Cornish fisherman who painted on the backs of boxes, and others inspired by and, in some cases, destroyed by their passion for art.

Though it would be an absurdity if I wrote a critical appreciation of Rembrandt, I have always felt an affinity with the Don Quixotes.

My hope is to point you in directions which may not have occurred to you. Elation is part of gallery-going. Appearing on *Gallery*, Sir David Attenborough told us that when he saw Piero della Francesca's *Baptism of Christ* in the National Gallery he simply felt 'blessed'. Going to see it the next morning I understood what he meant. As Sir Henry Irving implied, there is nothing wrong in not going to art galleries, but you would forfeit one of life's rewards.

Gallery Going

Going to a gallery is an art in itself. Enjoy yourself at leisure instead of attempting the headlong dash in which you attempt to see everything. If you live near one of the galleries described in this book, better by far to visit one room at a time and then return.

Maggi Hambling returns to this theme constantly. 'I really recommend going to a gallery to see three pictures in an afternoon rather than scuttling around and looking at thirty. So many people read the labels and think they've seen the picture.'

This stricture might sound forbidding if you are pressed for time in a gallery which you may not have the chance to visit again, but even then it is better to linger over the pictures which please you most instead of sticking to a comprehensive 'itinerary' which runs the risk of knowing the price of everything and the value of nothing.

'If you can go in quite openly to the National Gallery,' where Maggi Hambling was once the artist in residence, 'and allow a picture to leap off the wall and take you by the short and curlies, and give it the chance to work on you, that's what it's all about. A play *happens* – a television programme happens – you are entertained. Looking at a picture is quite a lot of hard work for *you*. Approach it in silence and let it speak to you. I would advise anyone going to our galleries to do so in an open spirit.'

Equally, gallery going should be a joy, an experience that is rich in pleasure and excitement. This is why I draw attention to the most interesting pictures in the galleries without attempting an inventory. And I have also chosen several galleries that are fun to go to regardless of their pictures, like the Sir John Soane's in London.

When an art gallery creates the right atmosphere, dispelling the cathedral reverence, the response from the public is immediate. With a skilful blend of old and new materials, the designers of the Burrell outside Glasgow, for instance, have made it so popular that it is now the biggest tourist attraction in Scotland. You will find no mention here of the Barbican or the Hayward, for these are concrete tombs hardly conducive to the appreciation of the paintings inside. They seem devoid of love. Other museums alienate the visitors who simply wish to learn more about art by an air of snobbery which suggests that they are not intended for them. A student on *Gallery* told me he was so delighted with a portrait by Frans Hals that he laughed aloud – an attendant hurried over to complain, 'You're not allowed to do that here, sir!'

I have been fortunate to visit so many galleries in the course of selecting pictures for the television series, for I should not have gone to them otherwise. The thought of going to Walsall or Accrington to see their paintings would not have occurred to me. This incentive has rewarded me and opened my eyes. Originally I headed for the famous Rembrandt or Impressionist, gradually finding equal pleasure from the lesser known work of British artists of whom I knew little or nothing at all.

The North
and the
Midlands

On His Holidays   J. S. Sargent   The Lady Lever Gallery, Port Sunlight

In the autumn of 1989 I travelled north on a journey which proved more astounding than a recent trip to Eastern Turkey. The north of England is another world.

'Where are you going?' people asked me, thinking in terms of Lanzarotte or Tenerife. They looked bemused when I told them, 'Birmingham, Walsall, Wolverhampton, Manchester, Salford . . . (my itinerary, as the Americans might say, was well prepared) . . . Liverpool, Leeds, Hull, York, Newcastle . . .'

I would urge anyone, particularly visitors from abroad, to use the art galleries as your reason for exploring the north of Britain, for you will be astounded by the discovery of unexpected art treasures in such settings as the Bowes Museum near Barnard Castle, and who would have thought that Accrington contains one of the finest collections of Tiffany glass in the world?

I set out on my journey in the fantastical spirit of visiting ancient Greece and as I left Lime Street station in Liverpool, confronted by those vast Classical municipal buildings, including the Walker Art Gallery, I might well have stepped back in time. There is a pleasant wistfulness in this anxiety to emulate the past, with local businessmen repaying the community for their wealth by contributing an art gallery, built in the Classical tradition, to enhance the future.

With the galleries as the justification for such a journey you have the opportunity to explore aspects of Britain that people either take for granted if they live there, or are unaware of. Northern people are straighter, kinder and more friendly, pleased to confide their life story within the first minute. The north is full of oddities: a pub in Liverpool of unbearable bleakness except for the promise of a sign which advertised, 'Exotic dancers – every Friday 3.00 to 3.30 p.m.'; a barman in a Manchester pub appearing in drag, complete with his moustache and a white wig, reappearing later as a male stripper in leather gear, spurred on by cries of lascivious encouragement from the mums seated at the tables round the tiny stage. The north may not be so lush as the west country where I live but the greater vigour is undeniable and the landscape as I passed through it by train has a sombre magnificence, with low lines of terraced houses on the hillside near Stalybridge, derelict, rusting factories and chimneys everywhere with whole towns built of the same brown brick – no wonder Lowry was attracted.

Southerners foster the myth of a north scarred by dark satanic mills, yet the cooling towers on the horizon near Scunthorpe, as you go from Leeds to Hull, have a peculiar grandeur, no town is half as littered or as filthy as London, and many of the new shopping centres have an imaginative elegance unknown in the south.

As for the galleries, here is the proof that art does not stop north of Trafalgar Square, here is the fulfilment of this book.

There is one warning I should give: when a gallery states that it closes at 5.00 p.m, be prepared to be shunted out a quarter of an hour earlier, as the staff depart with the desperation of a crowd fleeing from a fire. If you are still inside as the clock strikes five, you could well be locked in if they have not thrown you out, and protests that you have travelled several hundred miles will go unheeded. The latest time to arrive is 4.30 p.m. Otherwise, judging by my experience, you will be welcomed wherever you go.

Even so, it strikes me as museum madness that galleries close just as most people finish work. For them, the pursuit of happiness is an evening affair: going out to the theatre, opera, ballet or cinema, but this is virtually denied to art with a few honourable exceptions – in June, July and August, the National Gallery stays open until eight o'clock on Wednesdays.

Undeniably the expense of staying open is formidable, but galleries should find the means to do so and emulate the National Gallery's example on at least one evening a week. This will help in killing the stuffy image which implies that gallery-going is just for the fortunate few instead of a joy accessible to everyone.

'You ask me, what is the purpose of art? I can only reply, what is the purpose of love?' – Kenneth Clark.

Accrington

THE HAWORTH ART GALLERY

The Haworth Art Gallery was the former home of Miss Anne Haworth who died there in 1920, fulfilling the wishes of her late brother, a local JP with whom she shared the house, by leaving it with the grounds and their paintings to Accrington 'for the purposes of a Public Art Gallery, Museum and Park', with a sum to maintain them 'out of deep love for her native town'.

In the true spirit of the Collectors (see p. 227) this was a better memorial than a statue in a public square, and a means of reimbursing the community, for her father Thomas Haworth (1819–91) had done well out of Accrington by making a fortune from his cotton mills.

Today the mock-Tudor house, the thirteen acres of parkland and the paintings enhance each other. The house was opened as the town's Public Art Gallery in 1921 and its role as a cultural centre has developed with monthly exhibitions and showings of work by students and children. Of all the northern galleries, it is one of the friendliest.

The permanent exhibition is distinguished by one painting in particular, donated by the Mayor (1907–8), Alderman Higham – Vernet's *Storm on the French Coast*. Vernet had changed the name from the *Tempest*, possibly because he felt the longer title gave it extra weight, and because of this re-christening the picture became 'lost', rediscovered only when the Kenwood Gallery in London held a major Vernet exhibition and it was recognised as one of the artist's finer works. One look shows the influence on Rex Whistler's romantic mural at Plas Newydd.

There are several paintings to be enjoyed: *My Ladye's Palfrey* (1849) by John

Frederick Herring Senior; *Sunset* (1873) by Kuwassec; a *Coastal Scene with Figures* by William Shayer, Snr, and a shoal of Victorian watercolours.

The unique feature of the Haworth, however, is not in the field of painting at all but in glass. The Tiffany collection is internationally famous for the handmade coloured art nouveau examples of glass which were bought by wealthy Americans at the turn of the century.

Tiffany in Accrington? How did such an unusual marriage occur? The local connection is due to Joseph Briggs, an Accrington youth who sailed for the States at the age of seventeen to make his fortune. Starting as a foreman in the Tiffany Studios in New York, he ended as Art Director and personal assistant to Louis Comfort Tiffany, the son of the famous jeweller, who patented his glass lustring process.

Between the late 1890s and 1914 they produced some of the finest glassware the world has seen, technically and artistically brilliant: lamps, vases, tiles and windows all showed the distinctive Tiffany style. Then art nouveau fell out of fashion, replaced by Cubism and art deco. No longer popular, Tiffany collapsed. It was Joseph Briggs' sad responsibility to take the remaining stock, which had been worth hundreds of dollars each, to the rubbish tips of New York. Fortunately he had the foresight to bring back the best of Tiffany when he returned to Accrington in 1933 and gave half of it to the town, which explains this unlikely collection today.

Now Tiffany is back in vogue and the 130 pieces of glass in dazzling shapes and colours have a room of their own as they deserve. One of the most striking is a large glass mosaic of *Sulphur Crested Cockatoos* attributed to Briggs himself.

Barnard Castle

THE BOWES MUSEUM

In a country devoted to follies, few are so splendid as the Bowes Museum – a French château set in gardens and parkland laid out in the French style, housing one of the finest though least known collections in Britain.

If you are romantically inclined, you will savour the story of how this collection came about. John Bowes was a coal magnate with the luck to have seams of coal under his estate near Durham, and was also a shrewd businessman who made £100,000 a year, an astounding figure for the mid-1800s. Making Paris a regular base, he fell in love with a French actress, Mlle Joséphine Ernestine, who was no great beauty and allegedly of little talent though highly ambitious as a patron of the arts. Becoming his protégée, John Bowes bought her the Théâtre des Variétés and she had the means to commission plays in which she was cast, through tact rather than resemblance, as Madame Pompadour or one of the beauties of the age.

Josephine Bowes   A. Dury   The Bowes Museum

By 1850 John and Joséphine lived together in Paris and she retired from the stage the following year. They married in a civil ceremony in 1852.

As a wedding present, Bowes gave her the château Dubarry, an appropriate gift as this was the house which was occupied by Louis xv's last mistress, but most of their time was spent in Paris where they entertained on a lavish scale with parties for 150 guests and painting excursions to the coast and country.

In 1868 Joséphine acquired the title of the Countess of Montalbo and her life was complete apart from children, and it is this loss which may have encouraged her ambition to progress from a Salon in Paris to the establishment of a museum as their lasting memorial. To this end, she sold the château Dubarry in 1862 and used the money to buy the land near Barnard Castle.

Remarried in London in 1854, to make their contract legal, Joséphine Bowes became the epitome of respectability, not only collecting art but practising it herself, until her death at an early age after twenty years of bliss. Furthermore, her painting of one of their châteaux in France reveals a definite talent.

Surprisingly, the Bowes Museum was never their home, nor did they live to see its completion. John Bowes built the house in the French style, acquiring an art collection which was predominantly French, as a tribute to his beloved wife and a general act of benevolence. Usually buying directly from the artist, they had a shrewd agent and rarely paid more than £100 for a picture, and usually £10. He advised them to buy El Greco's *The Tears of St Peter* at the cost of a mere £8, and the two Goyas, *The Prisoner* and a portrait, for little more.

The Bowes collection has been added to over the years, and it now boasts 1,500 paintings, apart from the furniture and antiques. It is claimed that due to the French connection it has the finest array of French painting in Britain, with work by Boucher, Boudin, Fantin-Latour, Oudry and Vernet.

Quantity is no recommendation in itself, but the Bowes Museum is rich in major work, such as the small section of an altarpiece by Sassetta, *The Miracle of the Holy Sacrament*; *Crucifixion*, a massive triptych (1470–80) by the Delft painter known as the Master of the Virgo inter Virgines, whose *Pietà* hangs in the Walker Gallery, Liverpool; and two particularly fine Venetian scenes by Canaletto.

When you leave the Bowes Museum you are confronted by the French *parterre* on one side, and views overlooking Teesside on the other, and depart with admiration for the unlikely philanthropists, the coal mining magnate and his French wife.

(If the weather is good, make a day of it. The mechanical Swan made of English silver in 1770 operates twice a day – stretching its neck as it catches a fish in its beak – children will be enthralled.)

Bedford

THE CECIL HIGGINS MUSEUM AND ART GALLERY

Awarded the Sotheby prize for *Best Fine Art Museum in 1981*

This is one of the many galleries which are due to an act of benevolence. It is named after Cecil Higgins (1856–1941), member of a wealthy family of brewers in Bedford. Having no heirs, he sold the business in 1928 in order to collect ceramics and glass for a museum of art in his home, Castle Close. His ambition was completed after his death, when he left his collection to a board of trustees which opened the museum in 1949 in partnership with the North Bedfordshire Borough Council.

The Prisoner   Goya   The Bowes Museum, Barnard Castle, Co Durham

Cecil Higgins had the wisdom to leave his money in trust on condition 'that every item so acquired was approved by a national expert in the field'. Enhancing the collection immeasurably, the gallery has branched out into the field of painting, building up a fine collection of English watercolours and drawings over the subsequent twenty years – a time when it was possible to buy a watercolour for £2,000 which would be valued at £100,000 today.

Consequently, the quality is high, as the following purchases indicate: Constable, *Tree Study* in pencil; John Cozens, *Windsor Castle*, watercolour; Turner, *The Great Falls of Reichenbach*, watercolour; Henry Tonks, *Woman Walking on the Sand*, watercolour; Alan Reynolds, *Studies of Teazles*.

Two of the artists featured in this book are well represented: Edward Lear, with three studies; and Richard Dadd, with several scenes including one of *Bethlem Hospital*, 1853 (bought in 1961), where he was committed; and *Mother and Child*, an oil on canvas 19½ x 13 ins, inscribed R. Dadd 1860. This is a rarity and it is not known if Dadd painted this subject again. A halo of light transforms it into the Madonna and Child, though the beribboned hat and the ship on the horizon make it modern. A dark bird, its feathers so puffed up it is almost circular, adds a note of menace, though this is partly due to our awareness of Dadd's madness.

Bedford has the unusual distinction as well of a genuine Samuel Palmer and a fake Keating of Palmer's *A Barn at Shoreham* offering the chance to compare the two.

JOSEPH MALLORD WILLIAM TURNER

1775–1851

Turner is one of the few artists of undisputed genius, about whom words seem superfluous. It is impossible for me to do him justice with an illustration and a few paragraphs. His range was prodigious, from exact topography – like the watercolour of the *Cloisters, Salisbury Cathedral* – through the romanticism of Claude – to the later impressions that we admire today, which might have been splashed by the village pump. He left an astounding 20,000 watercolours and three hundred paintings when he died at the age of seventy-six, and his work can be seen in galleries throughout the country apart from the new Clore Gallery in the Tate. Consequently a Turner is hardly a rarity, yet one painting fetched a record £7 million when it was auctioned in 1984 and his work has never been so popular. Many would claim without hesitation that Turner is England's greatest artist.

Facts about the man are few. He was born in Maiden Lane off Covent Garden on 23 April 1775, only a year before Constable, who recognised his brilliance in a letter to Archdeacon Fisher in 1828: 'He is stark mad with ability. Turner has some golden visions, glorious and beautiful, but they are only visions, still they are art, and one could live and die with such pictures in one's house.' Turner's father was a barber and the bustle of Covent Garden's market was a sympathetic setting for the imaginative child, with the River Thames nearby, which never failed to fascinate. His talent was recognised at an early age, and he entered the Royal Academy Schools when he was fourteen. By the time he was nineteen he exhibited at the Academy, which supported him throughout his life. He became an ARA in 1799 and an RA in 1802, when he was twenty-seven; finally its Deputy President in 1845.

In spite of his individuality, Turner was susceptible to influence and grateful for it. Apart from the old masters he owed a special debt to the contemporary painter Thomas Girtin, with whom he worked for three years in the mid 1790s, washing in the colours on Girtin's outlines. He copied Girtin so faithfully that their work has been confused, and he was fortunate in having a friend of the same age with the same interests. The *Dictionary of Art & Artists* states that Girtin 'revolutionised landscape painting'. In the medium of watercolour he 'bridged the gap between the eighteenth-century stained drawing and the nineteenth-century watercolour painting' with the invention of using an absorbent off-white cartridge paper, abandoning 'the older monochrome underpainting in favour of a richer handling, with broad washes of strong colour often offset by dark blobs.' Turner acknowledged his debt for such innovation when his friend died at the age of twenty-seven: 'If Tom Girtin had lived, I should have starved.' Turner started as a watercolourist himself, exhibiting his first oil at the Academy when he was twenty-one – *Fishermen at Sea* (Tate) – which confirmed him as a master of that medium too. This typified the vortex that was such a feature of his work, with the swirling sea and tossing fishing boat lit by the moon, which breaks through clouds as dark as the foreground. It is possible to see the influence of Joseph Wright of Derby (1734–97) and his fascination with the dramatic intensity of light when fire or moonlight were involved, though he must have been a terrible nuisance on board.

Nearly fifty years later, *Snow Storm: Steam-Boat off a Harbour's Mouth* (Tate) perpetuated the theme with his example of another ship at the vortex of a storm and proved the lengths he was prepared to go to achieve it: 'I did not paint it to be understood,' he told Ruskin, 'but I wished to show what such a scene was like; I got the sailors to lash me to the mast to observe it; I was lashed for four hours and I did not expect to escape, but I felt bound to record it if I did.' Such is the madness of dedication.

In 1802 Turner travelled to the French Alps and Switzerland, where he was confronted by the full grandeur of nature. Standing up while he recorded them, he made hundreds of sketches of torrents, glaciers, crags and valleys, to be used in countless paintings in the future. Every impression was stored in his memory. When he stayed with one of his patrons, Walter Fawkes, in Yorkshire, he was so excited by a storm that he called to the son to come outside and admire it too. Seeing him make notes on the back of an envelope, the boy said he would bring some better material but Turner replied that the envelope served him well – 'He was absorbed – he was entranced. There was the storm rolling and sweeping and shafting out its lightning over the Yorkshire hills. Presently the storm passed and

A First Rate Taking in Stores   Turner   The Cecil Higgins Art Gallery, Bedford

he finished. "There," he said, "in two years you will see this again and call it *Hannibal and his Army Crossing the Alps.*"' Sure enough, this was the storm effect he used for the subsequent painting with that title.

On his return journey from the continent he stopped in Paris to see the art treasures in the Louvre which Napoleon had plundered during his conquest of Europe, and was particularly impressed by Poussin and the colours of Titian. Later, the classical influence of Poussin was replaced by the romanticism of Claude, evident in *Dido Building Carthage* (1815, National Gallery) which borrowed Claude's effect of looking *into* the sun, which was reflected on the shimmering water beside the quayside of the port.

Turner admired Claude to such an extent that he painted *Thomson's Aeolian Harp* as a tribute to the *Adoration of the Golden Calf* (both are in the Manchester City Art Gallery).

This was the poetic side of Turner, replaced by the impressions – 'portraits of nothing and very like' – which we favour today, like the famous image of a train forging through the landscape, *Rain, Steam, and Speed – the Great Western Railway* (1844, National Gallery) which prompted Kenneth Clark to yearn for more scenes of the new industrial age: 'In the 1840s smoking chimneys, furnaces and swathes of mist suited both his style and his pessimism better than the sunny enchantments of the Mediterranean.' It comes as a shock to be reminded by Lord Clark that 75 per cent of Turner's work was never shown in his lifetime or even seen until fifty years after his death, compared to the abundance now. As recently as 1939, fifty rolled-up tarpaulins in the cellars of the National Gallery proved to be the explosions of light and colour which replaced the literal interpretation of the subject. In the 1950s, when Francis Bacon introduced me to Turner's work, he had to take me to the *basement* of the Tate.

Clark should be allowed the last word when he states that there is 'nothing to distract us from the pure sensation. *They are modern painting.*'

Turner's work can be seen in galleries throughout the country, including:
Aberdeen, City Art Gallery
Bedford House, The Cecil Higgins Museum
Bowood House
Harewood House
Kenwood House
London, National Maritime Museum
 The Tate Gallery
Nottingham, Castle Museum
Petworth House
York, City Art Gallery

Birmingham
CITY MUSEUM AND ART GALLERY

If you have to go to Birmingham, you can find solace in this impressive building and the sympathy of the paintings, many the finest of their kind.

From the fifteenth and sixteenth century, you find the work of two great Venetians, Bellini's *Madonna and Child with Saints Peter and Paul and Donor;* and the *Adoration of the Shepherds* by Veronese. From the seventeenth and eighteenth century, Canaletto's view of the East Front of *Warwick Castle,* and the splendidly crowded picture of *The Fourth Earl of Manchester arriving in Venice in 1707* by the lesser known Luca Carlevaris.

I remember the shock – in the best use of that word – when I first saw *The Rest on the Flight into Egypt* by Orazio Gentileschi (1562–1647), an artist I had not heard of before but have looked out for ever since. In fact he was sufficiently admired in his time to receive an invitation from Charles I to visit London. Sadly most of his work there has been destroyed except for the ceiling which he painted for the Queen's house by Inigo Jones at Greenwich, now in Marlborough House.

The Rest on the Flight to Egypt   Orazio Gentileschi   Birmingham Museum & Art Gallery

His life was partly obscured by that of his daughter, though not for reasons which are wholly artistic, though she was a formidable painter herself. When she was fifteen she was raped by a close friend of her father, Agostino Tassi, also a painter, who then denounced her as a whore. Orazio petitioned the Pope and prosecuted Tassi, but the trial was as hideous an ordeal as the rape itself. Although it involved torture by thumb-screws, Artemisia never changed her story and Tassi was sent to prison for eight months. Her life was tainted by the scandal but her painting gained new power – she was elected as a member of the Academy in Florence at the age of twenty-three – and, understandably, a new violence can be seen in such pictures as *Judith and Holofernes*, in which she gained a sadistic revenge, delighting feminist movements today, as the two women saw off the man's head without a flicker of emotion, as if they are carving a chicken for lunch.

Inevitably, her father's life paled by comparison, yet it baffles me that this extraordinary picture in Birmingham is not better known. There are many versions of the subject and some are tiresome in their sentimentality, but Gentileschi's is devoid of sentiment, the face of the sleeping Joseph is creased by exhaustion, knocked out by the effort of their journey, while Mary is an attractive yet ordinary woman suckling the naked Jesus. The texture of the skin and the folds of the fabric are painted superbly, while the head of the donkey looms in disproportionate scale behind the wall whose cracks and pits on the surface are Dalinean. It is worth visiting the Birmingham Gallery for this alone.

As befits a major city, there is a wide range of work: Claude, Courbet, Degas, Renoir and Bonnard, and such twentieth-century British artists as Sickert, Steer, Spencer, Gwen and Augustus John, and Francis Bacon.

As you travel through Britain these become predictable names, but where Birmingham excels is in the Pre-Raphaelites, with Holman Hunt's portrait of Rossetti and *The Finding of the Saviour in the Temple* (see Emma Holt, p. 229); and Millais's study for the head of *Ophelia*, modelled by Elizabeth Siddall, Rossetti's wife. (It is claimed that she was made to lie in a bathtub in order to create the sensation of a body in water, which aggravated her consumption.) There is also Millais's famous *The Blind Girl*, first exhibited at the Royal Academy in 1856, and Rossetti's pen and ink of Tennyson (reading *Maud*) the Pre-Raphaelites' favourite poet.

Of special interest is the work of Ford Madox Brown, who was closely associated with the Pre-Raphaelites, perhaps too closely for his own advantage. Once the teacher of Rossetti, he is sometimes similar, as in *Pretty Baa Lambs* included here, with its bright colouring of the countryside yet stiff composition. The child apparently draped in a long night-dress justifies the nauseating title. In contrast *Work* has a welcome spontaneity, but this is in the Manchester City Gallery. Instead we have two landscapes, *An English Autumn Afternoon* and *Walton-on-the-Naze* (1859) which confirm his boldness as a landscape painter.

Birmingham also has the good fortune to possess his masterpiece, *The Last of England* (1855), a circular painting which becomes increasingly rewarding the more you examine it.

FORD MADOX BROWN

1821–93

> She grips his listless hand
> And clasps her child
> Through rainbow tears she sees a sunnier gleam
> She cannot see a void where he will be.
>
> Brown's poem on *The Last of England*

Ford Madox Brown was born in Calais and trained in Antwerp, Paris and Rome, where he met the Nazarenes, though he later escaped from their cloying influence. Settling in England when he was twenty-four, he remained in the tradition of Romantic historical painting practised by the Pre-Raphaelites and while he never became a member of the Brotherhood, one of his sketches had such an effect on Rossetti that he became Brown's pupil before moving on to Holman Hunt.

Like the Pre-Raphaelites, Brown painted out of doors and chose subjects with a contemporary theme such as the social structure depicted in *Work* and the poor conditions which drove people to emigrate, as in *The Last of England*.

Appearing on *Gallery*, Waldemar Januszczak commented that although 'We always have the view that the Pre-Raphaelites were very slushy, very sweet, it's important to remember that a lot of them were inspired by Ruskin, who was one of the great social reformers of all time. Ford Madox Brown was a great example of an artist with a social conscience.' Describing *Work* as one of the 'greatest pictures of honest labour ever produced', he interpreted *The Last of England* as 'an indictment of industrial England, an indictment of the north of England being turned over full of dark satanic mills. We are looking at people fleeing to a new horizon.'

Apart from the Gentileschi, *The Last of England* is my favourite picture in the Birmingham Museum because I covered similar ground in researching *Swans-downe*, my historical novel concerning a family who emigrate to Tasmania. I was familiar with the heartbreaking scene at Gravesend, with the bands playing, the passing ferry-boats sounding their sirens as the clipper turned into the Thames and the emigrants crowded the rails. I imagined the young looking forward to the open sea while the elderly looked back to England, the *last* of England, for they were unlikely to see it again, although the couple in Brown's picture are immersed in thoughts of their own.

Ford Madox Brown joined Holman Hunt and the Rossetti brothers at Gravesend on a bleak winter's day in 1852 to wave goodbye to their sculptor friend, Woolner, before he sailed for Australia. Brown was so moved by the departure that he started to paint it soon afterwards, using himself, his wife and their baby as models. It was painted in the open air on dull days to 'insure the peculiar look of light all around, which objects have on a dull day at sea'. He regarded the picture as 'in the strictest sense historical', as he wrote in his preface to the 1865 Piccadilly Exhibition, ' . . . in order to present the parting scene in its fullest tragic development [I have] singled out a couple from the middle-classes, high enough, through education and refinement, to appreciate all they are now giving up, and yet dignified enough in means to have to put up with the discomforts and humiliations incident to a vessel "all one class" . . . Absolutely, without any regard to the art of any period or country, I have tried to render this scene as it would appear. The minuteness of the detail which would be visible under such conditions of broad daylight I have thought it necessary to imitate as bringing the pathos of the subject more home to the beholder.'

There is more to the picture than initially meets the eye. At first I wondered if it would convey the same emotion if titled *Day Trip to Boulogne* until I studied it more closely and realised that such a label would be impossible. Look at the expressions – there is no day-trippery here, but dark foreboding, anxiety and fear. The more you look the more you discern: the tiny hand of the baby held in the mother's; her gloved hand entwining his; the cabbages strung from the rails to provide fresh food for the voyage.

Ford Madox Brown refers to other details which can scarcely be made out: 'an

The Last of England Ford Maddox Brown Birmingham Museum & Art Gallery

honest family of the greengrocer kind [making] the best of things with tobacco pipe and apples.' A young reprobate shakes his fist at his native land while his old mother reproves his 'foul-mouthed profanity'. It is just as well that Brown tells us this, for it would be hard to detect otherwise.

Although the picture is severe in its social significance it is saved from being a tract by Brown's passionate conviction and, surprisingly, by the shape, which should be so irrelevant yet which makes it instantly attractive. Why are pictures invariably straitjacketed by the conventional rectangle, though seldom a square? It is such a rigid tradition that one welcomes the rare departure: the oval miniatures of Hilliard; the octagonal enamel of Stubbs; or the irregular scraps of wood and cardboard used by Alfred Wallis. I appreciate that this is not an *artistic* point, yet the unconventional shape of *The Last of England* conveys the nostalgia of a locket, holding a memory of something – even a country – once loved.

Work by Ford Madox Brown can be seen in:
Nottingham, Castle Museum
Birmingham, Museum and Art Gallery
Manchester, City Gallery
             Whitworth Art Gallery
Wightwick Manor

Bradford

A famous lady novelist has suggested that if so many old buildings had not been destroyed, Bradford might qualify today as the 'Florence of the north'. This is surprising and so is the current transformation of this northern town into a centre for the arts. Already it boasts the *National Museum of Photography* (including film and television), and now there are two independent art galleries, one at Salt's Mill in Saltaire three miles from the centre, run by a fashionable entrepreneur Jonathan Silver, which contains pictures by David Hockney with whom he went to Bradford Grammar School. The other is managed by the equally fashionable Nicholas Treadwell, who has spent half a million pounds on converting a stone warehouse in the town's Little Germany into a leisure centre with an art gallery, theatre, video workshop and studios on the top floor for the use of artists. Treadwell declares, 'There is money in culture and as a cultural city Bradford has a tremendous future.'

CARTWRIGHT HALL ART GALLERY

Cartwright Hall in Lister Park is a memorial to Edmund Cartwright, the inventor of the power loom, and opened at the start of this century. Samuel Cunliffe-Lister offered his former home and paid towards the building described as 'French Baroque'. Notably, this is now the home for the International Print Biennial, with a number of prints displayed in the gallery.

    The collection also includes such old masters as *Flight Into Egypt* by Guido Reni, and work by Gainsborough, Etty and Ford Madox Brown, but is richer in more contemporary art: Sickert's portrayal of Leslie Banks and Edith Evans in *The Taming of the Shrew*; Wilson Steer; Spencer Gore; and the Bloomsbury Group represented by Duncan Grant, Roger Fry, and three paintings by the gifted, though short-lived Mark Gertler.

If Edmund Cartwright is Bradford's most illustrious son, David Hockney is probably the favourite, though the famous *Double Portrait* of his mother and father now hangs in the Tate.

The controversial cover of the 1989 Bradford and District Phone book, designed by David Hockney

Burghclere

SANDHAM MEMORIAL CHAPEL

One of the great war memorials in Britain, this is an extraordinary flight of the imagination. Stanley Spencer was fortunate in his patrons and few showed such faith as Mr and Mrs Behrend, who built him this chapel.

In spite of the religious subjects of so many of his paintings, his treatment was so innovative that few patrons would have commissioned him otherwise. The Behrends' faith proved justified and the chapel now contains the most exciting modern mural in the country, and I am not forgetting Sutherland's tapestry in Coventry Cathedral.

The mural, based on his experiences in Macedonia, is a personal memorial to a soldier killed in the First War. Starting with scrubbing the floors at Beauford Hospital, and culminating in the Resurrection, it is arguably his finest work.

Preparing his studies in 1922–3, he carried them out between 1926 and 1927. The Behrends supported him financially throughout this time and arranged for Stanley and Hilda his wife to live in a house nearby. Mr Behrend's patience must have been stretched, but he retained a sense of humour: when confronted with yet another painting as a possible purchase, he protested, 'Stanley, I can't do with any more graveyards!'

The chapel is found at the end of a straggling village, approached across lawns on a red-brick path with a wishing well halfway. The building itself is 1920s 'Institutional', but once you go inside you are greeted by side walls decorated waist-high to the ceiling, with eight panels showing army and hospital life, surmounted by murals of further troop activities such as resting by a river and washing clothes. Spencer himself was both the observer and the participant, recording such details as eating army 'wads and jam', which only a soldier could have known.

The main mural stretches from the floor to the ceiling behind the altar – a resurrection as soldiers rise from their graves to greet old comrades, the crosses tossed aside as if thrown up by an earthquake. Dead mules rear their heads and gaze towards the horizon which runs two inches from the ceiling, creating a perspective that draws one into this extraordinary vision.

STANLEY SPENCER

1891–1959

> I believe Christ talking is really me
> love-making to everybody
>
> > > Spencer

Spencer was a simple man living in a world of fantasy. Everything about him which seems odd to other people was natural to Stanley Spencer. He had no artifice. He was that rarest of artists – a true original.

Stanley Spencer was born at Cookham in 1891, a village he loved throughout his life. It could be argued that he never matured as a man, but he did so as an artist at an early age after he was accepted by Professor Tonks at the Slade School of Art, though he was incapable of passing the general knowledge paper.

Spencer had never been to London before and while he could manage the train journey he was so daunted by the underground and the walk down Gower Street that his father had to accompany him until he became used to it. He made friends with his fellow students C.R. Nevinson and Mark Gertler, but scurried back home the moment classes were finished, earning himself the nickname of 'Cookham'. His time at the Slade ended triumphantly with an award for *The Apple Gatherers*, based on his village, and the prize for the best figure painting of the year with his *Nativity*. Professor Tonks declared, 'In some ways he has shown signs of having the most original mind of anyone we have had in at the Slade and he combines this with great powers of draughtmanship.' His position as one of the foremost figures in British art this century was confirmed by the powerful *Self-Portrait*, a year later, which is now in the Tate along with *The Apple-Gatherers* and thirty-five other examples of his work.

In the First War Spencer volunteered for the army but as he was considered below the required physical standard he joined the Royal Army Medical Corps, scrubbing floors and performing other menial duties at the Beauford War Hospital at Bristol, which appealed to his streak of masochism and preoccupation with dirt. Always honest, he stated, 'I am on the side of the angels and dirt.'

Later he was sent to Macedonia, a tougher experience captured in the astonishing murals for Burghclere Chapel. The moment the war ended, Spencer completed the famous *Swan Upping* and two religious pictures, *The Last Supper* and *Christ Carrying the Cross* (Tate) in which he placed Christ in the context of Cookham.

This was Spencer's achievement, that he celebrated life on earth in heavenly terms. There is nothing offensive about *Christ Preaching at Cookham Regatta* from a wicker chair with bare feet and a sort of skirt, because that is how the artist saw him; nothing morbid about people rising from their graves in *The Resurrection*, for Spencer loved graveyards. Undeniably he was an oddity, preoccupied with filth, seldom changing his clothes or underwear, and startling the welders in the Clyde shipyards who noticed that he wore pyjamas underneath his bedraggled suit. At least that was in wartime with the need to keep warm, but people at dinner parties in later years were equally surprised to see his pyjama top peeking through, and his appearance was generally so scruffy that doormen took pleasure in barring him. He took an equal pleasure in making an appointment when he wanted to visit a gallery, coveting his sense of persecution by 'authority'. He was one of life's 'grievance collectors'.

His love life was equally bizarre. He married Hilda Carline in 1925 when he was thirty-four after knowing her for five years. Experiencing sex for the first time, he became obsessed by the *idea* of it as much as, if not more than, the reality – though in this he was hardly unique. Spencer's biographer, Maurice Collis, suggests that the 'Cookham Resurrection' was inspired by this discovery of sex – 'The meaning it carried of a paradisal love was the gate of heavenly love.' Hilda appears in the painting no less than five times, and Spencer twice, once in the nude in front of the porch. Collis points out that Hilda and Stanley are 'the presiding deities' yet the painting is in no way sacrilegious – 'In as much as it depicted an awakening to love.' The face of Christ even has a look of Hilda.

Although he remained in love with Hilda, they divorced in 1936. He planned to remarry her in 1943, although he was still married to his second wife, and when

Hilda died in 1950 after a mental breakdown, he continued to write to her as if she were alive. This was natural to him, for he was perpetuating his fantasy, starting his letters, 'Dear Hilda, ducky . . .'

The output of his letters was huge and most have not been printed because they are unprintable. Sometimes this unappetising side of Spencer enraged people to such an extent that they could stand neither the painter nor the paintings, which were often explicit. Even today the *Double Nude Portrait: the Artist and his Second Wife* (1936) has the power to shock when one sees it in the Tate, with Spencer in the nude crouching over his wife who looks unconcerned though his massive genitals are dangling on one side of her, with a raw leg of lamb on the other. The shock is to the credit of the artist but it is easy to imagine the effect such pictures had fifty years earlier on the less tolerant like Sir Alfred Munnings, who was replaced as President of the Royal Academy by Sir Gerald Kelly. After two of his pictures had been rejected by Munnings, Spencer resigned from the Academy in high dudgeon but Sir Gerald lured him back by hanging a number of his most

Travoys Arriving with the Wounded at a Dressing Station at Smol, Macedonia 1916
Stanley Spencer   The Imperial War Museum

important canvases in the annual exhibition of 1950. Spencer was mollified but Munnings spotted a painting in a dealer's window which he considered obscene and took his revenge, reporting it to the police and demanding a prosecution under the obscenity laws. Kelly returned from a visit to America in time to intervene and the case was dropped by the Director of Public Prosecutions, with a public apology to Spencer, who was left shaken none the less. As Collis explains, he was used to abuse but not to threats: 'Like many a great man, he was unworldly; he had a simple belief in goodness.' The painting was not obscene to him, but after this he was cautious.

To the public he remains a baffling figure: deeply religious, while depicting Christ in such an ungainly manner it is almost blasphemous. He shocked the society of the time with his scandalous private life, yet he was knighted by the Queen Mother in 1959, the year of his death.

I suspect that his appearance explains the lingering suspicion which surrounds him. He had none of the romantic aura of Augustus John, who was no less sensual but looked the true, rumbustious, bohemian artist. Instead, Spencer looks furtive in the *Double-Nude* as he peers through his glasses like a voyeur at his wife below. They resemble a suburban couple experimenting with pornography on a damp Sunday afternoon in front of a gas fire, though they appear joyless. Spencer's ability to convey seediness confirms his honesty as a painter, yet he was capable of naturalistic landscapes like *Engelfield House* (1951), which hangs at his museum at Cookham and he always strove to go further. After the conventionality of *Engelfield*, however, one is glad to turn to the stranger *Beatitudes of Love* (1937), which demands more from the viewer, and the naked, male *Sunbathers* (1935), which are also at Cookham.

While Spencer was simple he was far from stupid. His figures are frequently grotesque, swollen to the point of ugliness, yet there is no feeling that he did anything for effect. His mind was exceptionally alert, his ear for music was exact, and his paintings were entirely his own creation. Therein lies his genius, and he is one of the few British artists this century to whom that word applies.

Stanley Spencer's work can be seen in the following galleries:
Aberdeen, Art Gallery
Carlisle, Museum and Art Gallery
Cookham-on-Thames, The Stanley Spencer Gallery
Edinburgh, Gallery of Modern Art
Leeds, City Art Gallery
Liverpool, Walker Art Gallery
Newbury, Sandham Memorial Chapel
Nottingham, Castle Museum
Southampton, Art Gallery
York, City Art Gallery

Cookham-on-Thames

THE STANLEY SPENCER GALLERY

Surprisingly, this is the only gallery in Britain devoted to an artist in the village where he was born and spent most of his working life. Spencer's love for Cookham shows in the local scenes, which are instantly recognisable: the parish church, the river, Cookham Moor.

Cookham was also the setting for his heavenly visions. Appropriately, the gallery occupies the Victorian Methodist Chapel where he worshipped as a child, and contains documentation and even the pram in which he wheeled his equipment, as well as the paintings, 350 of which have been exhibited since the gallery opened in 1962.

The permanent collection includes such religious work as *The Betrayal* (1914), *The Last Supper* (1920), and *Christ Overturning the Money Changers' Table* (1921). There are also the Shipbuilding on the Clyde series from the Second World War, and his studies for the Sandham Memorial Chapel, based on his experiences in the First War.

Derby

JOSEPH WRIGHT

1734–97

Joseph Wright was such a local hero, with forty-five paintings and seventy-eight drawings in the Derby Art Gallery, that he was known affectionately as 'Wright of Derby'. Though one of our finest artists, Wright's reputation was almost entirely restricted to Derby until a few years ago when suddenly he became fashionable.

Born in Derby in 1734, the son of a successful lawyer, he moved to London when he was sixteen to study under a successful portrait painter called Thomas Hudson, who counted Joshua Reynolds among his pupils. This proved a happy apprenticeship and Wright stayed with him from 1751 to 1753, returning for a second tuition three years later.

Back in Derby, he benefited from his training by painting portraits which gave him the income to paint the less profitable subjects that interested him. These were the scenes of scientific experiment, which ultimately made him famous. Wright's particular trick or trademark was the intense light, which came from a solitary source such as the moon or a lamp, and which illuminated the cluster of people as they watched the experiment. The technique was undoubtedly brilliant though the pictures were unashamedly 'set-pieces', with carefully posed groups, lit meticulously, in the style admired by the Dutch in the seventeenth century.

While their artifice verges on the static, Wright was the 'first professional painter to express the spirit of the industrial revolution' and his work was bought by Wedgwood and Arkwright. When he was thirty-one, he exhibited at the Society of Artists in London and thirty-eight of his pictures were shown there over the next ten years, including his famous scientific painting now in Derby, *A Philosopher Giving that Lecture on the Orrery, in which a Lamp is Put in Place of the Sun*. An 'orrery' is a clockwork model of the planetary system.

This was followed by *An Experiment with the Air-Pump* (Tate) in which the detailed figures are life-size on a massive canvas measuring seven foot by nine.

Pictures by Wright were bought by Hartford and Yale in America, but it is only recently that his prices have rocketed here. In *The Times* in October 1984, Geraldine Norman revealed that his painting of *Mr and Mrs Coltman setting out to Ride* was due to fetch £1 million at a forthcoming auction at Christie's (the National Gallery bought it in November for £1,419,600), and it was rumoured that the interest came from America yet again. The picture had the added curiosity of 'a brilliantly delineated spaniel' beside Mrs Coltman on horseback, which might have been painted by George Stubbs, who was a personal friend. Describing Wright as 'a second division artist', Geraldine Norman added that the art world in Britain was staggered by this unforeseen elevation to the first division, though she pointed out that this is Wright's masterpiece, comparable to Gainsborough and Reynolds.

Yet his range was considerable, extending beyond his portraits and scientific experiments into landscape. A gouache of *Vesuvius* (1774) and *Landscape with Rainbow* (1794–5) are in the finest tradition of British landscape painting, and his *Rydal Waterfall* (1795), painted two years before his death, an actual breakthrough. The naturalism of the surrounding trees and foliage predates Constable, while the water is presented so stylistically it foreshadows Hockney. This was no accident. Writing to a friend, Wright explained: 'I was keen to produce an effect which I had never seen in painting of shewing the pebbles at the bottom of the water with the broken reflections on the surface.' He added: 'So highly finished is that little bit of nature, that to do it justice it should be painted upon ye spot.'

The Derby Gallery is in the fortunate position of discovering a treasure-trove in its extensive collection of their native artist, which will become even more valuable once his landscapes receive their recognition.

The work of Joseph Wright can be seen in:
Derby, The Derby Art Gallery
London, The Tate Gallery
Nottingham, Castle Museum

Huddersfield

ART GALLERY

Without meaning to patronise, Huddersfield is not the place where I would expect to find a fine collection of twentieth-century British art. The range is impeccable, with early work by Lucien Pissarro; *The Garden at Cookham Rise* by Stanley Spencer; and a *View of Ramsgate* by Sickert. There is, also, work by David Bomberg, Duncan Grant, and a still life of *Flowers* by Matthew Smith. More recent artists such as Frank Auerbach, John Bellany, Robert Bevan and John Minton are represented, too, along with Christopher Wood, Graham Sutherland and a series of watercolours by Wilson Steer.

Most spectacular of all is the early painting by Francis Bacon, *Figure Study II* (1945–6). The flatness of the title conceals an act of mysterious violence. An apparently naked figure, loosely draped by a herring-bone overcoat, mounted by an umbrella, leans over a palm his mouth wide open in a scream. The background is the colour of blood. What has happened? There is no telling.

To some extent, this is one of a pair, for *Figure Study I*, also 1945–6, has the same overcoat, delineated more boldly, and a hat with all the evidence of the human being absent. Instead, the 'shape' looms over a cluster of pale blue flowers.

By chance, this was one of the paintings on loan (from a private collection) chosen for the exhibition at the Marlborough Gallery which was held in honour of his eightieth birthday on 28 October 1989. The shock of these paintings was overwhelming as usual, but I was startled by the extraordinary beauty of *Figure Study I* and the contrasting delicacy of those small, blue flowers.

Echoing the torment of the *Three Studies for Figures at the Base of a Crucifixion*, painted in the previous year, these two studies haunt the memory and Huddersfield is fortunate indeed to possess such a memorable example of Francis Bacon's work.

FRANCIS BACON

1909–

> My ideal would really be just to pick up a handful of paint and throw it at the canvas and hope that the portrait was there. I want, very, very much to give the sensation without the boredom of its conveyance.
>
> Francis Bacon

Next to Stanley Spencer, Francis Bacon is the most important British artist of the twentieth century. The likes of Hockney and Hodgkin come nowhere near. Breaking through established barriers, Bacon is a true original. The disturbing world he draws us into is one of his own making and at times the recognition of ourselves is shocking. When future historians contemplate the malaise of the second half of this century, it is likely they will see us through his eyes.

Figure Study II   Francis Bacon   Kirklees Metropolitan Council, Huddersfield Art Gallery

This famous early Bacon was first shown at the Lefevre Gallery in 1946 and was subsequently donated to the Batley Art Gallery in 1952 by the Contemporary Art Society. A Bacon in Batley — the mind boggles. So did the minds of those in Batley, a northern town noted for its famous nightclub rather than its gallery. Sir John Rothenstein acknowledged this painting as one of Bacon's finest, pointing out that it was scarcely mentioned due to 'its belonging to a small and somewhat remote collection'. Apparently the painting was so disliked locally (so the artist himself has told me) that motions were put forward to the Council to sell it. These were defeated by the Director of the Batley Art Gallery at the time, Ronald Gelsthorpe, who believed in the painting's importance, and thanks to his perseverance it now hangs to greater advantage in Huddersfield.

Although he retains the power to shock, he remains comparatively unknown to the public and in this he is something of an enigma, despising the attentions of the media which Hockney courts so assiduously. That vital element of mystery explains why Bacon is misinterpreted as 'evil', while Hockney – probably the more popular artist – is easily understood.

The one artist who approaches Bacon is Lucian Freud, a close, former friend, but while Freud's work is distinctive, his purpose as a portraitist is so different from Bacon's, who encourages a painting to assume a life of its own, that the two are hardly comparable. Each man is unique. It has been my good fortune to know both these artists since I entered Soho in the early 1950s.

Bacon is in no respect an eccentric. A sacred monster, perhaps, and I included him in my book of the same name, but eccentricity implies an element of accident, and apart from the accident of paint which he twists to his advantage, there is nothing accidental about Francis Bacon. He is the most single-minded man I know.

Francis Bacon was born in a Dublin hospital on 28 October 1909. A distant descendant of his illustrious Elizabethan namesake, his parents were English and he was brought up in County Kildare where his father had a racing stable until the First War, when the family moved to London and his father worked in the War Office.

He was removed from a minor public school at Cheltenham because he was constantly running away, and given a weekly allowance of £3 by his mother. This was the end of both his education and his family life, for he had no sympathy with or from his father, who regarded his wish to become an artist as a tiresome self-indulgence. Bacon had two brothers who died at an early age and the only time he saw his father show emotion was on the death of the younger. Instead of tears for Francis, his father was disgusted by his laziness and penchant for dressing in his mother's clothes and decided to make a man of him by entrusting him to the care of a friend, a sporting gentleman who liked horses. Ironically, the friend also had a fondness for louche living and took him to Berlin in 1927. This was one of the decadent years of Berlin and a welcome antidote to home life. A lasting influence occurred very shortly afterwards in Paris, where he saw his first exhibition by Picasso, though it was seventeen years before this influence became apparent.

Back in London, Bacon drifted between jobs, acting in such a lackadaisical manner as a gentleman's gentleman that his employer sighed when he handed in his notice, 'I cannot understand why, as he never *does* anything.'

With characteristic candour, Bacon admitted that he lived on his wits: 'I used to steal money from my father whenever I could and I was always taking rooms in London and then disappearing – not paying the rent, not being able to pay it. What's called morality has grown on me with age. But in those days I managed to get by on petty theft and on living off people.' He has always been anarchic.

To understand Bacon's single-mindedness, it is crucial to appreciate that he was self-taught. He experimented as a designer and some modernistic furniture was illustrated in the *Studio* in 1930. He prefers to forget this phase, yet the sparseness of his early studio, the cubist rug, the tubular furniture and use of mirrors, has recurred in his painting, in his conveyance of the isolation of the human figure caught in an empty room.

He has stressed that nothing in his work mattered until 1945, but even if it was subconscious he was influenced by the Australian artist Roy de Maistre and particularly by Graham Sutherland. As early as 1934 he held his own show in a Curzon Street basement where his painting of a *Crucifixion* was noticed by Herbert Read and reproduced in his book *Art Now*. In 1937 he exhibited at Agnew's with other young British painters including John Piper and Sutherland. After this, his painting was virtually abandoned and most of his work destroyed. He knew the time was not yet ripe.

'I do what I do to excite myself,' he has said, adding, 'I have looked at everything in art.' Among the artists he admires are Rembrandt, Constable and Velasquez, whose portrait of *Pope Innocent X* provided the inspiration for his early series of Popes screaming in silence behind the glass and massive gilt frames, enclosed further by the horizontal lines which added to their caged despair.

Other images which helped him were the early photographs by Edward Muybridge of *The Human Figure in Motion* (1887) and the still of the nurse on the Odessa Steps, her glasses shattered and her mouth open in a scream, in Eisenstein's film *Battleship Potemkin* (1925).

In Monte Carlo after the war, Bacon was so poor – apart from luck at the Casino – that he painted on the reverse side of a used canvas and found the paint held so well on the rougher surface that he used it from then on, exploiting the accident. It was here that he resumed his friendship with Sutherland and when they shared a studio in London Bacon wrote to him asking him to spray fixative over a painting, adding that he felt he was on the point of 'doing something good'.

This shift came with *Three Studies for Figures at the Base of a Crucifixion* in 1944, shown in a mixed exhibition the following year at the Lefevre with Moore and Sutherland. It is now that the influence of Picasso's abstract shapes in 1927 is evident, though Bacon twisted them into figures which were almost human. 'Visitors tempted by the already familiar name of Graham Sutherland,' wrote John Russell, 'were brought up short by images so unrelievedly awful that the mind shut with a snap at the sight of them . . . these figures had an anatomy half-human, half-animal . . . they were equipped to probe, bite and suck . . . two at least were sightless. One was unpleasantly bandaged. They caused a total consternation.'

This was the turning point, but while Bacon was respected by his contemporaries in the art world he remained unknown to the public and so consistently hard up that once he asked me to sell one of his paintings, a study of the Velasquez Pope, which I succeeded in doing for the required sum of £150. It would sell for a million today. Though rivalry now jeopardised their friendship, Sutherland was loyal and introduced him to such patrons as Sir Colin Anderson and to Sir Kenneth Clark, whose manner was so cold that after he left Bacon's studio with a murmured, 'Interesting, yes,' Bacon exclaimed angrily. 'You see, you're surrounded by cretins.' That evening Clark phoned Sutherland: 'You and I may be in a minority of two, but will still be right in thinking that Francis Bacon has genius.' It must have been a traumatic moment for Sutherland, who saw his own success eclipsed.

A period followed with some of Bacon's most memorable images, even if he is dismissive of them now: *Figure in a Landscape*, hinting at assassination; *Study of Van Gogh*, a portrait of the artist at Arles. *Painting* (1946) – his titles are rarely descriptive – was bought by the Hanover Gallery where he exhibited and sold to the Museum of Modern Art in New York for £100.

Bacon's life changed dramatically ten years later when he joined the Marlborough, who dealt with his pictures as if they were big business, which they became. The gallery was instrumental in staging the first retrospective at the Tate in 1962, the first of three crucial exhibitions: the second at the Grand Palais in Paris in 1971; with another retrospective at the Tate in 1985, when he was acclaimed as 'Britain's greatest living painter', though there were a few dissenters such as Bernard Levin.

Certainly the association with the Marlborough hoisted his career on to a different and more lucrative level, but his life remained remarkably unchanged. I can think of no one less affected by success.

He lives in the same mews cottage where he has stayed for the last thirty years or more, and it still looks as if he is waiting for the decorators to arrive, with naked light bulbs and blankets instead of curtains, though the walls of his studio are ablaze with splashed paint in contrast to the austerity of his sitting room. He dislikes possessions. He has no car and frequently travels by tube. His excesses are no more excessive than before. This is the irony: that he divided his life between 'the gutter and the Ritz', consumed oysters at Wheeler's and signed the bill, followed by champagne at Muriel's afternoon club in Soho, expenses which he chalked up long before he could afford to. The champagne may be a better vintage now and the caviare returned if found too salty, and everything is paid for in cash (£50 notes); otherwise he treads his way through the old haunts in Soho with the same anonymity. At times I enjoy the fantasy of accompanying Toulouse-Lautrec on his way to the Moulin Rouge, except that Monsieur Lautrec would have been more conspicuous. Mr Bacon is so inconspicuous, in spite of his mesmeric personality, that he was once in a Soho pub where someone, hearing that he was a painter, offered him a job decorating his house. Flattered, Bacon did not disillusion the stranger.

A heavy drinker and impassioned gambler in the surprising venue of Charlie Chester's gaming club, his stamina has always been remarked on, appearing twenty years younger than his age, his hair dyed so skilfully that he says he has forgotten what colour it used to be. 'They say I look twenty years younger than my age,' he told me once, 'but even then I'd still be *old*!'

Walking with a deliberate gait, as if he has ventured on deck in a high storm, he enunciates each word carefully, investing it with utmost seriousness or hilarious humour, which tend to be lost on the printed page. When he says, 'I am just a simple iddy-yott,' it *sounds* the height of wit, and on one of his birthdays we had dinner at L'Escargot, where he expressed dismay when he saw my lamb served in a rich wine sauce. 'I do hope I don't have *gravy* on mine!' he exclaimed, reducing it to the feeblest gruel of some Dickensian workhouse, but you need to hear him say it, with his measured sentences and lilting intonation, to appreciate the fun.

He moves with equal ease in the pubs of Soho and the smartest *salons* of society, welcome wherever he goes. Yet he remains detached. When you turn round and discover he has vanished, you are not altogether surprised. Urged to live in Switzerland for reasons of tax, he groaned, 'Can you imagine anything more boring – all those *views*!' and though the concept of *Sir Francis Bacon* is entertaining, he has rejected all the honours offered him, though he is too polite to make his rejection public.

This admirable indifference towards the trappings of success is strengthened by bitter personal experience. On the morning after the first great retrospective at the Tate, a score of congratulatory telegrams included one which informed him of the death of his close friend, Peter Lacey, in Tangiers. Knowing that Lacey was ill he had wanted to fly out and see him, but had been thwarted by the preparations for the show. In Paris in 1971 as he waited at the top of the steps of the Grand Palais to welcome President Pompidou, surrounded by the pageantry of flags, guards of honour and bands, word was brought to him that his friend George Dyer had been discovered dead in his hotel in Paris, seated on the lavatory. There is doubt as to whether this was suicide or a stroke. Dyer was a charming but hopeless personality who had threatened to kill himself before. The foremost of Bacon's models, his image was reflected in numerous paintings at the Grand Palais and, by a brutal coincidence, one of the first works to confront the French President as Bacon showed him around was a portrait of Dyer seated on the lavatory. In 1973 Bacon commemorated Dyer in a posthumous triptych with the nude figure on a lavatory on the left, an anguished face in the centre beneath a naked light bulb, and the same figure heaving over a washbasin on the right: 'I suppose in so far as my pictures are ever any kind of illustration, this comes close as any to a kind of narrative.' It was sold by auction in New York in 1989 for £3.9 million.

Knowing the circumstances, the triptych has a compassion, almost a tenderness, and it is significant that Dyer's portrait was used as the poster for the second Tate retrospective in 1985. On this occasion the fates left Bacon alone and did not demand their sacrifice for triumph. Bacon was surrounded by friends on the night before the opening, including John Edwards, the young East Ender who has become one of his latest models and whose portrait was chosen for the poster at the Moscow exhibition in 1988.

In his eightieth year, Bacon is magnificent. His work is still preoccupied with the themes of human pain, despair and loneliness, for he has always been drawn to the darker side of life, though it was the image rather than the message which concerned him. In this he is constantly misinterpreted by critics, who see a terrible indictment of the twentieth century. It was not the anguish of the nurse in *Potemkin* which moved him but 'the beauty of that shot, the mouth, and I was excited by the idea of it being done in colour, the colour of the lips and the flesh and the tongue.'

His attraction to raw flesh is even simpler: 'You've only got to go into a butcher's shop like Harrod's food hall – it's nothing to do with mortality but it's to do with the great beauty of the *colour* of the meat.'

A documentary on television confused his screaming figures with the atrocities of Belsen. Although it had never been his intention to record historically, he aggravated the confusion when he added a swastika armband to a wounded figure in the right-hand panel of the *Crucifixion* (1965), explaining artlessly that he did so 'to break the continuity of the arm and to add that particular red ...' This exemplifies the theatricality which alienates, though it inspired Bertolucci to use Bacon's work as a background for *Last Tango in Paris*.

Other 'tricks' which critics regard as weaknesses are such mannerisms as the red arrows which point apparently pointlessly, and the naked torsos wearing cricket pads, which seem an irrelevance.

Yet Bacon has always known exactly what he was up to, even when he exploited the accident. In his first television interview in 1958, when I persuaded him to appear, he told me, 'Sometimes I have used subject matter which people think is sensational, because one of the things I have wanted to do was record the human cry – the whole coagulation of pain and despair – and that in itself is something sensational.' When I asked why he did not paint love and happiness as well, he smiled. 'They would be wonderful to paint also, I always hope I will be able to do that too. After all, it's only the reverse side of the shadow, isn't it?' He gave one of his inimitable shrugs.

No artist should be understood too easily and Bacon continues to exasperate his critics, which must be a healthy sign. I was present in the Trattoria Terrazza in Soho when James Birch asked him over dinner if he would be interested in exhibiting in Moscow, the first salvo towards the historic show there in September 1988 – an extraordinary honour for an artist frequently condemned in the West for his decadence. Bacon had the nous to sense this instantly, though he decided at the last moment to stay at home and avoid the inevitable protocol involving his presence at the opening, pleading one of his attacks of asthma, which plagued him that year, as his excuse.

Critics who disliked the early work for epitomising 'all the sickness of our sick period', were joined in 1989 by Richard Dorment, who condemned Bacon's new version of the *Three Studies for Figures at the Base of a Crucifixion* as 'pure evil'. When I told him this, Bacon feigned surprise: 'Really! I thought they were rather nice, myself.'

Yet, for a man who has loved food, drink and friendship, there is no sense of celebration as there is in the French Impressionists. For a man who will be remembered for his laughter, there is none of the wit of Lautrec. A superb colourist, who uses daring mauves and cyclamens and pinks, he admired Van Gogh so greatly that he painted his series of the artist on the road to Tarascon, yet he does not share Van Gogh's affinity with nature, though his few landscapes reveal how successfully he ventures in that direction.

Like the greatest of artists he compels you to look at life again, but while he shared Picasso's determination to extend the frontiers of art, he has restricted himself to variations on his favourite themes, whereas Picasso experimented in every form he could.

It is often said that Bacon's view of life is joyless, but he might reply that joy has nothing to do with it. He has said that he would like his pictures to look 'as if a human being had passed between them, like a snail, leaving a trail of the human presence and memory trace of past events as the snail leaves its slime.'

Whenever I return to his work I am stunned by the power. Eighty years old in October 1989, he remains the most enthralling man I know.

Francis Bacon 1989

I took this photograph of Francis Bacon outside the French Pub in Soho on 14 July 1989. Earlier that day we had been interviewed for Finnish Television, and as they were not transmitted, I quote some of the comments he made that morning after I mentioned the label of 'despair' which haunts his work.

'I don't try to paint despair. I love life.' This prompted me to raise another of those generalisations which he detests, expressing regret that someone with such a celebratory attitude towards life has never recorded that aspect in his work. He listened with exemplary patience: 'It's not my attitude, not my way of doing it. I'm a very limited artist. I portray what I can. After all, the fundamental thing about life is that it is a very short moment.'

'Then my question was silly?'

'Your question was silly. I don't try to paint despair but after the age of thirty what is there but death? That is not looking forward to despair but the realisation that there is the grave coming closer, closer, closer . . .' He said this beamingly, circling the air with his hand.

'What do you believe in?'

'*Nothing.*'

Yet he cares passionately. He abhors the obstinacy of Mrs Thatcher – 'This government would really like a dictatorship, they want to diminish freedom as far as possible' – and lamented the current commercialism in art: 'Prices are so ridiculous that people go to galleries because they are obsessed by money. Most people have no feeling about painting, why should they? They don't know good from bad, but they *are* influenced by the money. I long to see something new and exciting. It's very sad that there's nothing coming up at the moment anywhere, but you mustn't forget that at the end of the last century we had the Impressionists, and then Cubism and Picasso as a marvellous beginning to this century. Of course there must be laid-off periods – they cannot always be brilliant – but somebody new will come along and a new attitude will start again.' As for himself: 'I hope I'll go on working until I drop dead.'

The work of Francis Bacon can be seen in:
Aberdeen, Art Gallery
Huddersfield, Art Gallery
London, Tate Gallery
Manchester, City Art Gallery
          Whitworth Art Gallery

Kingston-upon-Hull

THE FERENS ART GALLERY

This gallery will be closed for most of 1990 due to an extension which will double its size when completed. Set in the main square where new buildings complement the old, this will be a good reason for visiting the town. Opened in 1927 and endowed by a local industrialist, the Rt Hon T.R. Ferens, the collection has been augmented carefully over the years with assistance from outside and local support. It now includes a range of interesting work and such masterpieces as the *Portrait of a Girl* by Frans Hals; the *Annunciation* by Francesco Maffei; and a further *Annunciation* by Philippe de Champaigne, bought for the Ferens by a local businessman.

Most provincial galleries have surprisingly little relevance to their locality, and though one wishes to avoid the parochial it is interesting to see the background and aspects of the history of Hull in the ship 'portraits' by John Ward, a fine local artist, and the later *Princes Dock, Hull* by Atkinson Grimshaw, one of the typical northern scenes by the artist who was born in Leeds. His city scenes were hugely popular in his time (1836–93), appearing in the Tate as well as Newcastle, Leeds and Preston, and could well become so again. *The Fish Market* by Joachim Beuckelaer, allegedly the first artist to paint this subject, depicts a stall in Antwerp but is equally appropriate here.

When I went to the Ferens in 1989 much of the collection was already confined to the basement in preparation for the extension, but I was given a guided tour by the Curator, Louise Carlton, which revealed a startling range of work, from the massive *Pride of Lions* by Rosa Bonheur to the small, untypical portrait by Spencelayh of a boy with his dead canary, *His First Grief*. This just avoids the sentimentality of *The First Born* by T.W. Elwell (see 'Popular Paintings' p. 236) which is probably the most popular work in the entire collection, along with Lady Butler's formidable *Return from Inkerman*.

Constable, Wilson, Hogarth and Sickert are represented, with a particularly absorbing Canaletto, *View of the Grand Canal*, where the water is devoid of the curly artificiality of his larger work, and the sky more subtle. For a moment I wondered if there could be a confusion with Guardi (also represented in the Ferens) until Louise Carlton explained that this is typical of Canaletto's earliest work, which I shall look out for in future.

A constant surprise in northern galleries is the excellence of recent and contemporary work: *Jerusalem* by Bomberg; *Top of the World* by the Yorkshire artist Edward Wadsworth; and the surrealist *Octavia* by Sir Roland Penrose, while sculptures include work by Epstein, Moore, Hepworth and Eduardo Paolozzi. Look out, too, for a blinding Bridget Riley and a 'clever' David Hockney, *Life Painting for Myself*.

Gerald Brockhurst, whose portraits have the glamorous realism of a Hollywood pin-up, tempered by a hint of menace, depicts a woman with a landscape behind her in *By the Hills*, and there is the rare chance to see a painting by Nina Hamnet, *The Student*, a portrait of Madame Dolores Courtney painted in 1917 when both women were involved in the Omega Workshop run by Roger Fry.

The Newlyn School are well represented by Stanhope Forbes with *At Their Moorings* and *Newlyn* (both 1906) and Walter Langley, the artist so admired by Tolstoy, with *Memories* painted in the same year.

Boulogne Sands: Children Shrimping by Philip Wilson Steer shown on the cover.

Leeds

CITY ART GALLERY

Apart from two country houses – Temple Newsam and Lotherton Hall – the main Art Gallery is housed in the Victorian building next to the famous Town Hall, which opened in 1888 with the gift of £10,000 from Queen Victoria's Jubilee Fund and which has been added to ever since until you find a superb collection in impressive, spacious surroundings today.

The collection is varied. Predictably, there are two scenes of urban Leeds by the local artist Atkinson Grimshaw, whose work can be studied in the book by Alex Robertson, the Keeper of the Gallery. Unpredictably, there is an unfamiliar landscape by the great engraver Gustave Doré of a *Sunrise in the Alps*.

Apart from major work by Guardi, Batoni, Mytens, Reynolds, Stubbs and Joseph Wright of Derby, the collection excels in paintings from the late nineteenth century up to the present day. Derain's *Barges on the Thames* is one of the best known and most popular; lesser known, though of equal interest, are works by Gertler, Augustus and Gwen John, Paul and John Nash, Wyndham Lewis, Christopher Wood, Carel Weight, Francis Bacon and Gilbert & George. Recent acquisitions include the new Glasgow Boys – Ken Currie's *In the City Bar*, and Steven Campbell's humorous *Men of Exactly the Same Size in an Unequal Room*.

Three artists are particularly well represented: thirteen paintings by Sickert, including one of the interiors of the *New Bedford*, and *Dieppe*; several by Wilson Steer, the alleged English 'Impressionist'; and Stanley Spencer's *Hilda*, *Separating Fighting Swans* and *Christ Entering Jerusalem*. Matthew Smith is represented by his masterpiece, *The Little Seamstress* (1919).

Three Men of Exactly the Same Size in an Unequal Room by Steven Campbell shown on the cover

MATTHEW SMITH

1879–1959

Although his work can be seen in galleries throughout Britain, the late Sir Matthew Smith is so unfashionable that he is virtually forgotten. As Vincent Price confirmed on *Gallery*, he is scarcely known in America except to a few collectors.

Conversely, eight of his paintings were included in the Royal Academy's exhibition of British art in the twentieth century, including his portrait of Augustus John, though John's own work was omitted. Apart from this recognition, his current neglect is surprising if you rank him among the ten leading British artists of this century.

Praise for Smith has come from the unexpected source of Francis Bacon, usually sparse in his compliments to other artists:

> He seems to me to be one of the very few English painters since Constable and Turner to be concerned with painting – that is, with attempting to make idea and technique inseparable.
>
> Consequently, every movement of the brush on canvas alters the shape and implications of the image. That is why real painting is a mysterious and continuous struggle with chance . . .
>
> I think that painting today is pure intuition and luck and taking advantage of what happens when you splash the stuff down, and in this game of chance Matthew Smith seems to have the gods on his side.
>
> (Tate Gallery Exhibition Catalogue)

When he made this splendid statement in 1953, Bacon may well have had himself in mind apart from his genuine sympathy for Smith's work.

Though Smith is usually thought of as an essentially English painter, he spent much of his life in France. He started work in Britain in an industrial job at the insistence of his father, who was a manufacturer, until he broke free to join the Art School of the Manchester School of Technology, followed by the Slade in London.

At the age of thirty-one he moved to Paris and came under the influence of Matisse during a brief spell at his school, before it closed in 1911. The influence of Matisse, a supreme colourist, and the other *Fauves* (Wild Beasts) such as Rouault, is evident in Smith's subsequent nudes and flower pieces, which are rich to the point of Mediterranean lushness.

Unable to stay in France in the First War, he moved back to London and to Fitzroy Street, where his neighbour was Walter Sickert, with whom he went on holiday, and where he became the lifelong friend of Jacob Epstein. Returning to France in the army, he was wounded, but was not discharged until 1919, when he settled at Grez-sur-Loing with his wife and two sons. His marriage, however, deteriorated after he met Vera Cunningham in Paris, who modelled for his series of nudes in the 1920s, and, afterwards, a nervous complaint led him to enter a Swiss sanatorium for treatment.

Although he exhibited with the London Group, he remained in France until after 1930 when he came to London in the Second War and lived in such anonymity that he was virtually a recluse.

Knowing that Roald Dahl was a loyal friend of Smith and a collector of his work, I invited him to appear on *Gallery* and included Smith's portrait of Augustus John as one of the paintings, to provide him with an opportunity to tell us about the artist personally.

Mr Dahl gave us a recollection which I find so moving that I include it here:

> I met him in the war, 1941 or 1942. I'd been flying a Hurricane in the RAF and was back on leave in London, wandering down Cork Street,

Dulcie   Mathew Smith   Southampton Art Gallery

when I saw a picture that bowled me over. It was the first picture I'd ever fallen in love with, and I went into the Redfern and asked who painted it, and they told me it was Matthew Smith. Can I see some more? They said we don't have any, so I said well, I'm going to see him – I was only twenty-five – and they told me you can't find him, nobody can find him. So I started a search all over London and it took me about two months going from one little studio to another, and finally I found him in the seediest ever hotel, up some stairs and I heard a tinny record of the Brandenbergs coming through the door, and I knocked.

   This chap opened the door, an old man in thick spectacles, pyjamas and stockinged feet with holes in the toes. And what I didn't realise at the time was the enormous impact this must have made on him, for there was this creature – ME – in RAF uniform with wings, and I did not know at the time that in the space of the last two months he had lost both his sons in the RAF – and that was fairly knock-out for him. 'Of course,' he said, 'come in, come in.' Probably he thought I had a message from one of them.

After this, they became friends and went together frequently to Paris. Dahl knew every picture that he painted and had them all in his own house at one time, until he found the artist another studio: 'We were friends until he died.'

Dahl's admiration for Smith does not prevent him from recognising a deterioration in the later work: 'Until he became three-quarters blind,' he explained, 'I rate him as a magnificent painter. The trouble was that he kept on painting for a further ten years and lost his sense of colour and design and everything else. And all those pictures went out on the loose, on to the market. A tremendous tragedy.'

The portrait of Augustus John shows Smith at the height of his power. Dahl says that Smith pointed excitedly at certain pictures, exclaiming: 'Look at that, isn't that wonderful?' and when Dahl asked him why, he'd say, 'He's not frightened of his paint!'

His study of John is fearless, painted in October 1944 when Smith stayed with John and his wife at Fryern and painted two other portraits now in Montreal and Newcastle, N.S.W., Australia. This picture was painted in three quarters of an hour, which helps to explain the surge of movement and the bravura of the brushstrokes.

John's verdict was arrogant: 'Another haemorrhage from Matthew,' especially so as his own portrait of Smith (Tate) looks insipid by comparison.

When people told Matthew Smith that his was the superior painting, he reacted with a characteristic *lack* of arrogance: 'Ah, but I had by far the more interesting subject!'

Other work by Matthew Smith can be seen in:
Aberdeen, Art Gallery
Cardiff, National Museum of Wales
Coventry, Herbert Art Gallery and Museum
London, Tate Gallery
             Guildhall Gallery
Southampton, Art Gallery

Port Sunlight
THE LADY LEVER ART GALLERY

Lord Leverhulme held the lofty view that he could increase the standards of his workmen by raising their ideals. It sounds somewhat patronising, though undoubtedly sincere. As the Chairman of the Merseyside Arts Committee has confirmed: 'Lord Leverhulme had strong personal views on the capacity of art to expand and refine the mind and the life of the individual.'

Conversely, he made his fortune from Sunlight Soap and repaid the community with his vision of a model village on the banks of the Mersey where he built his factory – 'houses in which our workpeople will be able to live and be comfortable; houses with gardens back to front, and in which they will be able to know more about the science of life than they can in a back slum, and in which they will learn that there is more enjoyment to life than in the mere going to and returning from work.' This extraordinary act of benevolence was enhanced by an art gallery to broaden their outlook – The Lady Lever Art Gallery, built as a memorial to his wife who died in 1913, which opened for his workers nine years later.

This was his showcase, built with Portland stone in the Classical style so popular before the First War, though slightly bizarre in such a setting. Inside it is everything a gallery should be: spacious, airy, and beautifully lit with natural light from the dome above. In the early days 150,000 people flocked here every year to gaze at the sculpture, Wedgwood pottery, Chinese porcelain, and eighteenth-century British furniture – as well as the paintings. These figures have slumped. Liverpool scarcely knows of Port Sunlight's existence though tourists leave amazed. It is well run by Merseyside Council so the lack of visitors is all the more regrettable and partly due to ignorance. Those who make the journey will be rewarded.

The art collection excels in the Pre-Raphaelites, who were prolific. Their paintings are scattered throughout the country, from City Museums like Birmingham to the William Morris Gallery in Lewisham; with private collections like Andrew Lloyd Webber's, although this is not open to the public.

Quantity is ultimately immaterial; quality counts, and in this respect Lord Lever's collection is triumphant, which is surprising since he was not the most discerning collector when he started in the 1880s, and bought a number of contemporary British paintings to be reproduced as advertisements for his soap. He was not alone in such commercialism; Millais was mortified when Messrs Pears bought *Bubbles*, but through good fortune or developed taste Lever acquired such Pre-Raphaelite gems as *The Scapegoat* by Holman Hunt; *The Garden of Hesperides* by Lord Leighton; and *Lingering Autumn* by Millais; as well as *The Blessed Damozel* by Rossetti – a formidable foursome.

Lord Lever's taste was predictable and literary for the time, with a sentimentality which subsequently went out of fashion but which is now gaining new popularity. Where Millais, for example, excels in a painting like the *Black Brunswicker*, of a soldier saying farewell, is that his sentimentality is unashamed, even proud. *Fidelity*, by Briton-Rivers, captures the expression in the dog's eyes to a point which *defies* sentiment.

As so often, it is Hunt who veers from one extreme to the other, from *The Scapegoat* (see p. 59) to *May Morning at Magdalen Tower*, with dainty pink clouds and pretty boys garnished with flowers. Yet his devotion to the subject is undeniable.

Those who find the Pre-Raphaelites unbearable can appreciate work by Constable and Richard Wilson; Turner's *The Falls of the Clyde* which is close to abstraction; and a rare self-portrait by Stubbs.

Asked for a personal favourite, the new director of Merseyside museums named the painting by John Singer Sargent of the thirteen-year-old son of his friend George McCulloch, a famous collector of Victorian art, with whom Sargent went fishing; *On His Holidays, Norway*. Fulfilling its title, Sargent has captured the freshness of the scene, the swirling water, and the boy's contemplative pleasure. It makes me wish to study Sargent's work more closely, and return to this delightful gallery near Liverpool.

WILLIAM HOLMAN HUNT

1827–1910

There was only one Pre-Raphaelite – Mr Holman Hunt

(anon, though quoted by and probably
attributable to, Evelyn Waugh
in his privately printed Essay on the
Pre-Raphaelite Brotherhood, 1926)

As Waugh explained in his Essay on Holman Hunt, to whom he was distantly related, Hunt's parents remembered the suicide of Benjamin Robert Haydon as 'a disturbing example of the difficulties of even a very eminent artist's life', and attempted to turn their son's 'aspirations from the studio to the warehouse'. In defiance of his well-meaning father, Holman Hunt refused to enter the City as a clerk, finding more sympathetic jobs for himself which included one with an employer who was an enthusiastic amateur artist and gave him encouragement. With this slight independence, Hunt spent most of his salary on painting lessons.

The crucial turning point was a visit to the Royal Academy's prize giving in 1843, when he met the young Millais, who won the Gold Medal.

'I say,' Millais exclaimed, 'are you not the fellow doing that good drawing in No. XIII Room? You ought to be in the Academy.'

The two were dissimilar. John Everett Millais was only fifteen, a year younger than Hunt, a beautiful, popular student beloved by his bohemian family, who gave him every support in contrast to Hunt's, even though they hoped that their son would be able to support them financially in his turn when he became famous.

The two young men loved each other on sight. Thomas Woolner, the sculptor who inspired *The Last of England* when he emigrated to Australia, accused them of homosexuality, and though this was wide of the mark they proved an incestuous group, falling in love with their models and those of their friends, yet so immersed in each other's company that their relationship could be misinterpreted even today.

Virtually adopted by Millais's eccentric family – his father played the violin in order to relax his son while he painted – Hunt found a new liberation and his own father was so impressed by his renewed confidence that he became more lenient.

Hunt soon established another relationship, with Dante Gabriel Rossetti, who was so precocious that he composed a blank verse drama at the age of five. Rossetti had written such an exaggerated letter of praise to Ford Madox Brown that Brown assumed it was ironic and arrived with a stick to beat him up. Instead, startled by Rossetti's genuine admiration, he gave him lessons for free.

Rossetti's respect for Brown remained undiminished but they were unable to work together and he went to Hunt instead. Within days he had moved into the studio which Hunt rented near Fitzroy Square, after the sale of a picture for £70 enabled him to leave the family home. In due course, Hunt became friends with Rossetti's brother William, and the suitor of Rossetti's sister, James Collinson. Returning after an absence in the country, Millais was decidedly miffed: 'Are you recruiting a regiment to take the Academy by storm?' Yet when he met Rossetti he succumbed to his charm as well.

In 1848, when Hunt was nineteen, he formed the Pre-Raphaelite Brotherhood with Millais, Rossetti and his brother, Collinson, and a protégé called F.G. Stevens. Of these, Hunt, Millais and Rossetti were the only artists of importance and at first they flourished. Hunt was able to sell his pictures and Millais received £150 and a smart new suit of clothes from three wealthy tailors for his painting of *Lorenzo and Isabella*, which showed consummate skill for a boy of twenty, even if the figures seem frozen in time. They signed their paintings with the initials PRB in the corner and it was Rossetti, with his penchant for intrigue, who betrayed them by revealing their significance.

The label had been applied accidentally after Hunt criticised Raphael at the Academy and another student laughed, saying 'Then you must be a *Pre-Raphaelite!*' Millais and Hunt had accepted the description readily, yet in secrecy. Now the truth was out and the Brotherhood – 'Indulging in the first thrills of rebellion' (Evelyn Waugh) – were regarded as revolutionaries determined to upset traditional values. Their declaration that painting had taken the wrong direction since Raphael and needed to return to the greater purity of the early Italians, seems innocuous today but it was regarded as heresy then. Attacking Millais's *Christ in the House of his Parents* (*The Carpenter's Shop*) (1849/50), Charles Dickens exploded into print in his weekly magazine, *Household Words*: 'In the foreground . . . is a hideous, wry-necked, blubbering, red-headed boy, in a bed gown, . . . (and) a kneeling woman so hideous in her ugliness, that (supposing it were possible for any creature to exist for a moment with that dislocated throat) she would stand out from the rest of the company as a monster, in the vilest cabaret in France, or the lowest ginshop in England.'

That a painting was capable of provoking such anger reveals the sterility of British art at the time, and this reflected the reaction of the Academics. Hunt and Millais were suddenly socially and commercially outcast, and Collinson resigned from the PRB. Holman Hunt commented, 'Our talk is deepest treason against our betters.'

Two men came to their defence. At the Royal Academy dinner in 1851, Prince Albert spoke of them generously, if only by implication, 'An unkind word of criticism passes like a cold blast over their tender shoots and shrinks them up.' Probably he had Dickens in mind when he referred to the vanity of professional

Cyril Benoni Holman Hunt   William Holman Hunt   The Fitzwilliam Museum, Cambridge

writers, 'who often strive to impress the public with a great idea of their own artistic knowledge, by the merciless manner in which they treat works which cost those who produced them the highest efforts of mind and feeling.'

Surprisingly, in view of Victorian snobbery, these words had little effect; it was an intervention by the respected critic John Ruskin which turned the tide of opinion in their favour once again. In a famous letter to *The Times* also in 1851, signing himself as the author of *Modern Painters*, Ruskin – ten years older than the Pre-Raphaelites – began with a qualification, 'I believe these artists to be at a most critical period of their career – at a turning point from which they may either sink into nothingness or rise to very real greatness.' He added that he did not know them personally and had a 'very imperfect sympathy with them', and no one who knew his work would suspect him of 'desiring to encourage them in their Romantist and Tractarian tendencies. They know little of ancient paintings who suppose the work of these young artists to resemble them ... They intend to return to early days in this one point only – that, in so far as in them lies, they will draw either what they see, or what they suppose might have been the actual facts of the source they desire to represent, irrespective of any conventional rules of picture-making; and they have chosen their unfortunate though not inaccurate name because all artists did this before Raphael's time, and after Raphael's time did *not* this, but sought to paint fair pictures rather than represent stern facts, of which the consequence has been that from Raphael's time to this day historical art has been in acknowledged decadence.'

In this begrudging way he praised the PRB for painting the truth, but a second letter a week later ended with the bolder declaration ' ... they may, as they gain experience, lay in our England the foundations of a school of art nobler than the world has seen for 300 years.'

This faith was vindicated the following year when Hunt exhibited *The Hireling Shepherd* at the Academy Exhibition, and Millais his *Ophelia*. Appalled by the rigid rules laid down by the Academy, Hunt embraced Ruskin's declaration to 'go to nature in all singleness of heart, and walk with her laboriously and trustingly, having no other thought but how best to penetrate her meaning; rejecting nothing, selecting nothing, and scorning nothing.'

This view makes sense in Ruskin's idolatry of Turner who *did* approach the truth, especially in his later work, yet that of the Pre-Raphaelites is frequently stilted and static by our standards today. It is exemplified by the bogus details in such pictures as *The Stonebreaker* by John Brett, with a jolly boy-workman in his bright red cravat and his puppy playing with his check-clothed cap. In revering nature through such love-struck eyes, they frequently made their rustic scenes look artificial compared to the freedom of the Impressionists. Sweetness was the vice of the PRB, the antithesis of nature.

Yet they saw themselves as the reaction to the 'dark satanic mills' of the Industrial Revolution, as William Morris wrote in *The Earthly Paradise*:

> Forget six counties overhung with smoke
> Forget the snorting steam and piston stroke,
> and dream of London, small and white and clean.

Turner and Gustave Doré saw differently, but Ruskin and the Pre-Raphaelites went to extraordinary lengths in their search for authenticity, with such naive idealism that Ruskin led a group of Oxford undergraduates to a 'back to the earth' outing armed with picks and shovels to see how the genuine labourers worked on the local roads.

Hunt lugged his gigantic canvas for *Rienzi* from Hampstead Heath to a friend's garden in Lambeth in order to paint a genuine fig tree, and carried back a palm from Kew.

The Scapegoat   Holman Hunt   The Lady Lever Art Gallery, Port Sunlight

He went to a further extreme in 1854 when he travelled for two years in Egypt and the Holy Land, the first of three such visits, in order to use the actual locations. There are two versions of *The Scapegoat*, which he painted on the banks of the Dead Sea at Oosdom, allegedly the site of Sodom and Gomorrah, and he was so obsessed by realism that three unfortunate goats died of exposure as this half-mad man, armed with a gun to ward off local tribesmen, painted the animals in the appalling heat. Returning to Jerusalem, he brought back sacks of salt mud in order to finish the feet, buying another goat which he placed in a tray of the earth. The earlier study had a rainbow symbolising God's covenant with man that the flood should never happen again. In the second, the rainbow has disappeared leaving a greater desolation, relating to the text from Leviticus: ' . . . the goat shall bear upon him all their iniquities unto a land not inhabited.' Poor goats. It would be nice to think that the skull and skeleton in the background may have been a memorial to his victims, though such a human touch seems unlikely.

By now the PRB had gone their separate ways. Seen off at the station when he departed for the Middle East, Millais gave Hunt a bag of sandwiches and Rossetti declared, 'so was the whole movement dissolved'. Far from being true to nature, Rossetti became highly mannered, while Millais astonished with such versatility that he might have earned more permanent respect without the Pre-Raphaelite label. His portrait of Ruskin is straightforward and ironic, as he fell in love with Ruskin's wife, Effie Gray, while he painted it and eloped with her soon afterwards, duly marrying her himself. A visit to Port Sunlight reveals the skill of Millais's paintings such as the *Black Brunswicker* with the sheen on the girl's satin dress as the soldier bids her farewell, while *Lingering Autumn* confirms his talent as a landscape painter. Regrettably, he is best known for *Bubbles* and *The Boyhood of Raleigh*. Ironically – in view of the early controversy – he became a President of the Royal Academy, and a baronet.

Holman Hunt was the only member of the Brotherhood to remain faithful to his principles, achieving a startling luminosity in his colours by using a white base.

In 1861 Woolner, who had returned disillusioned from Australia, introduced him to the Waugh sisters, Alice and Edith, the youngest of eight. Woolner married Alice while Hunt became engaged to Fanny Waugh – 'Every day I see the darling I discover some new merit in her,' and married her in 1865. In Florence, the following year, Fanny died six weeks after giving birth to a son. Grief-stricken, Hunt lost his religious conviction: 'I cannot say "Thy will be done" and bless God for this affliction,' though he gained courage in the knowledge that Fanny 'loved me beyond all measure'.

Due to a dry and fraudulent wet nurse, the baby boy named Cyril nearly died, saved only by a girl who, having lost her own baby, was put to bed with him.

Against the opposition of her family, Hunt married her sister Edith and they lived in illegal happiness until his death in 1910, when he was buried in St Paul's.

By then he had published the definitive work on the Pre-Raphaelites, received the Order of Merit, and had been venerated for such paintings as *The Light of the World* (there are two versions, in Keble College, Oxford, and St Paul's) which was sent on tour to Australia where people travelled from the outback, wept and fainted when they saw it.

Possibly influenced by his personal relationship, Evelyn Waugh, who hoped to write Hunt's biography (and what a treat that would have been) described *The Awakening Conscience* as 'perhaps, the noblest painting by any Englishman'. I have chosen the simpler and less characteristic portrait of his son Cyril, by now a confident and handsome boy, recovered from the traumas surrounding his childhood.

Works by Hunt can be seen in:
Sudley
Manchester, City Art Gallery
Birmingham, City Art Gallery
Wightwick Manor

Liverpool

THE WALKER ART GALLERY

When you leave Lime Street Station in Liverpool you are confronted by a darkened 'mock-up' (as film-makers might call it) of Ancient Rome. Among the municipal buildings in the neoclassical style, the Walker Art Gallery is overwhelming on the outside though more fun within. Indeed, there is a deliberate effort to make it so, with an unpretentious cafe on the ground floor, and special displays which are relevant to the community: the art of the Beatles; or the work of local children which persuades proud parents to enter portals which they would not normally dare to enter. The galleries are thronged.

The gallery was named after a wealthy brewer who reciprocated his appointment as Mayor of Liverpool in 1873 by donating the building to the city to be constructed at his own expense. It opened in 1877 based on the collection bought from William Roscoe, a self-educated lawyer, banker, writer and philanthropist of the eighteenth century, whose paintings included the *Pietà* by Ercole de Roberti (1450–96) originally part of several panels for an altarpiece in Bologna. A comparable work from the Netherlandish School is *The Entombment* by the Master of the Virgo inter Virgines, so named because of the artist's *Virgin amongst Virgins* in Amsterdam, echoed by his triptych in the Bowes Museum.

Added to over the years, this collection has a splendid range today, with such masterpieces as *A Green Monkey*, *Molly Longlegs and Her Jockey*, and a *Horse Frightened by a Lion*; amongst the finest work by Stubbs.

The self-portrait of the *Artist as a Young Man* by Rembrandt is deservedly well known, and so, in a very different context, is *And When Did You Last See Your Father?* by W.F. Yeames, of a boy in blue satin interrogated by a group of Roundheads. Note the '*And*', for if you produce a postcard and ask for the exact title, most people would omit it. I have won money on this!

To list the paintings would become too wearisome for the reader, so these are a few to look out for; Hogarth's dynamic *David Garrick as Richard III*, for they were close friends and Garrick collected Hogarth's work and dedicated a play to him. The head was painted from life and set later into the rest of the picture, with the result that Garrick is virtually neckless though none the less active.

Cranach's feline nude of *The Nymph of the Fountain* is as much a matter of taste as the florid, gargantuan *Samson* by Solomon, hung above the stairs and joined by Haydon's *Wellington at Waterloo*.

The Walker is rich in the Pre-Raphaelites, with many of their most important paintings: Millais's early *Lorenzo and Isabella*, skilfully painted yet curiously static, with the 'cast' avoiding each other's eyes; Holman Hunt's *The Triumph of the Innocents*; John Brett's *The Stonebreaker*, absurdly romanticised though praised by Ruskin; and Lord Leighton's sensual *Perseus and Andromeda* competing with the girls of Albert Moore.

A portrait of Edward Lear, described by Hunt as 'a child of the Pre-Raphaelites', was one of the studies in the Pre-Raphaelite Brotherhood exhibition in 1989. Drawings for larger pictures such as this and the loose sketch for the Christ Child in *The Triumph of the Innocents* were frequently stronger and more spontaneous than the finished work.

The Walker also excels in twentieth-century art with two of the finest Sickerts – the cheerful *Bathers at Dieppe*, and the darker interior of *The Old Bedford Theatre*. Robert Bevan, an artist who is neglected, is represented by *Under the Hammer*; Stanhope Forbes by work which is definitive of the Newlyn School – *Off to the Fishing Ground*; and John Minton's portrait of Robert Hunt, indicating why Minton is once again becoming fashionable.

Yet, superior and stronger than Minton is Lucian Freud's powerful *Paddington Interior* with Harry Diamond, Soho 'layabout' and now a talented photographer, standing by a wilting palm tree, captured to perfection down to the reflection in his glasses and the details of the street outside. Realistically painted from a distance, apparently spontaneous close up, and curiously evocative, this is one of the most popular pictures in the Walker Art Gallery. Another is Cézanne's brilliant, appalling *Murder*.

The John Moores Liverpool Exhibition to encourage contemporary art, is held here every two years. With an imaginative young director, Julian Treuherz, the future of the Walker promises new excitement.

EDWARD LEAR

1812–88

Famous for his *Book of Nonsense* and such classic verse as *The Owl and the Pussy Cat*, Lear epitomised the indomitable nature of the true Victorian. One of fifteen children, he overcame the asthma and epilepsy which marred his childhood. Short-sighted, he became a meticulous artist who needed a close-up molecular glass to sketch the details of the owls and parrots he saw in the zoological gardens, but which were so accurate that the Earl of Derby asked him to illustrate a book on Derby's own private zoo. While he was doing so, he wrote his Nonsense Verse to amuse Lord Derby's children.

An indomitable traveller, his paintings are largely the product of his journeys to the Mediterranean and the Middle East, which were the inspiration for his limericks too:

> There was an old man of Corfu
> Who never knew what he should do;
> So he rushed up and down till the sun made him brown
> That bewildered Old Man of Corfu.

Although he could be described as a *petit-maître*, his work has charm and

A View of the Pyramids, Gizēh   Edward Lear   Courtesy of the Fine Art Society

considerable delicacy, and his meticulous landscapes were absorbing to the Victorians before the age of photography. From 1836, at the age of twenty-four, to 1874, he spent only two years entirely in England. At the age of sixty he travelled to remote parts of Ceylon and India at the invitation of the Viceroy, writing with exultation, 'Let the inhabitants of the world be divided into two classes – them as has seen the Taj Mahal – and them as hasn't.' When he published his *Journals of a Landscape Painter in Greece and Albania* in 1851, Lord Tennyson wrote a poem for him, *To E.L. on his Travels in Greece,* and the score for Tennyson's poem *Tears Idle Tears,* which Lear had set to music, can be seen – as another form of tribute – in the foreground of Holman Hunt's *Awakening Conscience.*

It has been claimed that Lear suffered from depression and 'psychosomatic illness' which explains why he was constantly on the move. Admittedly he had much to be depressed about, a suppressed homosexual apart from his genuine handicaps; but the claim ignores his innate curiosity, his appreciation of travel, and inimitable humour. A classical scholar, Charles Church, who accompanied him on his first Greek tour, describes Lear's sense of fun: 'Travelling in company with Edward Lear, his truthful and delicate pencil made captive many an exquisite combination of poetic mountain and of broad plain, or he fearlessly sketched the wild palikari as they strutted in the bazaar or skipped down the mountain pass and stopped to drink at the wayside spring. As we journeyed, he would sing out some Italian air or chant with deep feeling some Tennysonian verse as "The Lotus Eaters", sitting on the yellow shore of the little bay of Aulis, or throw off some nonsense ditty, as in the mid-day halt by the hot sulphur-springs of Thermopylae:–

> There was an old man of Thermopylae
> who never did anything properly.

Encouraged to visit the Holy Land by Holman Hunt, Lear described his inadequacy on reaching Petra, in words which were far from inadequate: 'What art could give the star-bright flitting of that wild dove and rock partridge through the oleander bloom, or the sound of the clear river rushing among the ruins of the fallen city. I felt I have found a new world – but my art is helpless to recall it to others, or to represent it to those who have never seen it.'

Apart from a young barrister, Franklin Lushington, with whom he was unhappily in love, his constant companion was his faithful Greek servant Giorgio Kokkalis, who came from Corfu where Lushington was based, and stayed with him for thirty years.

Holman Hunt gave Lear lessons, and in his turn Lear was invited to teach Queen Victoria how to draw, yet in spite of such influential friends Lear was not well off, taking seven years before he found someone who would buy the picture which was probably his masterpiece, *Cedars of Lebanon*. After 1869 he complained to Holman Hunt, 'My life, or rather what I do with the rest of it, must be essentially topographical; I do not look to painting much in me at all.' And in 1873, the year before he stopped travelling, he confided to a friend, 'a sedentary life after moving about as I have done since I was twenty-four years old, will infallibly finish me off SUDDINGLY. And although I may be finished equally suddingly if I move about, yet I incline to think a thorough change will affect me for better rather than wusse.'

At one moment of disillusionment, he found comfort in creating work, 'which not only gives pleasures to its possessors at present but may continue to do so to hundreds of others for a century or more.' He died at San Remo and now, a hundred years later, his work not only continues to give pleasure but is much sought after, though he claimed he found it 'painful and disagreeable' to do.

THE TATE GALLERY

> I like myself art works which sort of ambush you, that in a sense take you by surprise because you can be in a place for some time and not even know that they are there, then suddenly you see them . . . I don't like art that dominates you, that is coming at you and is assailing you and is making an attack. I like work that is just there until it needs you and you need it.
>
> Carl André

In the splendid setting of the grand old Liverpool docks, with the River Mersey on one side and sailing ships with a Maritime Museum nearby, this is an exemplary restoration, though my taxi found it hard to identify and could not drop me outside. As there is 'full disabled access', I assume he was singularly ill-informed, but you may need to persevere. It is worth it, but I must admit to a slight disappointment when I was shown a gallery by a helpful assistant only to find it empty apart from some bricks, radiators and ventilators presumably left behind by the builders, though this was odd, for everything else was spotless. A closer look revealed that this was an exhibition devoted to Minimalism, and the bricks no less were little more than the controversial work of Carl André. At least I had seen them at last, face to face, brick to brick.

The other exhibition at that time was of Walter Sickert, and I was surprised to find several inferior paintings but not the invigorating *Bathers* or nostalgic *Old Bedford*, which hang in the Walker Gallery nearby.

Conversely, the permanent exhibition of sculpture upstairs is the best collection of twentieth-century sculpture I have seen and perfectly presented. Also, I am glad to report that the exhibition which succeeded Sickert, of the women in Degas's paintings, proved an unqualified triumph.

Manchester

THE CITY ART GALLERY

It is hardly surprising that Manchester possesses one of the grandest art galleries in Britain, worthy of a city which has always been a centre of the arts, especially when it commanded respect in the last century as England's second capital.

Now that the 'planners' have torn out the heart of the city, replacing it with a wilderness of graffiti-stained concrete, the gallery in Mosley Street provides a reminder of the former splendour, when Manchester was the largest textile city in the world.

The neoclassical building so beloved by the Victorians was an early though major work by Sir Charles Barry, designed for the Manchester Institution for Fine Arts to equip the local industries with a club, temporary exhibition gallery, life-class and lecture hall. It was completed in 1834 and the plaster casts of the Elgin Marbles which can just be seen above the entrance hall were donated by George IV. It became the Art Gallery in 1882.

When Timothy Clifford arrived as the new Director in 1978 the glory had gone. For the previous two years there had been no director at all, and Clifford had the gallery photographed at once to prove the dereliction of its leaking roof and tarnished rooms. Then he restored it as closely to the original as possible, a formidable undertaking as seventeen layers of paint were stripped to reveal the original colours, which then had to be analysed: an emerald green background below, terracotta and a rich dark green in the rooms above. The ornate, guilded hall was repainted, the statues and the Parthenon frieze with the Elgin Marbles restored.

Where Clifford excelled was in his attention to detail, scrapping the commercial stalls in the entrance, replacing them with Victorian furniture and potted plants. A blocked door which led to the earlier lecture hall at the centre of the staircase was filled in by a massive clock in a neoclassical case, with a security camera above, a clever combination of antiquity and the latest in technical invention.

The entrance hall to the gallery is one of the most resplendent, encouraging one to go upstairs to the landing where pictures are double-hung in the Victorian manner, which Clifford has adopted for the National Gallery in Scotland as well. When half-hidden, at least one has the need to see them more closely.

The result is a grand serenity as the Victorians intended, and the paintings are seen to their best advantage, many in their original frames.

The restoration is an astonishing achievement on the part of the local works department. Carried out at a cost of only £30,000, it is an example which other galleries could follow if they had the director to inspire them. With characteristic élan, Clifford explains: 'The great thing with provincial galleries is to inject some style, or there's the danger it could just become municipal tat. I spend my life taking risks.'

An unashamed élitist, he goes for the masterpieces rather than a quantity of second-rate work – 'That's what it's all about' – and in this pursuit he has acquired two fine Bellottos; Turner's *Thomson's Aeolian Harp*, accepted by the government in lieu of capital transfer tax; and the important work by Claude Lorraine which influenced Turner in his middle period: *Landscape with the Adoration of the Golden Calf*.

Above all there is Duccio's *Crucifixion*. Clifford fought to keep this for Manchester instead of letting it go to the Getty Museum in America; ironically, one of the donors who enabled this was Paul Getty's son.

The marble bust of Antonio Cerri (1635) by Alessandro Algardi is another major work, bought in 1981, and Clifford's final achievement before he left Manchester at the end of 1984 to go to Edinburgh was to build up the largest collection of Goya etchings outside London. They are among the most astonishing images ever made

– frightening, disturbing and beautiful fantasies of witchcraft, war and mystery.

Altogether, the Manchester City Art Gallery contains a formidable range of work, rich in variety, from the early portrait by Ter Bock of a sullen twelve-year-old boy – more convincing than Gainsborough's beautifully painted yet unlikely *Peasant Girl Gathering Faggots in a Wood* – to a popular modern work by David Hockney, a crayon of *Celia* – a sensitive drawing of a nude with just the eyes coloured.

On the way, *Ducks in the Stream* by John Herring Senior is as delightful as the title suggests, an appetiser leading to the main works in the Pre-Raphaelite and Renaissance Rooms, at the far end of which is the massive, magnificent work by George Stubbs still in the original frame: *Cheetah and Stag with Two Indians*. Approaching this gradually it confirms that Stubbs was greater than the label 'animal painter' suggested, and the Tate's Retrospective in 1984, too, proved his versatility. The superb cheetah, which wears a red collar, was a gift from the Governor of Madras to the Duke of Cumberland for his menagerie at Windsor. The mottled fur quivering in anticipation contrasts with the pure white drapery of the Indian keepers who are about to demonstrate its skill as a hunter by sending it in pursuit of the stag.

French Impressionism is represented by a fine Pissarro of a *Village Street* (1871), though the scene, as so often with Pissarro, is uneventful. I have a special fondness for the paintings he made in England with such titles as *Route de Sydenham*, while the train which steams into Dulwich Railway Station is even jollier.

There is an interesting contrast in styles between Gauguin's gentle *Le Port de Dieppe*, an early work, which is purely impressionistic in the style of Corot, and the later *Tahiti*.

The collection is enhanced by the thirty-five Turner watercolours and the outstanding selection of Pre-Raphaelites, many in the original frames, such as *The Hireling Shepherd*, which was designed by Holman Hunt himself and decorated with wheatsheafs. This is a prime example of his work due to the brilliance of the colour, painted three years after he founded the Brotherhood, when he urged the members to paint out of doors with a palette of white porcelain to ensure the clearness of the colours. Spiritual inadequacy is suggested by the half-eaten apple of the girl who is portrayed as a temptress, while the shepherd who has neglected his flock clutches a death's head hawk moth in his hand. Heavy symbolism, and the alleged criticism of the Church for ignoring its pastoral duty seems obscure, though Hunt fulfils his aim of showing us 'a real shepherd and a real shepherdess' instead of the usual Dresden china figurines. The landscape is in full sunlight with all the vigour of summer, unlike landscape painters before him, and while it is all rather pretty the details are impeccable.

Two other important Pre-Raphaelites are the *Captive Andromache* by Lord Leighton, still in its massive frame, which dominates one end of the room; and the complex *Work* by Ford Madox Brown, who was inspired by the sight of navvies digging up the drains in Hampstead while the gentry stroll about nearby. An impressive work, though it is hard to tell how much of the scene is intentionally humorous, it was bought by the City of Manchester in 1885 in approval of such values as honest toil, and also in recognition of the artist who worked on the Town Hall murals and lived in Manchester in the 1880s.

GEORGE STUBBS

1724–1806

Stubbs portrayed the English landscape with a loving simplicity, made all the more poignant today now that such a gentleness no longer exists. Not only did he evoke the essential English countryside but he did so with such exactitude that his patrons commissioned him to paint their horses, grooms and dogs, which they regarded with as much respect as they did their families.

His accuracy was due to his anatomical knowledge which was self-taught and gained through exhaustive research. Studying anatomy in York he lectured on the

Self-Portrait   Stubbs   Lady Lever Art Gallery, Port Sunlight

subject to medical students and painted portraits to earn his keep. After executing illustrations of human embryos for a book on midwifery, he travelled to Rome at the age of twenty in spite of his assurance that 'Nature is superior to art.' On his return journey, he witnessed an incident in North Africa – a lion devouring a horse – which influenced the rest of his life, or so it is claimed. He painted nine versions of the incident, including the oil in the Walker Gallery, Liverpool, and the circular composition in the Tate, which retains the power to shock. Painted over enamel on copper, it is extraordinarily vivid.

Dissecting horses back in England, stripping the flesh from the bones, the stink from his cauldron upset the neighbours even though he worked in a lonely Lincolnshire farmhouse. The knowledge he gained enabled him to produce his life's work, *Anatomy of the Horse*, published in 1766. An art critic, Sir Walter Gilbey, wrote, 'We might almost divide our British painters of horses into two periods – those who lived before Stubbs and those who followed him and profited by his monumental labours at the Horkstow farmhouse.'

Yet Stubbs was greater than a horse painter who was merely accurate in his portraits of animals. He caught the subtle nature of English country life, winning the support of such patrons as the Marquis of Rockingham and the Duke of Grafton, who wished to record their beloved dogs and horses for posterity. Stubbs's only equal was Gainsborough, his contemporary, who painted the wives of the landowners rather than the animals, while recording the countryside, too, when he was able to.

Always an active man, Stubbs walked his usual eight or nine miles on the day before his death, but woke in the night in excruciating pain. 'I fear not death,' he told his friends. 'I have no particular wish to live. I had indeed hoped to have finished my *Comparative Anatomy* 'ere I went, but for other things I have no anxiety.' He died an hour later.

THE WHITWORTH ART GALLERY

The Whitworth Institute was founded in 1889, named after a local engineering magnate Sir Joseph Whitworth (1803–87), who had little interest in art and was plainly down to earth, according to the description by Mrs Carlyle who visited Manchester in 1846 and wrote to her husband, 'Whitworth, the inventor of . . . many . . . wonderful machines, has a face not unlike a baboon; speaks the broadest Lancashire; could not invent an epigram to save his life; but has nevertheless a talent which might drive the genii to despair and when one talks with him, one feels that one is talking with a real live man, to my mind worth any number of the wits that go about.'

Whitworth invented a 'screw-thread' which made him so famous that he received honorary degrees from Oxford and Dublin, the Legion of Honour from

Napoleon III, and was made a baronet in 1869. Careful with his brass, he left a sum of £1,227,781 9s 1d, of which £157,000 was set aside for a posthumous Institute in his honour, with a committee which included C.P. Scott, the editor of the *Manchester Guardian*, establishing a 'worthy memorial of our late friend . . . a source of perpetual gratification to the people of Manchester and, at the same time, a permanent influence of the highest character in the directions of Commercial and Technical Instruction and the cultivation of taste and knowledge of the fine Arts of Painting, Sculpture and Architecture.'

In spite of these high ideals, which made amends for the profits he made from munitions, and the gift of the first oil painting of *Love and Death*, presented by the artist G.F. Watts, the artistic side of the Institute was neglected while the textile collection was enhanced, and by 1958 it had run into such financial difficulties that it was handed over to Manchester University, making it the modern equivalent of the Ashmolean or the Fitzwilliam.

Over the years the University has enhanced the art collection with the generous help of the Friends of the Whitworth and the National Art Collections Fund, bodies which all provincial galleries rely on, despite such setbacks as the governmental cut of 18 per cent from its University Grants in 1983, which reduced the University grant to the Whitworth accordingly. The philistinism of the Thatcher decade notwithstanding, the Whitworth celebrated its centenary in 1989 with a lavish catalogue, *The First Hundred Years*, which is glorious testimony to the collection assembled over the last thirty years.

The Whitworth is famous for its textiles and designs and one of the earliest is the Embroidered Panel from Egypt in the fourth century, dyed wools on linen ground, on permanent loan from the Manchester Museum. Wallpaper designs of the twentieth century include Voysey's *Fool's Parsley* (1907) and Edward Bawden's *Church and Dove* (1925). The tapestries include the work of William Morris and a number of works by Walter Crane, self-styled 'Artist, Designer and Socialist'.

The Whitworth Gallery today has the original red brick exterior which belies the spacious modern galleries inside devoted to the work of such artists as Nash, Moore, Alfred Wallis, Christopher Wood and Lowry. More recent artists' work includes pieces by John Minton, Michael Andrews and Frank Auerbach, with a portrait allegedly of Lucian Freud by Francis Bacon (1951) and a self-portrait by Freud (1963), representing the vaunted if mistitled 'School of London'.

Though much of this work is on the grandest scale, including Gilbert & George, there is a particularly satisfying gallery devoted to a Prints Collection, with work by Dürer, Mantegna, Piranesi, and *The Three Crosses* (1660–61) by Rembrandt; a watercolour of *The Stud Farm* by Stubbs; and Blake's famous watercolour *The Ancient of Days* (1824), in which the 'Creator', Urizen, encompasses the world.

In addition, look for the brilliant example of Picasso's Blue Period, *Poverty*, painted with pen, ink and wash in Barcelona in 1903; and the Japanese woodcut of a *Sudden Shower over O-hashi Bridge*, which made such an impact on Van Gogh.

Among the British wood-engravings, *Winter Morning* by Gwen Raverat is outstanding.

Newcastle

THE LAING ART GALLERY AND MUSEUM

Although there was no permanent collection to begin with, this has been assembled wisely over the years with further bequests, loans, and contributions from such official bodies as the National Art Collections Fund. The paintings range from Canaletto and Sir Thomas Lawrence to Adrian Wiszniewski, Steven Campbell and Richard Hamilton's *My Marilyn* (1965).

Recent works include Pasmore's *Girl with Mirror*; a full-length portrait of a woman by Bratby; Bomberg's beautiful *Bideford Bay*, included in the R.A.'s exhibition of twentieth-century British art; a Ken Kiff, *Echo and Narcissus*, of perplexing interest due to this artist's popularity among students; and a fine example of Christopher Wood, painted in the year he killed himself aged thirty – of a *Sleeping Fisherman*.

Correctly, there are several pictures on the grandest scale by John Martin (1789–1854), the leading artist of the North East, whose fantastical images (along with those of Francis Danby) and biblical scenes might well have inspired the film makers D.W. Griffiths and Cecil B. de Mille. His titles indicate his subject matter: *The Destruction of Sodom and Gomorrah* and *Belshazzar's Feast*, which was so popular when it was shown in 1821 that it had to be roped off to protect it from the crowds.

While his epics went out of fashion eventually, Martin was one of the most famous artists of his time. He is scarcely remembered today unless you search him out in the Tate, where you can see the three *Last Judgement* paintings, completed in 1853 a few weeks before his death, or go to the Laing Gallery where his work is still honoured and still attracts the crowds.

Nottingham

CASTLE MUSEUM

Here you find the unusual attraction of an Art Gallery in a Castle, once the fortress of King Richard and King John, besieged by Robin Hood and his merry men. Cromwell destroyed it, a new castle was burnt in the Reform riots of 1831, but peace was restored when it was opened by the Prince and Princess of Wales in 1878 as the first provincial museum devoted to the fine arts.

Although there is work by Richard Wilson, Henry Fuseli, John Martin, with the chance to compare Thomas Girtin's *Pinckney's Farm* with Turner's river scene showing *Nottingham* in the background, the importance of the collection lies in the watercolours by two of our finest exponents of this essentially English art: Paul Sandby (1725–1809) and Richard Parkes Bonington (1802–28) both of whom were born in the town.

They are well and justly represented by more than two hundred pictures each, though such a quantity should not eclipse the unique collection of watercolours by other English artists, reflecting the tremendous popularity of the art which was part of everyday life in the eighteenth century. Joseph Farington expressed his surprise that the Duke of Atholl had 'omitted to build a viewing shelter' for visitors to one of the waterfalls on his estate, as the artistic equivalent to a hunter's 'hide'. To enhance the landscape in the artist's eye, there were 'Claude glasses', dark reducing mirrors which helped to frame the view and see it in better perspective by removing the glaring colours, thus creating the more subdued effect of a classical composition by the French painter.

There is a particularly interesting watercolour by William Callow, done in his early twenties, of *The Quai de L'Horloge* in Paris, a brownish, panoramic impression which is both topographical and dreamlike too.

The leading watercolourists are Paul Sandby, who took part in the evolution of the art, and Richard Bonington who belonged to its maturity in his own, short lifetime.

Paul Sandby had no training yet he was considered to be the leading watercolourist in the third quarter of the eighteenth century, praised by Gainsborough as the only man of genius who painted 'real views from Nature' as against the contrivance of Claude.

His gouache of *A Moonlight Effect* is shamelessly romantic, with scudding clouds and a shimmering scene half lit by the moon peeping past the cliffs, sufficiently audacious to avoid the slur of staginess – just.

Sandby introduced the aquatint to England and in 1752 he moved to London where his elder brother Thomas was deputy ranger of Windsor forest nearby. His *Streetvendor* from *Cries of London* is reminiscent of Rowlandson, though he was born thirty years later than Sandby who therefore has the prior claim to the genre. Although the two brothers were employed as topographical artists to begin with, and Thomas's *View of Nottingham from the South* was the first work acquired for the Museum after it opened, Paul's range was the wider and the more imaginative. The underrated precursor of Constable, he became a founder member of the Royal Academy.

His work can also be seen in:
London The Victoria & Albert Museum
          The British Museum
          The Tate

Richard Parkes Bonington was short-lived though the more interesting. He went to France as a boy where he became a friend of Delacroix, who declared that Bonington was carried away by his own skill. This was meant as a compliment for it is the lightness and spontaneity which makes his work so attractive. The impression is conveyed of watercolours allowed to bleed into each other, exploiting the element of chance, turning the accident to advantage at a time when this might have been considered laziness.

Bonington's *The Undercliff* is a beautiful example, subtle yet strong, as figures surround a tumble of boats on a stormy shore. It is hard to conceive of any watercolour which has greater vigour.

His merging of the colours exploits the watercolour in a more exciting way than his conventional *Coast of Picardy* in the Wallace Collection, while his topographical watercolours of a tomb in Verona confirm his discipline. The initials RPB in *The Undercliff* have the figure 18 underneath indicating that it was painted in the year of his death, revealing the talent that would have blossomed.

Sandby and Bonington deserve greater recognition and there are signs of this already: in 1984 the British Museum bought Bonington's self-portrait with the help of the National Heritage Memorial Fund which contributed £45,000.

The Nottingham collection comes up to date with William Nicholson, David Bomberg, Lowry, Victor Pasmore, and a slick portrait by David Jagger called the *Jewish Refugee*. A typical scene by Charles Spencelayh depicts an old man wryly examining a slice of bread with a carving knife and ration book beside it, *His Daily Ration*. An old gipsy lady, dwarfed by a massive hat with black plumes, is one of eighteen works by Dame Laura Knight which are hugely popular.

Of past masters, conversely, there is work by Boudin, Ford Madox Brown, Nevinson, Sickert, Wright of Derby, Stanley Spencer and over seventy Turners.

Preston

HARRIS MUSEUM AND ART GALLERY

Yet another stupendous building in the grandiose style described as 'Greek Revival', a curious anachronism right at the heart of Preston and an excellent reason for pausing there. A central light-chamber rises 120 feet through three storeys and the walls of the third floor are embellished with scenes of Egypt. Altogether, the dimensions are so palatial that as you mount the broad stairs you might be going to the opening of a senate in Athens.

Robert Harris was a local man who bequeathed the considerable sum of £300,000 towards an art gallery in 1877, which explains the munificent scale of the building which opened under the management of the Town Corporation in 1895.

Richard Newsom, a banker and millowner, gave a further bequest of paintings which formed the basis of the present collection, enhanced over the years by a discerning eye. Unexpected purchases this century include *Dorette* by Gerald Brockhurst, whose portraits are coming back in fashion, a work with the realism of photography belied by a strange hypnotic quality and an undercurrent of anxiety. Charles Spencelayh (see p. 75) is represented by *Why War?*, probably his finest work, which could also be accused of being photographic until you

Dorette   Gerald Brockhurst   Harris Museum and Art Gallery

appreciate the meticulous detail in the carefully assembled 'set' with his gardener as the model. These happen to be two of the gallery's most popular exhibits.

The Art Gallery Committee also had the foresight to buy Augustus John's portrait of *Dorelia*, painted two years before his death when he was no longer fashionable and his work reputedly in decline. This portrait of his wife in her old age is reassuring evidence to the contrary; wise and loving and tender, it proves that this artist is too easily taken for granted.

Early work includes such masters as Dürer, Turner and Blake, but it is the unfamiliar aspect of more recent British artists that is particularly rewarding. Holman Hunt and John Sell Cotman, essentially English, are represented by watercolours completed in an alien land: *The Sphinx, Gizeh* and *Palace of Hyder Ali Khan, Rajah of Mysore* respectively, and both reveal the artists, literally, in a different, radiant light.

Walter Sickert is there, as usual, with one of his melancholy Camden Town bedsits, *Hubby and Marie* (1914), a study in claustrophobia. Less predictable, is the work of three women artists: Therese Lessore, Sickert's third wife, an etcher and watercolourist; *Swans, Cookham Bridge*, a striking picture by Hilda Carline, reminiscent of the work of her husband Stanley Spencer; and a delicate study by Dame Laura Knight of *Susie and the Washbasin*, a welcome change from the raddled old gipsy women for which she is famous.

Contemporary work is more sparse, with the striking exception of Lucian Freud's *Still Life with Sea Urchin*; *Crucifixion* by Carel Weight; and Rodrigo Moynihan's portrait of Gabriele Annan.

This is a gallery where you need to make your own discoveries rather than head for one or two outstanding works. A word of warning, however: the gallery has a wide range of events, holiday activities and temporary exhibitions, as well as a shop and the Rotunda Café, which are further assets; but these close at 4.15 sharp, so arrive in plenty of time.

CHARLES SPENCELAYH

1865–1957

> Dad went on his way and ignored any advice from other artists, in fact he was an isolationist.
>
> Vernon Spencelayh, his son.

Spencelayh's particular skill might be conveyed if I compare him to Norman Rockwell, whose meticulous scenes of American family life adorned the covers of the *Saturday Evening Post*. Yet Spencelayh is the more interesting, even if he is less famous than his American counterpart.

You will not find the name of Spencelayh in the Penguin *Dictionary of Art & Artists*. He was a loner and it is tempting to label him as another eccentric in British art, but he was staid and stolid, exhibiting at the Royal Academy for sixty-six years until his death at the age of ninety-two. Although the man who threatened to kick Picasso 'up the bum' is a dubious referee, Sir Alfred Munnings recognised the charm of Spencelayh's work: 'Give me a million pounds and I couldn't begin to do one little part of it.' Yet, although Munnings was the President, Spencelayh was never made an RA.

Why War?   Charles Spencelayh   Harris Museum and Art Gallery, Preston

His scale was minuscule but his span prodigious. He was born in Rochester in 1865 where his father, an engineer, was a friend of Charles Dickens, a literary association which may have influenced Spencelayh's later work. Spencelayh was far from naive. After studying at the National Art Training School at South Kensington (now the Royal College of Art), he moved to Paris where he exhibited at the Salon. A founder member of the Royal Society of Miniature Painters, he was described as 'the modern Meissonier of English domestic life', an artistic version of J.B. Priestley revelling in the portrayal of the lower middle classes with an undercurrent of humour.

When he lived at Chatham he painted a number of mayoral portraits but his speciality was the interior scene, which he prepared as scrupulously as a stage designer arranging a set, filling an entire room with junk which he used as props for such an occasion. Enlisting his aged gardener as a model, he took from six weeks to six months to complete a picture and these were sold for just a few pounds to begin with – 'Eighty years ago Dad got £3 to £5 with copyright', said his son – but the prices grew until a Manchester cotton merchant bought several for £600. Now they are becoming recognised as unique curios in British art. Bruce

Bernard, the art historian who first brought Spencelayh to my attention, calls him 'One of the most curious figures in the history of British painting, worth remembering for the remarkable solid document he left and for his extraordinary painting skill.'

Spencelayh's work can be seen in:
Kingston-upon-Hull, The Ferens Gallery
Nottingham, Castle Museum
Preston, Harris Museum and Art Gallery

Salford

MUSEUM AND ART GALLERY

Only a few minutes' drive from the centre of the city, this art gallery – which is next to Salford University – is worth visiting for two reasons: the reconstruction of a street in the last century, complete with period shops and the interior of a cottage with kettles on the hob, a stuffed cat by the hearth, and china laid out for tea – and the paintings of L.S. Lowry upstairs.

For some reason, the best of the art collection has an emphasis on war: *The Control Room* by William Roberts (1941); *Tool Inspection* by Henry Lamb; and a wartime *Coal-Mining Scene* by Graham Sutherland.

The two most popular paintings are a bizarre snow scene titled *Famine* (1904) by John Charles Dollman, in which a shrouded figure leads a pack of wolves, plus a few ravens, across an arctic waste; and the cosier shipwreck scene by Mrs M.D. Webb Robinson, *A Volunteer for the Lifeboat*, which was exhibited at the Royal Academy in 1892, and shows the welcome from some bearded old salts as a pretty young lad steps forward to join the lifeboat just off-shore. It is a prime example of a 'Popular Picture' (see p. 236).

The purpose, however, of going to the Salford Art Gallery is L.S. Lowry, who was born in a Manchester suburb on 1 November 1887 and recorded much of Salford life. The Lowry collection is an eye-opener providing evidence that he is a more complicated artist than most people assume if they only think of him in the limited scope of industrial scenes and matchstick men. The collection is far superior to the retrospective exhibition in the Royal Academy a few years ago.

Surprisingly Salford did not even possess a typical industrial scene until it acquired one recently, discovered in a local boardroom. Where it excels is in the early work, which shows his diversity, and this is well recorded in the catalogue edited by Michael Leber and Judith Sandling, published by the Phaidon Press and Salford Art Gallery.

Starting chronologically, the catalogue shows the early influence of his teacher, the French Impressionist Adolphe Valette, whose work is collected today by the Duke of Devonshire. When you see a Valette of Manchester, before he returned to

France, the similarity to Lowry's subsequent work is unmistakable, though Valette declared, admittedly with admiration, that Lowry was impossible to teach.

Valette's impressionistic influence is also seen in *Country Lane* (1914), and lingers, resurfacing in *The Empty House* (1934) and as late as 1965 in *A Ship*. Lowry's seascapes are as fascinating as the industrial scenes, reduced to a bare minimum in *The Sea*, which is divided into three layers – sand, sea, sky. He excels in his depiction of simplicity, though he was far from a simple man, with *The Bedroom, Pendlebury* (1940), *The House on the Moor* (1950), and the two blurred yet poignant figures in *Two People* (1962).

The popularity and fame of the matchstick men detract from the observation in his closer portraits which convey the hopelessness of many of his subjects: the pathetic *Man in an Overcoat* (sketch 1960) and people whose faces stare vacantly, probably because they were vacant.

Conversely, the portrait of his mother was painted with such tenderness that Maggi Hambling mistook it for Rembrandt when we showed a detail on *Gallery*.

A conventional self-portrait in 1925, of Lowry as a youngish man wearing a cap, was superseded in 1938 by *Head of a Man*, red-eyed, desperate, which reflected his own feelings at the time.

Though far from a late starter (his *Still Life* was painted in 1906 when he was nineteen) it took a long time before he gained recognition with his first one-man show at the Lefevre in London, in 1938. By then he was fifty-one, devastated by the illness of his mother who died the following year. His belated success was meaningless – 'It all came too late.'

All of the paintings mentioned above can be seen in the Salford Art Gallery, many donated by Lowry himself. In Salford's Retrospective in 1951, the city purchased thirteen works and he gave an additional fourteen, bequeathing a further four on his death to which the gallery added from his estate. Less than a dozen Lowrys have entered public collections since his death in 1976 and though most possess at least one example of his work, only six galleries have more than three.

Anyone interested in L.S. Lowry should go to Salford. Certainly I found him a more considerable and compassionate artist than I had appreciated before I went there.

L. S. LOWRY

1887–1976

That a Lowry industrial landscape should be instantly identifiable is proof of his originality – also of his limitations, *unless* one is aware of the other work so far removed from his matchstick men.

Without such versatility, the familiar industrial backgrounds would suggest a clever use of technique but an absence of passion. Lowry himself cultivated a bluff, untutored exterior, with welcome flashes of unexpected humour – 'Not all the art

The Funeral Party   L. S. Lowry   Salford Museum and Art Gallery

in the world is worth a good meat and potato pie' – which are surprisingly endearing.

Though such remarks suggest a carefree attitude to life and art itself, everything that Lowry did was calculated. Behind the 'plain' façade lurked a complicated man. Far from being gullible, he asked for the cheque in advance when he signed a series of prints, and when the sum proved smaller than agreed he signed them L.S. Low .., refusing to add the *ry* until he was paid in full. You can hardly be cannier than that.

Laurence Stephen Lowry was born on 1 November 1887 in Rusholme, a suburb of Manchester. When he left school he attended private art classes held by William Fitz in Moss Side, and for ten years attended evening classes at the Municipal College of Art in Manchester, after which he went to the Salford School of Art for a further ten years. Altogether he was an art student for close on twenty years – so much for the legend that he was largely self-taught. Also, he had the considerable luck of having Adolphe Valette as his teacher in charge of the life class in Manchester – 'If you can draw life, you can draw anything.' Valette's influence can be seen in his own studies of Albert Square, such as a man pushing a barrow, which pointed Lowry in the same direction.

In 1909 Lowry's family settled in Pendlebury five miles west of Manchester, part of the industrial suburbia which he detested at first until he became so obsessed that he stamped his signature upon it. First he recorded it in pastel, then he turned to paint to provide the necessary weight. In 1921 he held his first exhibition in the offices of an architect, and it was reviewed by the critic of the *Manchester Guardian*, who complained that the paintings were too dark. Lowry was so angry that he confronted the man with a painting on an entirely *white* background.

'Yes, that is much better!' said the critic disarmingly. To Lowry's credit he said he could have killed the man but saw the light. The use of a white background became his forté, though the colouring of some of his early work was exceptionally fine: the blue and black *Landscape in Wigan* (1925) and *A Manufacturing Town* (1922). There is a greater sensitivity in this early work with a less meticulous use of paint, exemplified in *Peel Park, Salford* (1927) and the *Yachts at Lytham St Annes* (1920).

One of his first pictures, painted in 1912, of a mill and a woman dressed in a shawl (*Mill Worker*) reveals a genuine sympathy for the subject unlike the subsequent, posturing figures. Admittedly, some like *Father Going Home* (1962) are deliberately, if heavily, humorous.

If Lowry was ever young and affectionate, it was a short spell, but there is such evidence in the work of his early twenties, especially in the portrait of his mother (1909) which is drawn with love. But once he dealt in background he needed to fill it with figures – 'A street is not a street without people, it is as dead as mutton', and he saw them as objects. 'I am haunted by the loneliness of those characters made desolate by one set of circumstances or another,' he explained. Probably because of his objectivity, he was able to paint such pictures as *The Cripples*, telling his biographer Mervyn Levy that 'Cripples are funny to look at.' After Levy said that no scene could contain so many cripples, Lowry persuaded him to go on a bus ride to see how many they could count.

Lowry was never the childish painter that his admirers would like him to be. His 'simplicity' was deceptive. Developing his style, he struggled to make his pictures 'come right' as if they were painstaking exercises. 'There will be no passable forgeries of Lowry's paintings,' said a famous artist. 'They are too difficult to be worth the effort.' In fact, several forgeries have been exposed since then, for the clumsy imitations are instantly suspect.

Although he was exhibited in Manchester, Japan, and Paris from 1926 to 1930, his talent was largely ignored until a dealer gave him an exhibition in 1939. This made him famous. Too much of an introvert to be labelled eccentric, Lowry was odd enough to appeal to the media. He did not smoke, he did not drink, and is supposed to have died a virgin though he liked his young girl companions to dress provocatively and left a quantity of surprisingly erotic work. He never went abroad, owned neither a car nor a television set, and admitted he had never been in love. The few artists he admired were a very mixed bunch – Ford Madox Brown; Rossetti; Dali; Magritte; Münch; Lucian Freud; Paul Delvaux and Alfred Munnings.

His paintings speak in defence of this strange, lonely figure. I prefer the warmth of his early work, and though his great, imaginary, industrial scenes are admirable they become monotonous when seen *en masse*, eclipsing the splendid seascapes and the tenderness of the early portraits. Compared to them, his final work seems mechanical.

Perhaps he lost heart after the death of the mother he adored. 'She did not understand my paintings,' he admitted poignantly, 'but she understood me and that was enough.' Lowry died in 1976 at the age of eighty-nine.

Work by L.S. Lowry can be seen in galleries throughout the country including:
London, The Tate Gallery
Manchester, Whitworth Gallery
York, City Art Gallery
Salford, Museum and Art Gallery

Sheffield

THE GRAVES ART GALLERY
MAPPIN ART GALLERY

The Sheffield City Art Galleries are divided between the better known Graves, endowed by Doctor Graves, and the Mappin Gallery which has a greater emphasis on modern work, with the whole collection shared between the two.

It includes early work by Carracci and Pittoni, while the French School is represented by Corot, Millet, Daubigny and Bastien-Lepage, and the engraver Gustave Doré, though the most valuable works are probably the Cézanne, *Bassin du Jas de Bouffan* and a gouache by Bonnard.

The art of the British watercolour is best seen at the Mappin with work by Constable, Cotman, Gainsborough, Turner and Samuel Palmer; the Pre-Raphaelites are represented by Burne-Jones, Holman Hunt and Arthur Hughes, with later work by Sargent, Wilson Steer, Stanley Spencer and the almost obligatory scene of Dieppe by Sickert.

There is contemporary work as well by Hockney and Kitaj, but the outstanding work of this century is Gwen John's simple, poignant empty room in Paris where she lived in the rue du Cherche Midi, painted 1907–10, *A Corner of the Artist's Room*. The height of subtlety, there is little more than an umbrella and shawl leaning against a wicker-work chair and a small vase of flowers on a table underneath the window, yet it is redolent in atmosphere.

One of the favourites of the Assistant Keeper, Anne Goodchild, is the painting by Christopher Wood, *La Plage*, bought from the collection of Rex Nankivell. It is part of the touring exhibition of Wood's work exhibited at the Graves Gallery in January 1990, which provided the opportunity to assess this artist's work, which has been neglected until now.

In 1989, the Graves also played host to a remarkable exhibition devoted to paintings from the Chantrey Bequest 1883–1985 – 'Within These Shores'. Francis Chantrey, a sculptor of national importance in his time and highly successful financially, was born in Norton village, a mile outside Sheffield, in 1781, and so true to his roots that he was buried there at his request on his death in 1841.

His bequest has been described as 'among the most imaginative and generous for the nation' with the emphasis exclusively on British art, and has been added to meticulously over the years.

GWEN JOHN

1876–1939

Gwen John is enjoying the posthumous reputation of a sad, even a tragic personality. I suspect, however, that she was the type of woman who welcomed the role of victim and used her shyness as ammunition rather than defence. She lived her last years in Paris in a shabby room, eating little, devoting herself to her numerous cats, but she could have sold more paintings had she wished to or been prepared to exhibit them more frequently.

To be fair she had a genuine grievance as the part-time mistress of the great sculptor Rodin. Their relationship lasted for ten years and at one point she wrote to him twice a day, even after they separated. Two thousand of these letters are now in the Rodin Museum. It seems that he was the only man she loved and that he treated her callously, but it is easier to love than be loved and she may have preferred this role. 'People are like shadows to me,' she said, 'and I am like a shadow.' Certainly she was overshadowed by her brother, Augustus, but he was so ebullient that he overshadowed everyone.

George Melly quoted the painter Clifford Hall, who was sent to Paris with a message for Gwen John and found her a different personality from the one he imagined: 'She was rather forthright, very forceful, they went to a café for a drink and had a good laugh.' This makes one wonder if the myth was contrived. 'People cast painters into certain roles,' Melly pointed out. 'Augustus the great womaniser, she the shy little mouse painting her nuns and cats.' Such 'mice' can be made of steel.

To call yourself 'God's little artist' hardly smacks of modesty. Intensely private and completely disciplined, she revealed the truth in her splendid self-portrait in the National Portrait Gallery, which stares at the watcher defiantly, with unmistakable humour in her self-confidence. It was painted in 1900 when she was only twenty-four. Already her greatness as an artist is apparent and her expression conveys her certainty. Always generous artistically (if not financially) where his sister was concerned, Augustus conceded, 'The little pictures to me are charged with feeling.'

Born in 1876, two years before her brother, they studied together at the Slade under Professor Tonks. Afterwards she moved to Paris where she remained

A Corner of the Artist's Room   Gwen John   Graves Art Gallery, Sheffield

throughout the First War, though Augustus came to see her in December 1914 to persuade her to return. They exhibited together at the New Chentil Gallery in 1926 and she bought a cottage in England the following year, leaving for Paris to sell 'one or two pictures' to help pay for it. She never returned, not even for her father's funeral in 1938.

In the early days she studied under Whistler, whose influence can be seen in her work, and eked out a living as a model for other artists, including Rodin. She became a Catholic in 1913, which was one reason for staying on in Paris and explains her portraits of the nuns in a nearby Dominican convent. She was a loner and lived simply, rejecting the patronage of dealers who were anxious to sell her work.

She died when she was sixty-three. She was on her way to Dieppe in 1939, probably returning to England rather than endure a second war in Paris, when she collapsed and was taken to the Hospice de Dieppe where she died. Characteristically, she had left provision for her cats.

Today, as Augustus predicted, her rarer talent is recognised as superior to his.

> Few on meeting this retiring person in black, with her tiny hands and feet, a soft, almost inaudible voice, and delicate Pembrokeshire accent, would have guessed that here was the greatest woman artist of her age, or, as I think, of any other.

Work by Gwen John can be seen in:
Aberdeen, City Art Gallery
Birmingham, City Art Gallery
Cardiff, National Museum of Wales
Edinburgh, Gallery of Modern Art
Sheffield, Graves Art Gallery

Walsall

MUSEUM AND ART GALLERY

Walsall! The name is hardly glamorous, yet this proved the first reward of my journey north. I imagine that few people would go to this town north of Birmingham purely for pleasure, unless they wish to see the extraordinary and little-known Art Gallery. Until recently this was housed in the badly lit and slightly forlorn setting upstairs in the Central Library, though the surrounding streets are attractive and Walsall itself is surprisingly sympathetic, with a long pedestrian walkway lined with smart shops. In 1990 the art collection came into its own right at last, when it was moved to a listed house opposite.

The variety of the paintings is astonishing, including a portrait of his sister by Degas; an unusual landscape by Monet; Gainsborough; Turner; a Boudin watercolour and a lively oil of a naval lieutenant by Joshua Reynolds. Probably the best-known work is the drawing by Van Gogh with the English title *Sorrow*, which he referred to in a letter to his brother Theo: ' . . . in my opinion (it) is the best figure I have drawn yet.'

There is also a drawing by Millet and a striking colour etching by Rouault, *Trois Croix*.

The explanation as to why all these treasures came to be in Walsall is that the Garman/Ryan Bequest of 1973 enhanced the paintings already in Walsall's possession. Garman was the maiden name of Sir Jacob Epstein's widow, whose father was a local artist Theodore Garman. Miss Sally Ryan was a wealthy American sculptress and a poor painter judging by her *Nasturtiums*, who collected Epstein's work.

This accounts for the plethora of Epstein which reveals his surprising range: a handsome bust of T.S. Eliot; sketches in chalk such as *Men with Mice and Birds*; and a study of his famous tomb to Oscar Wilde in the Père-Lachaise cemetery in Paris, which was either his own design or that of Charles Holden who was responsible for the plinth – which is cleaner in line than the finished result.

Of similar interest is the maquette for the *Madonna and Child* in Cavendish Square in London, one of Epstein's most famous sculptures, and a blazing oil, *Autumn Landscape*, of Epping Forest (1933).

Epstein's daughter Kitty is celebrated by her father, with his sculpture *Head of Kitty with Curls* (1949) and a portrait in pencil when she was ten years old; also by her husband Lucian Freud with his *Portrait of Kitty* (1948). As Freud's first wife, she was the subject of numerous portraits including *Girl with Roses* (British Council) and the outstanding *Girl with a White Dog* (Tate). The heads of their children, Ann and Annabel Freud (1952), sculpted by Epstein, are in the Walsall collection.

Apart from antiquities, the collection includes the work of 135 artists including Rembrandt and Dürer and a surprising self-portrait by Thackeray. Making a selection for the fourth series of *Gallery* was difficult with such a wealth to choose from: I have a particular liking for Renoir's etching *La Danse à la Campagne*, allegedly of Suzanne Valedon and Renoir's brother Edmond; also the figure which Modigliani gave to Epstein in Paris; but I was particularly impressed by the small oil painting by Géricault, *Étude d'un Homme Nu*, and decided on this for our 'painting of the week' from the Walsall Art Gallery.

Until recently this gallery has been neglected and the annual attendance little more than 30,000. With the new premises, the Garman/Ryan collection should receive the attention it deserves.

Originally there were three drawings of *Sorrow* and judging by a letter sent to his brother Theo, this is one he sent to him. The model was Clasina Maria Hoornick (Sien) with whom Van Gogh was living at the time.

Sien was pregnant when he met her in the Hague and he considered it his responsibility to look after her and her children, but though he planned to marry her, they parted after a year. In July 1882, he wrote, '. . . I want to do drawings which can *touch* some people. *Sorrow* is a small beginning . . . (he mentions three landscapes and continues) In those there is at least something straight from my own heart. In either figure or landscape I should wish to express not sentimental melancholy, but serious sorrow. In short, I want to progress so far that people will say of my work, "He feels deeply, he feels tenderly" – notwithstanding my so-called roughness, perhaps even because of it.

Sorrow   Van Gogh   Walsall Museum and Art Gallery

'What am I in most people's eyes? A nonentity, or an eccentric and disagreeable man – somebody who has no position in society and never will have, in short the lowest of the low. Very well, even if this were true, then I should want my work to show what is in the heart of such an eccentric, of such a nobody.

'This is my ambition, which is, in spite of everything, founded less on anger than on love, more on serenity than passion. It is true that I am often in the greatest misery, but still there is a calm, pure harmony and music inside me.'

Wolverhampton

MUSEUM AND ART GALLERY

This pleasant neoclassical building, with spacious, well-lit galleries inside, opened in 1884 due to the acumen and benevolence of a local industrialist, Philip Horsman, who donated £5,000 towards an art gallery and then won the contract to build it.

Horsman, and another local man, Sidney Cartwright, a tin toy manufacturer, bequeathed their paintings which have been added to over the years. The collection today is surprisingly varied, including work by Gainsborough, Turner, Zoffany and Francis Danby whose *Wreck of the Hope* is one of the more popular paintings.

The most popular of all is predictably sentimental though humorous, of *The Dismayed Artist* who returns with his canvas to complete his picture of the rustic smoke-stained parlour to discover, to his dismay, that it is being whitewashed in his honour. The artist in the picture is Frederick Daniel Hardy himself, followed by his brother George, another member of the Cranbrook Colony of artists who lived in Kent. His paintbox and easel can be seen on the left, labelled 'F.D. Hardy/Cranbrook and Chari(ng Cross) to Staplehu(rst)'. The picture is much loved, and Wolverhampton has the largest collection of the Cranbrook School in Britain.

However, the most surprising feature of the Wolverhampton Art Gallery is the selection of contemporary art: Andy Warhol's *Jacqueline*, a silkscreen on canvas of Mrs Onassis; Roy Lichtenstein; Gilbert & George – *Good*, a cross of red roses and the heads of four boys; Peter Blake and Richard Hamilton. Recent additions are work by Steven Campbell and Adrian Wisznieuski.

There is a surrealistic work, *Atomic Flower*, by Humphrey Spender, who is better known as a photographer, and another by John Banting, one of several versions of *The Card Players after Cézanne*.

Two works interested me in particular: Richard Wilson's *The Falls of Niagara*, because it is so untypical; and *Queen Victoria in Windsor Home Park* by Sir Edwin Landseer which I had not seen before. It was one of several versions made from sittings between 1838 and 1839 and in spite of her admiration for the artist, was rejected by the Queen on grounds of etiquette – there was no female companion on horseback to chaperone her as there should have been, rather than the carnage of dead deer at her feet, which reflects Landseer's extraordinary brutality as well as his sentimentality.

York

CITY ART GALLERY

Founded in 1879 as an offshoot of the Industrial and Fine Arts Exhibition thirteen years earlier, this was a minor gallery until it was bombed by the Germans in the last war and reconstructed afterwards. It received a bequest in 1955 from F.D. Lycett Green which considerably enhanced the previous collection, predominantly the work of the local artist William Etty, with paintings such as the *Toilet of Venus* and the portrait of *Mlle Rachel*.

Silver Dollar Bar   Edward Burra   York City Art Gallery

Today there is a massive collection of varying quality: a good Sickert of Venice, a bad one of a butcher's shop; a *Nocturne* by Whistler, except that it is 'finished by Walter Greaves' which, admittedly, gives it an added interest, and Greaves's own *Japanese Figures on the Chelsea Embankment* (1876) (see Greaves, p. 118).

Earlier work includes a masterpiece by Melendez, *A Still Life with Lemon and Nuts*; Frans Snyder's *The Game Stall*, a disconcerting mass of dead birds; the *Portrait of a Man* by Jan Van Scorel; and a small, untypical landscape by Richard Dadd. If you like the overwhelming imagery of John Martin, he is seen at his wildest in *Christ Stilleth the Tempest* (1852), while Francis Danby follows in pursuit with his *Sunset*.

In this century, Paul Nash is represented by the haunting *Winter Sea*, painted after the First War and previously shown on Gallery; *Silver Dollar Bar*, a watercolour by Edward Burra; a *Café Scene* by Victor Pasmore; and the powerful *Betrayal of Christ* by Carel Weight.

Such a list merely creams the collection, though I hope it indicates the rewarding mixture of old and new.

RICHARD DADD

1817–86

When I started this book I had no idea of the vein of eccentricity which runs through British art. The French Impressionists, for example, seem a sober and stolid lot in contrast to the peculiarity of the British.

Of all our painters, Richard Dadd is the maddest. Literally so. His obituary was published in the *Art Union* in 1843 when he had another forty-three years to live, for by then he was dead to the outside world: 'The late Richard Dadd. Alas we must so preface the name of a youth of genius that promised to do honour to the world; for although the grave has not actually closed over him, he must be classed among the dead.'

Yet there were redeeming elements even in his madness. The start of his life held promise. Dadd was born in Chatham, the fourth of seven children, where his mother died when he was seven years old. His father remarried, his second wife dying a few years later after bearing him two sons. Robert Dadd was a respected member of Chatham society, devoted to his children, and Richard enjoyed a happy childhood, starting to draw after leaving school at thirteen. The family moved to London where Robert set up as a gilder of picture frames off the Haymarket, a sympathetic atmosphere for his son, who was admitted to the Royal Academy Schools when he was twenty. His professor, Henry Howard, must have exerted a considerable influence, though not necessarily to his pupil's advantage, with his studies of fairies: *The Contention of Oberon and Titania* and *Fairies on the Sea Shore*.

Richard Dadd quickly revealed an exceptional talent so it was natural that he should be recommended as the travelling companion for a wealthy patron called Sir Thomas Phillips, who needed a young artist to record his grand tour of Europe and the Middle East, anticipating the 'holiday snaps' of today.

It seemed the ideal arrangement with 'the knowledge that the young artist's powers as a draughtsman, and his amiable qualities as a man would render him charming in companionship as he would be efficient as an artist.' In fact, it proved a disaster.

The wealthy patron and his acolyte set off on their marathon journey in the summer of 1842. Sir Thomas was indefatigable, dashing up the Bernese Alps, crossing eighty-five miles in two days – switching from rail to foot to charabanc and boat, reaching Corfu, where Dadd was entranced by the 'deliciously villainous faces . . . oh, such heads! enough to turn the brain of an artist.' Onwards to Smyrna, down to Beirut and Damascus, finally pausing in Egypt.

It has been claimed that Dadd suffered from extreme sunstroke in Egypt and that this caused his madness. It is more likely that the sun precipitated an illness which had shown itself already, for he wrote to a friend before their arrival of having 'lain down at night with my imagination so full of wild vagaries that I have really and truly doubted my own sanity.' For Dadd this must have been a hideous moment, still sufficiently sane to try to ward off the incipient madness that was devastating the rest of his family. Out of seven of his brothers and sisters, four were to die insane. Though the sunstroke exacerbated, it was not the cause of his illness.

The return from Egypt proved a nightmare for the travellers. Writing to the friend in London who had recommended him for the post, Dadd confessed that he had never passed 'six more miserable days' in his life. He saw evil in everything; devilish spirits pursued him up the coast of Italy in the guise of an old woman, there was evil in the Vatican, or in a priest who did not understand what he was saying. Sir Thomas appeared to play for the Captain's soul in a card game on board ship, and he was sufficiently alarmed by Dadd's reaction to call for medical assistance in Paris, whereupon Dadd disappeared and fled to London, arriving at the end of May 1843.

The change was obvious to his friends. Dadd was gloomy, watchful and sometimes violent as he protected himself from the spirits which were still in pursuit. Outwardly he struggled to preserve a façade of normality which must have demanded a supreme effort, for when he left his lodgings his landlady found the carpet strewn with the shells of three hundred eggs, and discovered portraits of his friends which he had slashed at the throat.

Touchingly, his father clung to the hope that this was simply a case of sunstroke which would pass. Refusing to accept the doctor's advice that his son should be committed, he accompanied him to the country, and while they walked in a park Richard produced a razor and cut his father's throat. Forearmed with a passport, he escaped to France, which implies a curious element of calculation. Two days later his younger brother was sent to Kensington House Asylum and later that same day Dadd was arrested in a stagecoach on the way to murder the Emperor of Austria, after attacking a fellow traveller with an open razor. Deported to England, Dadd was committed to the criminal lunatic department of Bethlem Hospital, better known as Bedlam, now the Imperial War Museum. And, ironically, it was here that his fortunes improved. He was just twenty-seven years old.

At first he lost all interest in painting but he was blessed by the enlightenment of the Bethlem doctors: Dr Edward Monro, a collector with a keen interest in art; the young Dr William Hood; George Henry Haydon, and, particularly, Sir Alexander Morison, who was one of the two resident consultant physicians and a recognised authority on the treatment of mental disease. Noting that 'Dadd is an extraordinary artist', he realised that it would help Dadd to overcome his 'block' if he resumed painting and encouraged him to do so, amassing a collection of the drawings himself. I have seen the original portrait of Sir Alexander (sold by the Royal College of Physicians in Edinburgh) in which he poses with top hat before the background of one of his Scottish estates. It was based on a sketch provided by one of Morison's daughters, who are depicted in the setting as two fishwives. An astonishing painting – tender, slightly mysterious, beautifully painted, with none of the affectation of the Pre-Raphaelites. Perhaps in gratitude, the elderly man is painted with gentle compassion.

With new incentive and without the pressure of time, Dadd continued to paint, entering a world of his own fantasy. The doctors' encouragement was one of genuine admiration as well as a form of therapy, and Dr Hood owned thirty-three examples of Dadd's work, including the famous *Oberon and Titania* which is now in America. Still more famous is *The Fairy Feller's Master-Stroke*, painted the following year in 1855 and completed later. It now hangs in the Tate and depicts an

Sir Alexander Morison   Richard Dadd   National Galleries of Scotland

abundance of fairies in minute detail, a legacy of Professor Howard's interest in fairyland enhanced by Dadd's obsession, tinged by madness.

Surprisingly, his work is meticulously painted with none of the wild brush-strokes one might expect. His biblical and historic scenes, such as *Mercy* and *David Spareth Saul's Life*, have the authenticity of Leighton or Holman Hunt, though they are less pretentious. *A Mother and Child* (1860) is photographic in its realism, apart from the golden halo which suggests that this is a *Madonna and Child*. As so often in his work, a ship lies at anchor in the background, an echo of his boyhood days at Chatham. Only a few of his paintings relate directly to his madness, such as *Agony-Raving Madness*, one of the series of *Sketches to Illustrate the Passions*, an obvious portrayal of a chained lunatic. Other sketches are even more disturbing: the depiction of *Murder* as seen in the story of Cain and Abel; and the haunting image of insanity in *Crazy Jane*, in which the mad woman is painted with the utmost delicacy even though the model for the face is plainly that of a fellow male patient. There is a puzzling watercolour, *The Child's Problem*, with the sinister head of a child appearing behind a table littered with chess pieces and various symbols, while an elderly man sleeps in a chair wearing curious headgear.

In such pictures Dadd achieves the fantastic imagery which sane artists strive for. To return to *The Fairy Feller's Master-Stroke*, which took him six years to complete and is acknowledged as his masterpiece, however tiresome the subject matter, every figure has a symbolic purpose: the man with a white beard is a magician holding a club for hitting the smaller fairies on the head; Queen Mab's carriage is drawn by female centaurs with a gnat as coachman; and the 'feller', with his back to us, raises his axe to split a hazelnut and break the magic spell that everyone is under. The more you look the more you will find, even a 'tinker, tailor, soldier and sailor' at the top. Perhaps only someone who inhabited a similar world of fantasy could paint this so convincingly. Dadd wrote a long poem to explain it, of which this is the last verse:

> But whether it be or be not so
> You can afford to let this go
> For nought as nothing it explains
> And nothing from nothing nothing gains.

Polonius would have been baffled by such cleverness.

As conditions improved in Bethlem, so did Dadd, though he never recovered his full sanity. In 1866 he was transferred to the new countryside asylum of Broadmoor, which was free by comparison. Unfortunately his designs for the theatre there have been destroyed. Richard Dadd was buried in Broadmoor's cemetery in 1886.

Work by Richard Dadd can be seen in:
Bedford, The Cecil Higgins Art Gallery
London, The Tate Gallery
York, City Art Gallery

Scotland

Rev. Robert Walker   Henry Raeburn   National Galleries of Scotland

Scotland – the ultimate reward for travelling north. The art galleries more than stand comparison with those in England. Apart from the masterpieces to be found in the Scottish National Gallery on The Mound in Edinburgh, there are constant surprises everywhere. Which southern gallery equals the popularity of the Burrell, with the bonus of Pollok House a stroll away? As for the collections in castles or stately homes, those in Bowhill near Selkirk and Drumlanrig Castle near Thornhill, both owned by the Duke of Buccleuch, are incomparable.

Furthermore, there is an attractive new vigour to Scottish art, both in the rediscovery that there *is* such a thing, with a prospective gallery devoted to Scottish art, containing more than 1,000 paintings by such artists as Raeburn, Ramsay and Wilkie; and in the new Glasgow School, which I shall refer to separately.

Coinciding with the Edinburgh Festival in 1989, the Royal Scottish Academy devoted an exhibition to William McTaggart, described by the organisers as the 'peer' of nineteenth-century landscape painting (not excluding the Impressionists). You would need to have been a very dull dog indeed not to have been infected by the general enthusiasm, although the gallery attendants were as bemused as I was by the adulatory crowds thronging the exhibition. Seeing McTaggart's wee bairns in such cloying pictures as *Corn in the Ear* and *Spring* I had to agree with the charming girl at the pay desk where I bought some postcards, who exclaimed, 'But he's *terrible*, isn't he!' Admittedly the later storms are a welcome antidote to the sicklier stuff, but the girl had a point.

By contrast, around the corner in the National Gallery on The Mound, there was an absorbing, provoking exhibition to enhance El Greco's *Allegory*, recently acquired for the gallery, largely through the effort of its Director, Timothy Clifford.

Aberdeen was my final stop, with an astonished look at Landseer's *Monarch of the Glen* in Dundee on the way.

Aberdeen

ART GALLERY

Founded in 1884, Aberdeen has one of the finest collections of nineteenth- and twentieth-century paintings in Britain. They have been chosen with care, often to show the artist at his or her best, as in Boudin's *Leaving Port*, with his inimitable vigour of sea and sky; Gwen John's *Seated Girl Holding a Piece of Sewing*, tinged by the artist's melancholy; and the thrusting *Pope-Study after Velasquez* by Francis Bacon, which I believe is the same picture that I sold on behalf of the painter for £150 shortly after it was painted in 1951. There is also the freshness of Sir John Lavery's *The Tennis Party* (1885) which is understandably popular and encourages one to assess this artist again and search for more of his work.

There is a perfect still life of white flowers by Fantin-Latour; and a study by the influential French painter, Bastien-Lepage, of a child *Going to School*. Turner's vaulting interior of *Ely Cathedral* confirms his topographical genius, with a soaring sense of height and space.

It is interesting to see examples of a famous artist's work which are *less* typical, and here we have Stanley Spencer's cheerful beach scene, *Southwold*, complete with breakwaters and striped deck chairs and holiday makers bracing themselves on an outing to the seaside. Compared to Christ pottering around Cookham, or the lugubrious portraits of himself in the nude, this is wonderfully refreshing. Another surprise is *The Blue Pool* by Augustus John, of a girl whose face is little more than a smudge, reclining with a bright yellow book against a background of cliffs and water, a pleasing composition at the least.

Correctly, the Aberdeen artist, William Dyce, is represented by *Titian's First Essay in Colour*, a highly allegorical work typical of the Pre-Raphaelites, which was praised by their champion Ruskin though it is lifeless compared to Dyce's splendid *Pegwell Bay* in the Tate; and by Robert Colquhoun's *Woman in Green* (1949), an oil on canvas.

ROBERT COLQUHOUN

1914–62

A wild Scot, Colquhoun was the stuff of legend, devoting his life to art, drink and his lover Robert Macbryde. 'The two Roberts', as they were known affectionately to their friends, chose to live in England, where they were cared for by the Canadian poet, Elizabeth Smart, and lived together openly at a time when homosexuality was illegal. Soho was their refuge yet it aggravated their addiction to drink, which in turn weakened the discipline so vital to their work. Alien to conventional society, they appeared as doomed, heroic figures and this tended to eclipse the seriousness of their work.

That Colquhoun, in particular, should have been omitted from the Royal Academy's exhibition of British Art was disgraceful.

Like most reprobates, the two Roberts were deeply puritanical and would have loathed the glamorisation of their relationship which is bound to happen, yet it can be claimed that this was a case of 'love at first sight' when they met at the Glasgow School of Art in 1932. Macbryde was born in 1913 at Maybole in Ayrshire; Colquhoun at Kilmarnock, twenty miles away, a year later. After their meeting they lived together for most of their lives – prizes and scholarships took them to Italy and France, and they were staying in Paris when war was declared. Colquhoun enlisted as an ambulance driver, which sounds an extra hazard for the wounded, but Macbryde was rejected as unfit. He wrote to the army canvassing for his friend's release, which came about naturally when Colquhoun collapsed from a heart attack and the couple were reunited in London in 1941.

I met them ten years later. Of the two, Macbryde was outwardly the gentler and livelier, while Colquhoun smouldered with sardonic resentment. Macbryde kept home, whenever they had one, ironing the shirts and washing the dishes, accepting the lesser role as 'servant of the great master'. He did so uncomplainingly, anxious to promote the work of his friend to the detriment of his own.

In the 1940s their future looked good. They were befriended by the shipowner Sir Colin Anderson; Peter Watson, the wealthy patron of Horizon; such artists as John Minton, John Craxton, and Keith Vaughan; and the poets George Barker and Dylan Thomas. Departing from the neo-Romanticism of such English artists as Sutherland, they concentrated on figures in a semi-abstract style, influenced by Picasso and the Polish artist Jankel Adler, with whom they became lifelong friends. Their exhibitions were well received at the Lefevre and their lives were exuberant. Then the fashion changed towards either a total abstraction or a total realism, and they fell between the two. Worst of all, Duncan MacDonald, who had supported them with shows at the Lefevre, died. The new director was less sympathetic: the two Roberts were 'out' in almost every sense.

Colquhoun's latent pessimism, expressed in his paintings of old women, cripples and alarming animals, was evident as the two Roberts wasted their afternoons in the Caves de France, an immensely sympathetic, bohemian rendezvous in Dean Street where people drank their dreams away.

Then their luck changed with the promise of a retrospective at the Whitechapel Gallery, on condition that Colquhoun produce several new pictures, which the Gallery was prepared to commission. I sensed Colquhoun's excitement: 'It should mean a new lease of life. It may seem a bit early to have an exhibition like this, but the moment a painter has this kind of show there's a next move. I want to do something that looks like something,' he declared vaguely. 'The canvases are going to be bigger than ever before.'

'Yes?' I leant forward eagerly. 'And why are you making them bigger?' Colquhoun looked surprised. 'Because it's such a big gallery, of course!'

The two Roberts vanished from Soho. Sober and industrious they completed the new work and left for a well-earned holiday. While they were away, thieves broke into their studio, stole or destroyed anything of value, and, probably because there was so little of value to steal, mutilated the paintings. Simultaneously, the council evicted them due to demolition of the property. So the Roberts returned to the doorsteps of pubs, waiting for opening time. Little wonder that Colquhoun smouldered, though he did so with anger rather than bitterness, while Macbryde remained defiant. Asked by the dandy-writer, Maclaren Ross, if he prepared apologies for the people he'd been rude to the night before, Macbryde thought this over: 'Mebbe thinking up a new lot of rude things to say, next time we're drunk.'

Beneath the scowl, they were the gentlest of men. 'Make it with love and keep it simple,' Colquhoun told his students, which could be his epitaph. He died from a heart attack in 1962 in the arms of Macbryde, who was left inconsolable and moved to Dublin to stay with friends. Staggering back from the pubs four years later, he was struck by a car and killed.

Robert Macbryde is represented at the Aberdeen Gallery with *Still Life – Vegetables*.

Work by Robert Colquhoun can be seen in:
Aberdeen, Art Gallery
Coventry, Herbert Art Gallery and Museums
Edinburgh, Museum of Modern Art
London, The Tate Gallery

Glasgow

THE WILD GLASWEGIAN BOYS

Throughout this century, Glasgow's reputation has been tarnished by the image of the Gorbals, the tough, rough slum area dominated by the razor-slashing villains who were the local heroes. Vice and violence are more exploitable than virtue and this was the reputation fostered by journalism, film and even reputable writers. Glasgow's innate culture was ignored in favour of Edinburgh's prim and proper façade as the cultural capital, enhanced by that idiotic label, 'The Athens of the North'.

A sharper scrutiny would have revealed Glasgow's vigour: the genius of the architect and designer Charles Rennie Mackintosh (also a considerable painter); the acumen of such collectors as Burrell and McLellan; the elegance of Pollok House; the collection of Whistler's furniture, porcelain and paintings in the university; and the swagger of the early Glasgow Boys, emulated by John Duncan Fergusson, whose first retrospective opened in Glasgow in 1948.

Today Glasgow is vindicated. By contrast, Edinburgh's attitude towards the annual arts festival has been condemned by Dr Jonathan Miller as 'grudging, mean spirited and unwelcoming. They don't just bite the hand that feeds them, they spit on it as well. I sometimes think they deserve to have the whole festival taken away from them and just be left to rot.'

If sections of the festival do move away, they will head – and are already heading – to Glasgow, to share in the renaissance which has been encouraged by the discerning City Council. For once, the planning has been so imaginative, while restoring the best of the old, that a Glasgow Tourist Board opened in 1984 to celebrate the transformation. Tourists to Glasgow! Who would have thought it? Certainly not those who lived in Edinburgh. Furthermore the city has now received the honour of being designated the Cultural Capital of Europe in 1990.

Glasgow's artistic revival is a triumph, though Glaswegian sophistication was there all the time, as the galleries and printmakers could bear witness. Today's surge forward, which has happened so quickly, has been aided by the new generation of Glasgow Boys, a powerful group of young men, most of whom are friends and studied at the Glasgow School of Art: Steven Campbell; Adrian Wiszniewski; Peter Howson; Ken Currie; and now Stephen Conroy. There is nothing to approach their vigour in the south.

My first impression in 1985, when their work was shown at the Air Gallery in London, was immediate and I was somewhat shocked. Earlier that morning I had visited the three-day annual sale in the Smith Gallery, Covent Garden and though many of the pictures were pleasant I feared for the future of artists capable of such insipidity. There were no such doubts with the 'wee hairies'. Like them or not, their strength was undeniable. Writing in *The Sunday Times*, Marina Vaizey realised their potential: 'While each has a recognisable individual style, idiom and technique [they] share several characteristics. Their imagery is packed with incident, crowded with people. It is expressionist in flavour, rich in social comment: not café Deutschland, but pub Glasgow. It is fantastical, heroic, larger than life, but rooted in the ordinary. Spectators, hungry for readily communicated emotion, and delighted by the lack of inhibition, are intrigued, amused and moved.'

Today this Glasgow School is part of the international art market and work by Wiszniewski and Campbell in particular can be seen in numerous provincial galleries, as well as in the Tate and the New York Museum of Modern Art.

With such a closely-knit group, the label of a School is justified. They are much the same age – Wiszniewski and Howson were born in 1958 – shared studios and came under the influence of Alexander Moffat (born 1943), who has taught at the Glasgow School of Art since 1979 and who did them proud. His impressive portrait hung beside their work in *Scottish Art Since 1900* at the Scottish National Gallery of Modern Art in 1989.

In contrast to the doctrines in the south, Moffat taught them that art should have something to say. In the case of Campbell and Wiszniewski it is sometimes hard to understand what it is they are saying, but Ken Currie's work is brazenly political, with his murals on the history of the Scottish Labour movement for the People's Palace, while Peter Howson's tremendous *Heroic Dosser* speaks for itself. Stephen Conroy is enigmatic – that is his forte – but his posed scenes disclose a social comment too. They are all the antithesis of the passivity of abstract art.

STEVEN CAMPBELL

1953–

If there is a leader of the Scottish pack, it is Steven Campbell. A few years older than the rest and the first to be commercially successful, he established his reputation in New York after he won a Fulbright Scholarship in 1982. Staying on, he explained, 'If you aren't international you aren't anywhere, and New York is the international art capital of the world.'

One can imagine the impact he made there: a Scottish Gully Jimson on the

Stephen Campbell 1989

rampage, alarmingly direct, thickly accented, thickly hirsute, like a Highland bull about to charge, with a face that looks blasted by the elements. This could be fearsome without the sense of humour which is evident in such titles as *Men of Exactly the Same Size in an Unequal Room* (when they are clearly disproportionate) or *The Building Accuses the Architect*. When I told him that Francis Bacon insists that there cannot be humour in art, he groaned, 'I wish you hadn't told me that. I admire Bacon so much; but there is humour in everything I do.'

To this cause he turns the world upside down, as puzzling as Alice's descent through the looking glass and just as surreal. This humour is tempered by the sense of threat, of tweed-clad Man embroiled with Nature, who appears to be taking some revenge. This has led to the description of 'an anatomist of catastrophe', though Campbell sees himself in a lighter vein, even if his claims are grandiose: 'I decided to invent Modern Scottish Art, as I called it. I invented it by doing it – I started working on all these semi-Gothic Scottish things with a slight P.G. Wodehouse inflection. The moors and the mountains, the checks, the tweeds and the hunters, that sort of thing.'

When they were at the School of Art, Ken Currie came first in a competition and Campbell second, receiving the Bram Stoker award of £60. As Stoker was my great-uncle I expressed a particular interest, surprised to learn of this Glaswegian connection which was so unexpected. Campbell had never heard of Stoker before but the prize inspired him to buy a copy of *Dracula*, which he read mesmerised in the New York subway, which seemed a suitably menacing setting, and has relished the novel ever since. The combination of Bertie Wooster and Count Dracula is irresistible and explains a lot.

Plainly the toughness of the Glasgow background has infused Campbell's work as well as that of his contemporaries. He left school at sixteen and worked as a maintenance engineer in a steelworks for the next seven years. When he was twenty his grandmother gave him a book on Toulouse-Lautrec – 'not an art book, but gossipy stuff, scandal' – which inspired him to visit art galleries. 'After that my interest sort of turned into an obsession. When I was at the steelworks I was so pissed off with life that anything seemed a great alternative. I went to night school to get the qualifications to go to art school. When I finally got there I went wild. I went at it like someone possessed.'

Such exuberance is the virtue of the Scottish artists: 'Scottish cockiness, humour, push and panache all help. I don't think English artists have the temperament for this new expressionist stuff. The Scots really go wild at their thing, the philosophy is "bang it all out and get into the light."'

In 1986, now handled by the Marlborough (his paintings sell for around £15,000), he returned to Glasgow where he lives today. I met him at the Edinburgh Festival in 1989, where I had travelled with the HTV director Ken Price on a tour of the north, to invite him to appear on Gallery. He agreed at once, making no stipulation, demanding no fee, so long as he could have a good outing in the process and bring Adrian Wiszniewski as the other guest.

On that first meeting at the City Café and Bar in Edinburgh (a more refined setting than the infamous City Bar in Glasgow, but still boisterous) Campbell's exuberance was everything I had hoped for. He was instantly friendly and accessible, unusual and fun, and dressed in tweed plus fours with a hank of hair falling down one side of his face. Without the good humour of his wife he could well be troublesome (which I like), and when one of his little girls started crying because she hurt her hand on the railings outside the Café where I photographed them, he leant forward confidingly: 'It could be the vibes,' he explained. 'She always gets anxious on my behalf when she feels that I'm about to become *aggressive*!'

ADRIAN WISZNIEWSKI

1958–

Wiszniewski's father was a refugee from Poland, which explains the name, although he was born in Glasgow and studied first at the Mackintosh School of Architecture and then the Glasgow School of Art. Receiving numerous scholarships, he exhibited at the Air Gallery in London in 1984 and a year later his work had been bought by the Tate.

Wiszniewski could be described as the Glasgow School's 'Romantic', depicting dreamy, elongated young men, some of whom are based on himself. Although they seem to be wearing velvet suits it is claimed that he wore a dark suit and tie when he painted, a possible reaction to the hard upbringing in the Castlemilk overspill on the outskirts of the city. Once he became a postgraduate at the Art School, free materials were provided in abundance, enabling him (and Campbell) to paint on a grand scale, blazing forth in swirling oils and vivid colours.

His world has been described as 'Arcadian' and the languid first impression he gives is heightened on closer inspection by a feeling of 'suppressed sexual desire', to quote the handsome catalogue for *Scottish Art Since 1900*. That is probably too glib for such a complicated artist. He is someone who becomes more interesting every time I see him and his tribute to El Greco at the Scottish National Gallery's exhibition in 1989 was particularly exciting, even if the message of his *Attack of a Right-Wing Nature* eluded me. It was startling yet somehow entirely apposite to see a Glasgow Boy in such a context.

PETER HOWSON

1958–

His work is a contrasting mixture of delicacy in the drawings and brutality in the massive, later oils such as *The Heroic Dosser*. Born in London, Howson moved to Glasgow at the age of four and interrupted his studies at the Art School by two years' travelling, which included service in the Scottish Infantry. These experiences inspired such paintings as the *Regimental Bath* (1985), in which a naked soldier seems in danger of rape, and *Closing Time at the Cally*, where he worked as a bouncer.

In contrast to the harshness of such work, and a few conflicting reports, he proved a charming, diffident man when I turned up unannounced at his Glaswegian basement flat. His masculine world celebrates boxers, footballers, soldiers and drunks in bars with such ferocity that it might be an indictment too, though the evident sympathy for *The Heroic Dosser* refutes this. By comparison, many of his drawings have a tenderness which suggests that of all the Glasgow Boys, he retains the greatest promise. A calmer man today, with large golden curls which give him the appearance of a menacing angel, he attributes the transformation to a happy marriage.

Death of Innocence   Peter Howson   Courtesy of the Flowers East Gallery

STEPHEN CONROY

1964–

The youngest of the Glasgow Boys was acclaimed when he took part in *Vigorous Imagination* at the Edinburgh Festival while still in his final year at the Glasgow School of Art. Dealers pursued him and he signed a contract which led to such legal complications that a writ was issued preventing him from selling or exhibiting his future work without their agreement. With the dealers reserving such rights, his work was not shown at all – a shattering setback for the promising young artist.

Breaking the surface once more in 1989, he did so with a considerable splash, propelled by the Marlborough Gallery, who had sorted out the legal problems and who can smell success before they make it happen. Suddenly he had joined the

Healing of a Lunatic Boy   Stephen Conroy   National Galleries of Scotland
Courtesy of the Marlborough Gallery

ranks of Bacon and Steven Campbell, also handled by the Marlborough. Moreover, the two years' abeyance in the wilderness might have done him good, for this first one-man show was a *succès fou*, with forty-nine works sold at prices ranging from £5,000 to £20,000 before the private view was over. The Marlborough promotional brilliance had triumphed again, ensuring Conroy commercial success while exposing him to a harsher scrutiny than before. Some critics thought he was overrated, but the majority agreed that he had yet to prove himself. One made the devastating if obscure comment that it looked like 'restaurant art'. Richard Dorment, however, had no hesitation in the *Telegraph* in claiming that this was a rare event, 'the emergence of a major new artist on the British scene. I have no reservations about calling him the most considerable figurative painter to emerge in Britain in the 1980s.' Dangerous praise for an artist in his mid-twenties, so unassuming that his hands trembled on his opening night, preferring beer to the inevitable champagne when Miss Beston of the Marlborough, and Francis Bacon, took him to the Colony in Soho.

Compared to the others his work is meticulous, carefully planned – often using models – and deliberately derivative, as in *Further and Better Particulars*, which is influenced by Degas's drowsy *Cotton-Broker's Office at New Orleans*, except that Conroy's men seem frozen in time, ciphers waiting in silence to be activated.

Two of Conroy's paintings were included in *Scottish Art Since 1900: The Enthusiasts* and *Healing of a Lunatic Boy*, the second of which I chose for Gallery. Both are characteristically enigmatic and the latter most disturbing. Sickert is another obvious influence, but Conroy has yet to break out with the high-kickers or music hall singers to be so jolly.

The Oslo Art Gallery bought a Conroy from the Marlborough exhibition but the Tate refused. When I asked Nicholas Serota why, he smiled, 'There would have been an outcry if we *had* bought it at this stage.' But I expect that Conroy will be in the Tate before the decade is out.

THE PEOPLE'S PALACE MUSEUM

This bastion of Glasgow's socialism, built appropriately in cheerful red sandstone, was intended as a cultural centre for the people of the city's East End, and was opened in 1898. It is primarily a historical museum, recording the development of the local Labour Party and such heroes as James Maxton, who devoted his life to the cause of Home Rule, was imprisoned in the First War for opposing it, and elected as MP for the Independent Labour Party in 1922.

The socialist theme is evident in the art gallery, with portraits ranging from early, much-loved labour leaders like Jimmy Maxton up to the present day with Jimmy Reid. Yet the picture gallery upstairs was formed with loans from the municipality to start with, including contributions from that embodiment of capitalism, Queen Victoria, who assisted with the inaugural exhibition.

Ken Currie, the first of the new Glasgow Boys to be shown on *Gallery*, is represented with such statements as *War*, a striking composition in the best of the political tradition. The old Glasgow Boys, however, are absent, due to their indifference to Glasgow's industrial past and their preoccupation with the present.

A colourful, full-length portrait of the comedian Billy Connolly by John Byrne is understandably popular, while the local artist and novelist Alasdair Gray has composed a collage from the contents of the handbag of one of the Palace's volunteer workers, with a ticket for an Elton John concert, a disco ticket, personal snaps and so on. In addition, there are thirty of his own paintings and drawings, for Gray is another local hero, older than the new Glasgow School, though supportive, and curiously neglected in the south.

Some of the most attractive features of this constantly surprising museum are the panoramic paintings by John Knox of early Glasgow, and the unassuming, friendly atmosphere is captured by the delightful primitive of a lady greengrocer behind her counter in a corner-shop with paper-wrapped cones of sugar loaves behind her, the bonneted embodiment of everyday life in the 1790s.

A Glasgow shopkeeper of the 1790s   anon   People's Palace Museum, Glasgow Green

ART GALLERY AND MUSEUM

This is one of those cathedral-like museums where the atmosphere is equally awesome, or would be without the brilliance of such paintings as Van Gogh's portrait of the Glaswegian art dealer Alexander Reid, so fresh that it might have been painted yesterday.

Salvador Dali photographed by the author in 1951,
with Christ of St. John of the Cross behind him,
bought by the Glasgow Art Gallery and Museum

The gallery developed from the personal enthusiasm of a local councillor and coachbuilder, Archibald McLellan, who started to collect in his twenties with such a museum in mind. Although he built a suitable exhibition gallery in Sauchiehall Street, he was so deeply in debt at his death in 1854 that the local council assumed responsibility for its maintenance until the present gallery was opened in 1902.

As usual the original collection was enhanced by further gifts and bequests, making it one of the finest in Britain today, too diversified for more than an indication here. Look in particular for Lippi's *Madonna and Child*; the fragment of Giorgione's *Head of a Man*; and Rembrandt's *Man in Armour*.

While large contemporary abstracts by Bruce MacLean seem curiously ill at ease in such solemnity, the Impressionists and Pre-Raphaelites adapt as usual, with notable work by Monet, Renoir, Sisley, Cézanne and Degas.

The most surprising, and incidentally the most popular work is Salvador Dali's *Christ of St John of the Cross*, which caused a sensation when the Glasgow Art Gallery had the courage to buy it for £8,200 in 1952, the highest price ever paid by the gallery for a work of art. The directors were accused of wilful extravagance, but they showed remarkable foresight, for the painting is worth several million pounds today. Then, the work was considered so blasphemous that a vandal attacked it physically a few years after it was bought and the picture had to be restored. Even today, the *Dictionary of Art and Artists* describes it as 'crude sensationalism'.

By chance I was the first member of the public allowed to see it, when I photographed Dali for *Picture Post* in 1951. In the late afternoon when the sun's glare was softening, with shadows cast on the rocks outside his house at Port Lligat near Cadaques in northern Spain, Dali beckoned to me and led me conspiratorially inside, past a stuffed white bear in the hallway, to his studio. 'My Christ is not yet finished, but sufficiently advanced. You shall be the first to see it.' The canvas was still wet, Christ caught in the same light we had left outside. In a startling feat of perspective, his foreshortened body floated above the familiar rocks, with the deceptive light at Port Lligat giving the illusion that the distant shore was suspended in space, a trick which Dali made surreal.

'My wish,' Dali told me, 'is that my Christ should be as beautiful as the God he is.'

POLLOK HOUSE

The triumph of the Burrell eclipses the faded splendour of Pollok House nearby. The crowds who descend from their coaches would never think of strolling down the pleasant tree-lined avenue, through parkland once owned by the Stirling Maxwell family, who bequeathed it to the city of Glasgow along with Pollok House and their art collection in 1960, because they do not know what lies at the other end.

While the Burrell thrives on publicity, Pollok House is a quiet, gracious building supposedly designed by Adam and completed by his son, which retains the reticence of a family home, complete with furniture and polished floors which are so immaculate that the paintings seem to hang on sufferance.

Yet the visitor, taken unawares, is liable to be astonished by these pictures. There are superb examples of Spanish art, notably El Greco's *Lady in a Fur Wrap*,

A Lady in a Fur Wrap El Greco Pollok House, Glasgow

painted in 1577 but so 'modern' it might be a portrait painted by Sargent; Murillo, Velasquez; and two small, horizontal oils by Goya of *Boys Playing at Soldiers*, which must be priceless. When I showed these on Gallery, the panels were overwhelmed, previously unaware of their existence.

British art is distinguished by six works by William Blake, including *Adam Naming the Beasts* and *Eve Naming the Birds*. Painted in tempera, they are less overpowering than Blake's more dramatic, visionary subjects, and reveal a delightful, almost naive simplicity.

WILLIAM BLAKE

1757–1827

Occasionally a talent illumines like a flash of lightning and 'genius' is indisputable. Original and shocking in his time, Blake's soaring vision is instantly recognisable today, so it came as a surprise on *Gallery* to hear him criticised by Maggi Hambling, who conceded that he was 'a great poet' but finds his work no more than 'illustration'. Waldemar Januszczak, then the art critic for the *Guardian*, said that Samuel Palmer, one of Blake's disciples, succeeded in fusing the message with the paintwork where Blake failed – 'there is a sense of control missing, the rationale is thrown out of the window, which I find annoying.'

Their attitude amazed me. If there was an English artist whom the panel would praise unreservedly, I thought it would have been Blake. To criticise him for a lack of anatomical accuracy (which was one of the complaints) seems to miss the point. Plainly his romanticism is out of fashion, though it was significant that the young Scottish student, Francis Convery, stated unequivocally that Blake was simply 'the best British painter'. When pressed that this was a 'definitive' judgement, Convery confirmed that it was what he intended, adding, however, that it was not only as a painter but as a poet and designer too.

That *literary* diversification was exactly what Maggi Hambling objected to, but Geraldine Norman (then the salesroom correspondent for *The Times*) agreed with the student: 'I think that poetry and art and painting come from the same source. Blake seems to me to be a child of nature – the dreams he put down on paper have an extraordinary quality. I don't understand them, but they come straight off the page at me – something very vivid and spiritual.'

Blake lived in poverty for most of his life, starting as an engraver. When he was a boy he spent hours in Westminster Abbey drawing details for a publisher and the impressions of those grey, recumbent figures carved in stone above their tombs are echoed in his later work. Another inspiration came from the prints he handled as a dealer.

While he engraved for others, Blake published his poems, which he also engraved and illustrated, doing the colouring by hand. *Songs of Innocence* (1789) was followed by *Songs of Experience* five years later. The famous watercolours for the *Book of Job* were produced between 1820 and 1826, the result of a commission obtained on his behalf by young admirers who rescued Blake and his wife from penury. His patron, John Linnell, a painter himself, provided Blake with work for the rest of his life, and he enjoyed the comfort in his old age of being surrounded by a group of young disciples who called themselves 'The Ancients', and included Palmer.

When he was sixty Blake learned Italian and read Dante. The late Lord Clark considers the hundred watercolours illustrating Dante as the masterpiece of Blake's last years, suggesting that he recognised an intellect which was equal or superior to his own, and found a new serenity in doing so. *The Whirlwind of Lovers* is literally that.

What is difficult to recognise is that Blake was a religious man devoted to biblical subjects while at the same time seeing them as something awful, with the Creation as a crime against humanity. *Adam Naming the Beasts*, at Pollok House outside Glasgow, is for me one of the most beautiful biblical scenes, conceived with an innocent, primitive quality at variance with his more complicated work. A curly-headed Adam stands under an oak tree, stroking the massive scales of a serpent which is wound around him, while cattle and horses and a placid solitary lion parade across the background. It is a moment of calm. Yet the earlier scene of man's creation is horrifying when seen in *Elohim Creating Adam* (Tate), with Adam screaming in agony, his legs trapped by a gigantic worm, and God depicted as a bearded figure with massive wings, on top of him. *God Judging Adam* (Tate), a colour print finished in pen and watercolour, which belongs to the prolific output in 1795, is another condemnation of the God of the Old Testament. *Nebuchadnez-zar*, one of his most disturbing images, shows man as a wild animal, probably based on the illustration of a werewolf by Cranach.

Blake's vaulting imagination was the antidote to the Age of Reason, expressed in another magnificent image, *The Ancient of Days* (British Museum), of an old man measuring the world with compasses, apparently seen by Blake in a vision. The biblical reference, 'He set a compass on the face of the depths', might have inspired him too.

Blake refused to draw from life, for he regarded realism as unimportant. His technique was his own: a complicated use of watercolour and the eggyolk of tempera which has worn badly, due to flaking. Though his biblical scenes and versions of the Fall of Man are tinged with a sense of doom, he was a happy man, especially in his early years when he declared, 'Joy is my name.' Above all, there is the redeeming quality of his compassion. In the picture of Abel's body discovered by Adam and Eve, we see Cain clasping his head with grief as well as guilt, appalled by what he has done. Eve slumps over the body of her murdered son while Adam reels back, aghast. The dark clouds pursue the murderer, the sun throbs, even the shape of the mountains cry vengeance. It is a terrible concept of anguish in the highest sense, wholly comprehensible and elating too. 'When the sun rises do you not see a round disc of fire somewhat like a guinea?' Blake asks in his *Descriptive Catalogue*. 'Oh no, no, I see an unnumerable company of the heavenly host crying "Holy, holy, holy is the Lord God Almighty".' Blake, of course, is the author of 'Jerusalem'.

True simplicity is one of the highest peaks in art and hard to reach. Blake was simple by nature – once he was found in his garden naked, playing at Adam and Eve with his wife – and the following description is revealing of the man. It is an entry in her diary by the perceptive Lady Charlotte Bury, who went to a dinner party in 1820 which was attended by Blake and Sir Thomas Lawrence, the most successful artist of the day and the President of the Royal Academy:

> Besides Sir T . . . there was another eccentric little artist by name Blake; not a regular professional painter but one of those persons who follow

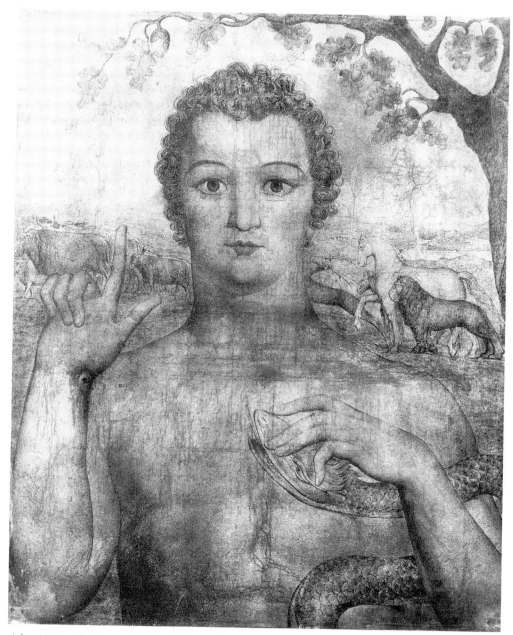

Adam Naming the Beasts   William Blake   Pollok House, Glasgow

the art for its own sweet sake and derive their happiness from its pursuit. He appeared to me to be full of beautiful imaginations and genius . . . Mr Blake appears unlearned in all that concerns this world. He looks careworn and subdued but his countenance radiated as he spoke of his favourite pursuit . . . I can easily imagine that he seldom meets with any one who enters into his views; for they are peculiar and exalted above the common level of received opinions.

I could not help contrasting this humble artist with the great and powerful Sir Thomas Lawrence . . . Mr Blake, though he may have as much right from talent and merit, to the advantages of which Sir Thomas is possessed, evidently lacks that worldly wisdom and that grace of manner which makes a man sure of eminence in his profession and success in society. Every word he uttered spoke the perfect simplicity of his mind and his total ignorance of all worldly matters.

The work of William Blake can be seen at:
Aberdeen, Art Gallery
Brighton Pavilion
Cambridge, Fitzwilliam
London, The Tate Gallery
         The British Museum
Manchester, City Art Gallery
Petworth House
Pollok House
Walsall, Museum and Art Gallery

THE HUNTERIAN ART GALLERY

Since it is part of Glasgow University, the Hunterian might be overlooked by visitors who are unaware that it has two outstanding assets: the best collection of the Scottish architect Charles Rennie Mackintosh (1868–1928), including a reconstructed interior of his house – a striking contrast of white walls and black furniture; and the finest collection of James McNeill Whistler (1834–1903), which is rivalled only by the Freer Gallery in Washington DC.

The museum's founder was a famous teacher of anatomy, William Hunter, who left his collection of medical specimens, manuscripts and paintings with the request that it should form part of a medical school devoted to anatomy. When this idea was greeted with governmental indifference he left his collection on his death in 1783 to his nephew Matthew Baillie, who gave it to the university. Since then it has been enriched by such bequests as Whistler's, due to his niece and trustee Miss Birnie Philip, with additional work by Rembrandt, Bernini, Stubbs and Chardin. The Glasgow Boys and the Scottish artist McTaggart also feature, and there is a comprehensive history of printmaking, with the staggering number of 15,000 items ranging from the fifteenth century to Picasso, which makes the Hunterian the largest print collection in Scotland.

The Whistlers include eighty paintings, one hundred pastels, including his first efforts as a child, and several hundred drawings and watercolours, as well as letters, documents and Whistler's own furniture and Chinese ceramics. The decorations for the Butterfly Cabinet were designed by Godwin, and one of the loveliest items is the *Screen with Old Battersea Bridge*, by Whistler himself, which I chose for *Gallery*. The screen consists of two hinged panels in gilded frames which are decorated with petals and Whistler's emblem of a butterfly in the top right-hand corner. The reverse side, by the Japanese woman artist, Nampo Jhoshi, a contemporary, reveals the Oriental influence on Whistler, with Japanese paintings on silk in the Chinese style and inset with Chinese characters, dated as late as 1867. The obverse has distemper and gold paint on brown paper laid on canvas. The two facets link Whistler's aestheticism of the late 1860s with his

Blue and Silver Screen with Old Battersea Bridge   James McNeill Whistler
Hunterian Art Gallery, University of Glasgow

nocturnes of the Thames painted in the 1870s. The university's catalogue elaborates: 'The embellished frame and the bright gold moon and clock face speak the same kind of language as the flowers and birds on the reverse of each panel. But although the composition of arched bridge, moon and river derives from good Ukiyo-e precedents, it is also a view of the Battersea reach of the Thames.'

Equally, *A Bridge in Edo* (Tokyo) by Hiroshige was an even greater influence on Whistler' depiction of Albert Bridge, which was being repaired. In a letter to a gallery proprietor in December 1872, Whistler mentioned that the screen was nearly complete and was intended for his leading patron, a shipowner called F.R. Leyland. Presumably they quarrelled, a regular occurrence with Whistler, for the screen was not delivered and he kept it for himself, showing it at his first one-man exhibition in Pall Mall in 1874. As photographs of his Paris studio and London houses confirm, it stayed with him for the rest of his life. The essence of Whistler's art, he developed the subject later in his famous *Nocturne in Blue and Gold: the Battersea Bridge*, now in the Tate.

The largest collection of the works of Charles Rennie Mackintosh confirms his genius. The house was salvaged before the demolition in 1963 and has been reconstructed with the interiors as Mackintosh intended, with the additional interest of several watercolours.

La Rue du Soleil Charles Rennie Mackintosh Hunterian Art Gallery, University of Glasgow

JAMES ABBOTT McNEILL WHISTLER

1834–1903

The English are wary of Whistler. We are suspicious of expatriates anyhow, and Whistler did not fit. He had not even fitted in America where he was born, attending the highly disciplined military academy of West Point until he swung to the other extreme and left for Paris to study art. He was twenty-one and became a friend of Fantin-Latour, Manet and Degas. Four years later he veered off to London and made this his home. Though never wholly accepted, his brush captured the subtlety of the River Thames as no Englishman had before him, certainly not Canaletto, who transformed the city into Venice.

One has the feeling that Whistler loved the Thames all the more because it was new to him. As Tissot caught the quality of London's squares so exactly that one can sense the musty smell of autumn and the damp-packed leaves in *Les Adieux*, Whistler detected the mystery of the river which eluded others, and, in his turn, made it mysterious.

This ran against the fashionable tide of the Pre-Raphaelites, for whom the subject and the story were everything. Their respective titles illustrate the difference: *Work* by Ford Madox Brown; *Nocturne in Black and Gold* (1877) by Whistler. It was this Impressionist interpretation which provoked the blistering attack by Ruskin, the champion of the Pre-Raphaelites and the most influential art critic of his time: 'I have seen and heard much of Cockney impudence before now,' he remarked ironically about the American, 'but never expected to hear a coxcomb ask 200 guineas for flinging a pot of paint in the public's face.' Whistler sued, and the trial was celebrated for the following exchange:

'Do you really ask that for two days' work?'

'No, I ask it for the knowledge of a lifetime!'

Whistler was awarded the insult of a farthing's damages, and the costs of the trial made him bankrupt, although he had enough spirit to persuade the bailiffs to act as butlers should anyone call at his house.

The Victorians liked outrageous behaviour but they felt that there was something caddish about his antics, such as throwing his brother-in-law through a plate-glass window; attacking a man on Waterloo station; dashing off to Valparaiso to take part in a local war – an act of bravado which ended disastrously. How the media of today would devour him!

Then Whistler made the mistake of looking foreign. Max Beerbohm described him neatly as 'Tiny – Noah's Ark – flat-brimmed hat – band almost to top-coat just not touching ground – button of the Legion of Honour – black gloves – exquisite hands, long and lithe – short palms.' One begins to understand why some Englishmen looked askance.

Added to this was his association with Oscar Wilde, which started in friendly rivalry, changed to jealousy and finally became a venomous hostility on the part of Whistler. The trouble was that Whistler had wit but little humour, while Oscar had both and enjoyed a joke at his own expense. One of their exchanges is famous though the preamble is less familiar: the art critic for *The Times*, Humphrey Ward, had gone to a Whistler exhibition and had pointed out that this picture was good and that one bad. 'My dear fellow,' exclaimed Whistler, 'good and bad are not terms to be used by you. But you may say "I like this" or "I don't like that", and you will be within your rights. Now come and have a whisky; you're sure to like *that*.'

'I wish I'd said that,' said Oscar.

'You will, Oscar, you will!' said Whistler with a resounding laugh.

He was twenty years older than Wilde and began to resent the younger man with his undoubted charm who was replacing him as the centre of attention. For him, praise had to be undiluted so he took objection to a comment by Oscar in 1885, although it was intended generously: 'For that he is indeed one of the greatest masters of painting is my opinion. And I may add that in this opinion Mr Whistler himself entirely concurs.' Oscar mocked the artist's pretensions after one of his famous 'Ten o'Clock' lectures, when Whistler described the riverside of the Thames as if he had appropriated it for himself:

> And when the evening mist clothes the riverside with poetry, as with a veil, and the poor buildings lose themselves in the dim sky, and the tall chimneys become campanile, . . . and the whole city hangs in the heavens, and fairy-land is before us – then the wayfarer hastens home; the working man and the cultured one, the wise man the one of pleasure, cease to understand, as they have ceased to see, and Nature, who for once, has sung in tune, sings her exquisite song to the artist alone.

This was too much for Oscar: 'There may have been fogs for centuries in London. I dare say there were. But no one saw them. They did not exist till Art had invented them.'

The point is, however, that Whistler had seen them, conveying the various moods of the Thames in meticulous engravings and impressionistic oils. Ever the dissatisfied egotist, he resented Wilde's flippancy and after a year of silence attacked him in print, accusing Wilde of being a plagiarist who had stolen Whistler's own ideas: 'How was it, that in your list of culprits, you omitted that fattest of offenders – our own Oscar?'

By now Wilde's saving grace of humour had evaporated, and perhaps he was hurt by the reference to his corpulence: 'It is a trouble for any gentleman to have to notice the lubrications of so ill-bred and ignorant a person as Mr Whistler . . .'

Whistler responded gleefully: 'At bay, and sublime in his agony, he certainly has for once borrowed from no living author, and comes out in his own true colours – as his own "gentleman".'

The badinage did not enhance Whistler's reputation as a serious artist. In his heyday he was as much the object of parody as Wilde himself: one of the Victorian songsheets by Concanen, for a roundelay entitled *Quite Too Utterly Utter*, shows

Whistler with his hands clasped in ecstasy, admiring some gigantic sunflowers planted in blue and white urns. Such notoriety diminished his standing and though his skill as a draughtsman was undeniable, he did not enjoy the popularity of the English artists whose pictures told a story.

Yet in contrast to his poor reception in his adopted city of London, his *White Girl* was the triumph of the Salon de Refusés in Paris in 1863, although it had been rejected by the Royal Academy the year before, a decision that won the approval of the critic of the Athenaeum: 'We are certain that in a very few years' time he will recognise the reasonableness of its rejection. It is one of the most incomplete paintings we have ever met with.' The *Daily Telegraph* was even haughtier, urging Whistler to 'paint cleanly, like a gentleman'.

The White Girl and the comparable *Symphony in White No. II*, of two ladies in white beside a white sofa (Barber Institute) indicate the growing preoccupation with the use of paint, so that even the famous portrait of his mother is really titled *Arrangement in Grey and Black No. I.*

Inevitably, his disillusionment with the English grew. This did not extend to the Scots who honoured him in 1903 with a Doctor of Laws degree, conferred by the University of Glasgow. Too ill to attend the ceremony, he wrote to the Principal, 'I would like to have said to these gentlemen, as a reassurance in their generosity, that, in one way at least, the Gods have prepared me for such dignity: in as much as they have kept, for me, the purest possible strain of Scottish blood – for am I not a McNeill – a McNeill of Barra?' It is sad that the expatriate clutched at these slender roots so pedantically, and died that same year hating the country of his adoption.

England's indifference was Scotland's gain and the finest collection of Whistlers outside America can be seen in the Hunterian Gallery. The catalogue cannot resist the comment: 'Whistler was being recognised formally as a great artist, and by a Scottish institution, when the English had officially ignored him for forty years. In the last ten years before his death, Whistler began to ignore the English, refusing to paint their portraits and criticising their politics (his later sitters were almost always American, French or Scots; and he was ardently pro-Boer). He quite convinced his heir Miss Rosalind Birnie Philip, sister of his wife Beatrix, that, whatever happened to his estate, it was not to go to an English collection.'

Unlike many trustees, Miss Birnie was true to his wishes, even refusing to lend any of his work to the Memorial Exhibition in London in 1905, though she did so readily for similar exhibitions in Paris and Boston. Remembering the honour conferred by Glasgow, she donated the best of his paintings and drawings in 1935, stipulating that none should leave the university under any circumstances. After her death in 1958, the Hunterian acquired the whole estate – a vast collection including Whistler's furniture and Chinese ceramics, and the beautiful Chinese screen which we showed on Gallery. There are also delightful sketches made when Whistler was a child.

The estate was restricted to Whistler's London house and studio, so the Hunterian has added work to enhance it, including a copy after Ingres and a Courbet-like portrait, painted by Whistler during his first years in Paris.

Because of Miss Birnie's strict instructions, the bequest cannot be lent for other exhibitions – Whistler bore his grudge against the English to the grave.

WALTER GREAVES

1846–1931

This is a case of genius killed by talent. If it had not been for Whistler, Greaves might have become an important painter. Unfortunately Whistler helped him develop and Greaves idolised his 'master' to the fatal point of imitation.

Though Greaves was a simple Chelsea boatman – or *because* of that simplicity – he painted an extraordinary picture when he was only sixteen, *Hammersmith Bridge on Boat-race Day*, which hangs in the Tate. With unusual vigour and splashes of colour, it suggests that Greaves was potentially our finest *naïf*, but it was painted before he was Whistler's pupil and lost his naivety.

A review in *The Times* of a posthumous exhibition in the 1940s, concluded that 'instead of producing the long succession of strange and original works that might have been expected, Greaves spent much of his time learning the tricks of Whistler's trade, a pursuit in which a worse artist might have been far more successful. It is a horrible story . . .' Although Greaves' riverscapes are interesting

Hammersmith Bridge on Boat Race Day   Walter Greaves   The Tate Gallery

in their own right, they are diminished by the incomparable delicacy of the nocturnes by Whistler which preceded them.

There is another reason why Greaves' work is little known today: many of his pictures have disintegrated because he was too poor to afford canvases, and had to repair old ones as best he could, using the paint which covered his father's boots.

To be fair to Whistler, his admiration and affection for Greaves was genuine, apart from finding it convenient to have a handyman around the studio and someone to row him across the Thames. Because of Whistler's domination, however inadvertent that might have been, Greaves never showed in public until he was given a one-man show in 1911 when he was seventy, suddenly 'hailed as a new and in some respects a greater Whistler' and a 'remarkable case of late recognition of a genius' to quote the anonymous critic in the *Chronicle*. Although a popular figure in Chelsea, he lacked the confidence or conceit to promote his work himself, calling on friends with etchings and watercolours, which he sold for five shillings. Residents were glad to buy his watercolours of buildings threatened by development, but they were motivated by nostalgia rather than a belief in Greaves as a master in his own right.

Ultimately, after his glorious beginning, Greaves provides a poignant footnote in the history of British art. His loyalty to Whistler remained intact; in his old age when he was committed to a workhouse, he was so anxious to look like Whistler, as well as paint like him, that the matron had to prevent him from dying his white hair with boot polish in order to emulate Whistler's ebony locks. There is something magnificent in such a lifelong passion.

Work by Walter Greaves can be seen in:
London, The Tate Gallery
Oxford, Ashmolean Museum
York, City Art Gallery

THE BURRELL COLLECTION

> The collection, to the collector, is the important thing
>
> > Sir William Burrell

The wealthy Glaswegian shipowner, William Burrell, personified the Englishman's concept of the Scot: dour, canny, and, shall I say, *careful* with his money – which is why he had it.

Sir Kenneth Clark suggested that if he had been prepared to pay more for individual works of art, his collection would be priceless today. Yet his collection is the perfect complement to the other Glaswegian galleries, who excel in their different ways, and any collection which includes Degas's pastel of the *Jockeys in the Rain* and Bellini's *Virgin and Child* is worth visiting.

Where Burrell was fortunate was in the architects chosen in 1971 to house his collection, which he and Lady Burrell had given to the city of Glasgow nearly thirty years earlier. The delay was due to his stipulation that the building should be sixteen miles outside the city centre in order to avoid pollution. This was a wise precaution, and enabled Barry Gasson and Associates, who won the competition, to take advantage of the space offered them in Pollok Park. The result, opened by the Queen in 1983, has been an unqualified success. The Burrell is proof that a visit to an art gallery need not be an intellectual penance but a joy. The evident excitement of the visitors who descend from their coaches explains why this is now the most popular tourist attraction in Scotland.

The designer's aim sounds simple – a blend of old materials and new – yet how seldom does the promise on the plan materialise. The combination of sandstone, timber and glass gives a sense of airiness and light, though some of the inner rooms are comparatively dark, and Barry Gasson was audacious to the point of bravura in his use of massive stonework such as in the *Hornby Castle Portal*, originally installed for William, Lord Conyers (1468–1524), with lavish heraldic carvings stretching high above the gateway.

If Burrell was cautious with his money, he was profligate with his foresight, having bought the medieval stone doorways, arches and windows which Gasson has incorporated, from the collection of the American newspaper tycoon William Randolph Hearst.

Barry Gasson, who was awarded the OBE and won every conceivable museum award in consequence, including the Stone Federation Award for Natural Stone, has acted with panache throughout: a gallery with Egyptian antiquities seen against a woodland background through glass; the high, vaulted roof of the Oriental Daylit Gallery conveying similar light at dusk; and the row of medieval stained glass inset into the glass panels along the South Gallery.

Where he has been impeccable is in reflecting Burrell's personal enthusiasms for medieval stone and glass and tapestries, for Burrell's interests were not confined to painting, but included Roman glass, Persian rugs, Chinese pottery and ceramics dating from the fourth century BC. There is even an example of south Italian earthenware with a red design which suggests Picasso on a first impression.

Perhaps it is the diversity of the Burrell Collection which makes it so popular, and though he rarely spent more than £20,000 a year, with Frans Hals' *Portrait of a Gentleman* his most expensive purchase at £14,500, surely this is the yardstick of the true collector – discernment rather than cost – and in this respect Sir William's taste is highly individual. The work by the Scottish artist Joseph Crawhall was acquired due to a personal friendship with this 'Glasgow Boy', and includes 132 watercolours and drawings with *The Flower Shop* and *The Girl on a Bicycle* (plus dachshund). I find it endearing that this gruff shipping magnate's taste ranged from the monumental stonework destined for Hearst to a humorous watercolour by a personal friend.

Jockeys in the Rain Edgar Degas The Burrell Collection, Glasgow

His collection of paintings is equally unpredictable. In this he was guided by Alexander Reid (later of Reid-Lefevre, London) whose portrait by Van Gogh hangs in the Glasgow Art Gallery. The prizes of the collection are Géricault's *Prancing Grey Horse*, which influenced Delacroix's *White Horse*; Boudin's *The Empress Eugénie on the Beach at Trouville* and Cézanne's *Le Chareau de Medan* once owned by Gauguin. Almost as remarkable as the self-portrait of Rembrandt is the portrait of a blood-bespattered *Dog* by Jean-Baptiste Oudry (1686–1755), who became the court painter to Louis XIV, painted the Royal Hounds, and may be underrated accordingly. The painting of the dog's china water bowl is astonishing in itself.

The paintings by Degas prove his versatility, with the *Jockeys in the Rain* an interesting parallel to Van Gogh's *Rain at Auvers* (Cardiff), for, influenced by Japanese prints, the rain falls in straight lines in both.

The portrait of *Duranty* reveals another facet, and though *The Rehearsal* deals with the familiar subject of ballet dancers he kills the sweetness of the subject – the girls in tutus with pink bows – by the boldness of his composition. A staircase winds to the left and all that we can see are legs descending and a figure virtually obscured. On the right, the old wardrobe mistress attends to one of the dancers,

The Dog   Jean Baptiste Oudry   The Burrell Collection, Glasgow

who is sliced in half – another influence from the Japanese, as well as from the less intended cut-off of the camera. The striking feature is the empty space right in the foreground, which most artists would have filled. 'It's the kind of arrogance,' said Frank Whitford on Gallery, 'of someone who so supremely knows what he is doing that in his way he changes art because all compositional rules are irrelevant.'

In 1946 Sir William Burrell gave £450,000 to Glasgow towards the cost of housing the collection. In 1984, the year after it opened, the millionth visitor came to see it. Attendance today is second only to the Tate in London.

Edinburgh

> How often in going through the great Florentine galleries our own came to mind and made me realise how many fine things there are in it. Indeed, in proportion to its size, we have more things of varied excellence than most galleries, and we have but little padding.
>
> Sir David Young Cameron, Scottish painter and
> Trustee of the Scottish National Gallery for
> the last twenty-five years of his life.

THE NATIONAL GALLERY OF SCOTLAND

After his splendid restoration of the Manchester City Gallery to its original glory, down to the smallest details of light fittings and the colours of the walls, Timothy Clifford moved to Edinburgh as the Director of the Scottish National Galleries, including the National Portrait Gallery and the National Gallery of Modern Art.

Showing me around the National Gallery in Edinburgh soon after his appointment, Clifford expressed dismay at the haphazard selection and display, with a plethora of work which was frankly second rate. With typical determination, in the face of considerable criticism at the time, he cut the chaff and refurbished the galleries painstakingly, returning to the original design by William Playfair, with the double-hanging of pictures on two levels, the crimson Victorian felt wall covering and green carpeting. Today this is seen as wholly acceptable and proof of his success is evident in the attendance figures which have increased by 65 per cent and are now in excess of 300,000 visitors a year. The public respond gratefully to the reinstatement of the original entrance hall and staircase by W.T. Oldrieve, and the small room with seven Poussins where the marble floor and three-branched lamps are taken from details in the paintings. That is dedication.

In his Introduction to the handsome catalogue published in 1989, Timothy Clifford refers to the 'main holdings' of Western European and American paintings and the predominant work by the old masters: Raphael, Titian, Rubens, Rembrandt and Velasquez up to the Impressionists and Post-Impressionists.

Ultimately, a gallery thrives on quality, which is one reason why Clifford fought (unsuccessfully) for the retention in this country of such a masterpiece as the Mantegna, and the National Gallery in Edinburgh excels in this respect.

The foundation stone was laid by Prince Albert in 1850 and the building opened nine years later, designed by Playfair in the classical tradition. In spite of this illustrious beginning, and paintings acquired on the advice of the Scottish painter (and close friend of Benjamin Robert Haydon) Sir David Wilkie, the Gallery was handicapped by a lack of funds, receiving no financial support from the treasury. Donations enabled the purchase of William Etty's massive triptych of *Judith and Holofernes* 'then regarded as a triumph of contemporary historical style' (to quote Timothy Clifford); Van Dyck's *Lomellini Family*, and the magnificent Gainsborough full-length portrait of one of his haughty ladies, *The Hon Mrs Graham*. The brewer, the Rt Hon William McEwan MP also came to the rescue, buying two portraits by Frans Hals, including the interesting *Verdonck* of a man with a jawbone, and Rembrandt's *Woman in Bed*. Another benefactor, W.A. Coats, partner in a thread-manufacturing firm, donated thirteen Corots, five Boudins, and seven Géricaults. The great, early, signed Vermeer of *Christ in the House of Martha and Mary* was presented in his memory by his two sons in 1927.

Under pressure, the treasury finally agreed to a grant of £1,000 a year for the purchase of new work, but this was totally inadequate. In 1919, the situation was saved with a gift of £55,000 from the son of a shipowner, James Cowan Smith, on condition that the gallery hung a portrait of his favourite Dandie Dinmont terrier called *Callum* and provided for another dog, *Fury*, should it survive him. Wisely, the trustees agreed to these extraordinary provisos and Fury was duly placed in the care of Mr Wing, a coachman, while the gallery benefited from the interest on Cowan Smith's generous gift, which enabled them to buy such fine work as Constable's *Vale of Dedham* in 1944.

Financial restriction could have prompted the purchase of more but lesser work, and although the gallery has this too, the financial limitations appears to have made the acquisitions all the more discerning.

Outside the National Gallery in London and the Royal Collection, the gallery probably contains the finest collection of Italian paintings in Britain, with the early panel by Lorenzo Monaco of the *Madonna and Child* and Verrocchio's serene painting of the same subject described by Clifford as 'quintessentially fifteenth-century Florentine, full of tranquil grace and purity'. Understandably, this is one of the most loved paintings with the public.

The collection is enhanced immeasurably by the loan from the Duke of Sutherland of three works by Raphael, five by Titian, and one Tintoretto. Of these, the Raphael of the *Holy Family with a Palm Tree* (1506–7), allegedly once in the possession of the Duke of Urbino, is sublime. It is worth visiting the gallery for this alone, like Piero's *Baptism* in London's National Gallery.

Venus Anadyomene, also on loan, is the famous nude by Titian, while Tintoretto's *Deposition of Christ* was bought with the aid of the National Heritage Memorial Fund in 1984.

The prime example of Scottish art is *The Painter's Wife* by Allan Ramsay. In fact she was his second wife and eloped with him to Italy where he painted this superb and loving portrait.

The most recent, major acquisition is El Greco's *Allegory*, sold in lieu of death duties with the assistance of the NHMF, another triumph for Clifford's persistence. This remarkable work was the *raison d'être* for the exhibition during the 1989 Festival, which was structured around it, with modern tributes by Adrian

The Painter's Wife   Allan Ramsay   The National Gallery of Scotland

Wiszniewski and John Bellany. The meaning of the picture is unclear – an intent monkey, a boy lighting a candle, a leering, loutish man who might have been the animal's keeper – but the figures were current at the time. El Greco's self-portrait, painted when he was still a boy, is plainly the central figure in *Allegory*, with an alternative version owned by the Earl of Harewood in which the monkey is chained. This echoes the two tragic monkeys by Pieter Bruegel the Elder, chained on a window ledge overlooking Antwerp and the River Scheldt. A monkey also appears in Dürer's *Virgin with Child* in University College, London.

Explanations for this 'problem picture' suggest a diabolical association, with the blowing on fire as a symbol of sexual passion, while the monkey represents art – 'art is the ape of nature' – as well as representing vice. Is this in fact a picture of lust? I have no idea, though it is entertaining to surmise.

In conclusion, closer to our own time, works by the Impressionists include superb pieces by Pissarro, Monet's simple *Haystacks: Snow Effect*, three Degas, Gauguin's famous *The Vision after the Sermon* (also known as *Jacob Wrestling with the Angel*), and two contrasting works by Van Gogh: the peaceful *Orchard in Blossom*

(1888), followed by the wilder *Olive Trees* (1889), which has greater excitement.

The paintings mentioned are no more than a hint of the wealth of this great collection in the splendid new setting which allows for no distraction.

SCOTTISH NATIONAL GALLERY OF MODERN ART

Surprisingly, for the building was a hospital for destitute children built in the 1820s, this is one of the most delightful galleries in Britain and I can think of few where the paintings are so well displayed. It opened in 1984 and retains that freshness, with sculptures in the parkland to welcome the visitor as he approaches.

This is the place to head for if you are interested in Scottish art, for the collection of twentieth-century Scottish painting is unequalled. If some of the names are unfamiliar, you may well wonder why – F.B. Cadell's striking *Lady in Black* (1921); J.D. Fergusson's *La Terrasse, le Café d'Harcourt*, and the still life and *Man Laughing* by S.J. Peploe would be equally at home in the Tate.

The meticulous detail in *A City Garden* by James McIntosh Patrick explains why this artist is receiving belated recognition in his eighties, even though he is still more popular north of the border. His charming *Springtime in Eskdale* is, however, one of the favourites in the Walker Art Gallery in Liverpool.

Colquhoun and Macbryde are represented by outstanding examples of their work, and the New Glasgow boys are much in evidence too. *Allegory*, a triptych by John Bellany, reveals this artist at his most imaginative in his treatment of the crucifixion.

Always associated with his architectural design and furniture, there is a splendid wooden bookcase by Charles Rennie Mackintosh, and also one of his considerable watercolours, *Le Fort Maillert* (1927), belonging to the Glasgow School of Art, which he designed in art nouveau style between 1897 and 1902, and which is recognised today as one of the finest modern buildings in Europe.

Opinions on the very latest work will depend on your personal taste, though the abstracts are more interesting than usual; if John McLean's *Escalator* (1988) is a series of daubs, they are rather attractive daubs; Gwen Hardie's *Fist* (1986) has considerable power; and Kate Whitford's *Red Spiral* (1986) is jolly, though I doubt if she would thank me for saying so. Born in Glasgow in 1952 her work, which started as minimalist and is strictly non–figurative, is an interesting complement to the stark realism of the Glasgow brotherhood.

The South

A Soldier on Horseback   Anthony Van Dyck
Christ Church Picture Gallery, Oxford

Cambridge

THE FITZWILLIAM MUSEUM

The Fitzwilliam is one of the oldest public museums in Britain, founded in 1816 by the Seventh Viscount Fitzwilliam of Merrion, who bequeathed his collection to the university, 'for the purpose of promoting the increase of learning and the other great objects of that noble foundation'. In addition, he donated a crucial £100,000 to house his treasures. A competition for the building work was won by George Basevi (1794–1836), whose plans were selected from thirty-six rivals in the Classical and Gothic styles. The museum opened in 1848 but remained a backwater in the snobbish life of the university, with 'respectably dressed' members of the public admitted on only three days in the week.

In 1908 C.S. Cockerell took over as Director and found it a 'pig sty'. By 1937 he had 'turned it into a palace' through his tenacity, and his presence at a sickbed, lingering for last bequests, was dreaded by the rich as a sure sign of impending death. With these and public appeals he completed the transformation which confronts us today – one of the most unexpected collections in one of the most imposing buildings.

The lavishly illustrated brochure supports the claim of the current Director, Michael Jaffé, that it is 'the finest small museum in Western Europe', appealing to 'hundreds of thousands of visitors'. On my visit I was joined by a swarm of French children who descended, chattering, like locusts – one of the pleasures or penalties of Cambridge in the tourist season.

Everyone should be able to find a painting to fall in love with – there are at least a dozen I should like to absorb each day. Apart from superb antiquities, such as the painted wood figure of an Egyptian *Official* dated twenty-third century BC, you meet with constant surprise, like Degas's little-known version of *David and Goliath*, an early work with the naked figure of David in the foreground about to let loose his sling, and a small Goliath in the background. There is also Holman Hunt's charming portrait of his thirteen-year-old son with a fishing rod, in a typically sumptuous frame. There is an unusual landscape by Gauguin; an avenue of trees by Van Gogh, *L'Allée en Automne*; and Renoir's lovely *Le Coup de Vent*, in which the gust of wind can be sensed as it crosses a blurred valley.

More recent works include Picasso's cubist *Head of a Woman*; a large portrait of Sir William Nicholson, which makes one ponder yet again on the talent of Augustus John, now so unfashionable; and a Nevinson watercolour, ink and pencil of *Looking Through Brooklyn Bridge*.

A further treasure is Derain's *Portrait of Isabel*, which has the added interest that Isabel Lambert (later Isabel Rawsthorne) also modelled for Giacometti and later for Francis Bacon, who painted her portrait in triptych as well as the famous painting of her *Standing in a Street in Soho*.

An interesting range of Sickert includes a typical scene at the *Old Bedford* music hall and a lesser known portrait of Hugh Walpole; while Edward Lear is well represented by the large oil of *View of the Temple of Apollo and Bassal in Arcadia*. Samuel Palmer's masterpiece *The Magic Apple Tree* is discussed elsewhere.

Yet the old masters linger particularly in the memory, such as Frans Hals' *Portrait of a Man*, who looks as if he is suffering from the night before and wonders if it was worth it. The painter Patrick Procktor, one of the guests on *Gallery*, told me, 'One painting I have always loved since seeing it is *The Annunciation* by Domenico Veneziano. Berenson only has a paragraph about the artist, but it is certainly a gem of the purest beauty. So much of gallery going when one is young is learning about art and artist with its necessary tedium and toil, but the unalloyed pleasure of this small panel remains with me as an ideal.'

Frank Whitford recommended the small oil by Dürer of *St Jerome and the Lion*, kept under glass and covered with a cloth, which helps to explain its extraordinary freshness and the startling colour of the blue robe. Like Bellini's version in the Ashmolean, this is perfection. So is the still life, *A Bundle of Asparagus*, by Adriaen Coorte (1683–1705) which glows with life. It was given to the university by Sir Frank Brangwyn, but I cannot find the artist, Coorte, mentioned in my reference books, possibly because the art of the still life tends to be underrated, though it excels here also with Fantin-Latour's *White Cup and Saucer*.

How ashamed I am to have studied at Pembroke College further down the street, yet never set foot in the Fitzwilliam. What an opportunity I wasted.

AUBREY VINCENT BEARDSLEY

1872–98

A Beardsley drawing makes such stylish use of black and white that once seen it is never mistaken – that is his strength, along with the added sense of decadence, hinting at forbidden pleasure, which is so attractive to the young.

Beardsley's mastery of his languorous subject matter places him among the finest illustrators. If he had not died at the age of twenty-five he might have astounded us by a greater versatility as he matured. Such theorising is pointless, though it should be recognised that the morbid element in his work was heightened by the tuberculosis which burnt him out too soon. On the evidence of what we have, his was a rare if minor talent.

Beardsley was born in Brighton in 1872 and went to school there before moving to London at the age of sixteen. By the time he was nineteen his talent was so unmistakable that Burne-Jones told him, 'Nature has given you every gift which is necessary to become a great artist. I seldom or never advise anyone to take up art as a profession but in your case I can do nothing else.' For the next seven years his brilliance shone. New methods of reproduction complemented his particular use of black and white and his drawings became widely known if not admired. He detested the bluff hypocrisy of Victorian morality, and was considered decadent by the people he despised. As the art editor of the notorious *Yellow Book*, he contributed to the first issue, which scandalised London. His erotic illustrations for Oscar Wilde's *Salome* in 1894 caused a sensation and contributed to the book's success. They were denounced by *The Times* as 'fantastic, grotesque, unintelligible, repulsive'. High praise, and neither man was bothered by the controversy until Wilde was brought to the Old Bailey the following year.

In fact, the two men were not the best of friends, although Beardsley implored Wilde to let him make the translation of *Salome* from the French original. Wilde gave way reluctantly and was so displeased by the result that he gave the work to Alfred Douglas, whose name appeared as the translator. Meanwhile, Robert Ross persuaded Wilde to allow Beardsley to do the illustrations, which Wilde disliked with equal intensity: 'They are too Japanese, while my play is Byzantine. They are like the naughty scribbles a precocious schoolboy makes on the margins of his copybooks.' While this was a perceptive comment, Beardsley's illustrations are as famous today as the text itself. However badly he behaved in the eyes of respectable society, Wilde considered himself a man of honour and Beardsley's drawings came uncomfortably close to revelation: 'They are cruel and evil, and so like dear Aubrey, who has a face like a silver hatchet, with grass-green hair.' Wilde also described Beardsley as 'the most monstrous of orchids'.

Never so generous as Wilde, Beardsley did not forgive his rejection of the translation of *Salome*, nor the subsequent criticism of his illustrations, and when John Lane published the *Yellow Book* Wilde was noticeable by his absence as a contributor. In his turn, Wilde called the book, 'horrid . . . loathsome . . . dull . . . a great failure . . . not yellow at all. Dear Aubrey is always too Parisian; he cannot forget that he has been to Dieppe – *once*.'

Beardsley, however, proved too alarming even for John Lane and was sacked after four issues – '*The Yellow Book* turned grey in a single night' – and while it staggered on for nine feeble editions, Beardsley started a rival, *The Savoy*, which ran for eight. As Hesketh Pearson remarked in his biography of Wilde, 'it might just as well have been called *The Beardsley*, for he was the life and soul, at least the body and death of it.'

Referring to Beardsley's hostility to Wilde after his exile to France, Pearson remarked that 'A little more of Wilde's humanity and a little less of formal Christianity would have prevented Aubrey Beardsley behaving as he did.' Beardsley had become a Catholic and was trying to renounce both his sins and his more disreputable relationships. Visiting Dieppe in March 1897, he wrote to a friend that 'some rather unpleasant people come here', and when he saw Wilde approaching him on the quay he slipped up a side street to avoid him. Wilde was hurt though characteristically forgiving, but Beardsley was unable to afford such magnanimity in his new-found religion and wrote to Leonard Smithers in December agreeing to contribute to a forthcoming magazine provided that 'Oscar Wilde contributes nothing . . . anonymously, pseudonymously, or otherwise . . .' Beardsley died three months later, though Wilde managed to slip into the next century.

Ironically, Beardsley's name is for ever associated with that of Wilde, and it might have amused Oscar that 'Dear Aubrey' has become a symbol of decadence, enhanced by the photographs of the effete young man with the foppish bow tie.

Philip Core, the American artist and critic who lived in London and died from AIDS in November 1989, suggested in his book, *Camp*, that Beardsley escaped from his genteel, middle-class background into a secret life of transvestism, conveniently cross-dressing with his sister (whom Wilde described as a 'daisy' compared to Aubrey's orchid-ness), with whom he may have had an incestuous relationship. Core quotes from Beardsley's pornographic novella *Under the Hill* in evidence: 'I am going to Jimmie's ... dressed up like a tart and mean to have a regular spree.' *The Night Piece*, in the Fitzwilliam, Cambridge, takes on a suspect

A Night Piece   Aubrey Beardsley   The Fitzwilliam Museum

quality when viewed in this androgynous light, for there is a suggestion in the face that 'she' is in fact a young man.

The narcissism of Beardsley's work and the constant representation of dressing-up in *The Toilet of Salome* and *The Lady of the Camellias at her Dressing Table*, confirm Core's theory that Beardsley was obsessed with costume and make-up.

When I chose the *Fat Woman* from the Tate to be shown on *Gallery*, I expected to receive the drawing of the large lady with the voluminous hat and black-gloved hands resting on a white table which holds a solitary bottle. This seemed typical of his style, though less art nouveau than the famous cover for the *Morte d'Arthur*, the work for which is he is usually remembered. Instead, the Tate sent a rarity of greater interest, an oil painting of a woman (possibly the same) wearing a mask. Her identity is intriguing because of the suspicion that she was the wife of his friend Whistler, which explains why the *Fat Woman* was omitted from the first issue of the *Yellow Book* when Lane spotted the resemblance. The oil portrait is a flattering atonement, interesting as an oil only because Beardsley's importance lies in his greater skill as a draughtsman.

KETTLE'S YARD

This unique modern gallery is a modest antidote to the grandeur of the Fitzwilliam. While it is maintained today by the university, Kettle's Yard was the personal creation of Jim Ede, who was obsessed by the idea of 'a living place where pictures could be seen in a domestic setting'. To this end he bought several condemned slum cottages and transformed them into a home for himself and his wife Helen, the setting for a casual gallery with furniture, paintings and sculpture next to natural objects like pebbles and driftwood. This could have been precious but the gallery's charm and lack of reverence made it instantly popular. 'Had I been rich I could not have done it,' said Ede, 'though I am rich in experience.' There is no need to whisper in Kettle's Yard.

Jim Ede has devoted his life to art, studying at Leys School in Cambridge before he became an assistant at the Tate Gallery, where he met Ben Nicholson around 1924: 'He opened a door into the world of contemporary art and I rushed headlong into the arms of Brancusi and Braque; not losing, however, my rapture over Giotto, Angelico, Monaco and Piero della Francesca.' The use of *rapture* conveys the enthusiasm which he brought to his own collection. Thanks to Nicholson he made contact with the Cornish primitive painter Alfred Wallis and two years later began to receive his paintings, 'They would come by post, perhaps sixty at a time, and the price fixed at one or three shillings according to size. I once bought as many as twenty but usually could not afford so many.'

One hundred paintings by Wallis; forty-four by Ben Nicholson, ranging from *Apples and Pears* (1927) to *Jug* (1967); and the sympathetic self-portrait of his friend

Christopher Wood, who died at the age of 29, form the nucleus of Ede's art collection. This is enhanced by the sculpture of Gaudier-Brzeska, much of whose work was rejected by the Tate after he was killed in the First War, but was bought up by Ede to save it from being destroyed. The drawings, so brilliant in their simplicity, and such sculpture as the famous *Bird Swallowing a Fish* (1914) confirm his potential greatness. Kettle's Yard has the largest collection of Gaudier-Brzeska's work after the Tate and the Musée National d'Art Moderne.

Leaving the Tate in 1936, Ede travelled in France and North Africa, returning to England in 1956. His ambition was fulfilled the following year when the President of the Cambridge Preservation Society recommended the conversion of the four slum dwellings, and an extension was opened by Prince Charles in 1970.

A few years later, Jim and Helen Ede left for Edinburgh, where she died in 1980. Approaching his centenary as I write this, Jim Ede leads a reclusive life, although he is devoted to the cause of a hospice for elderly people.

Inevitably, the original homely atmosphere of Kettle's Yard has diminished, but the gallery remains as popular as ever.

ALFRED WALLIS

1855–1942

The only English primitive of any consequence, and indeed one of the most interesting and overlooked English artists of this century.

Edwin Mullins

In 1928 the two young artists Ben Nicholson and Christopher Wood passed the back door of a cottage in St Ives and glimpsed some paintings nailed roughly to the wall. From that moment they helped to promote the work of Alfred Wallis, bringing it to the attention of Jim Ede at Kettle's Yard in Cambridge.

Wallis was a true primitive. Unlike the sophisticated artist with enough skill to pass himself off as a *faux naif*, Wallis had innocence but he was not naive, nor was there a hint of falsification.

A rag-and-bone man, Wallis was seventy-three when the artists met him, having started to paint 'for the company' after the death of his wife six years earlier. It was fortunate that these particular painters discovered him, for they appreciated his talent instantly. Indeed, his influence upon them shows in their subsequent work. Others might have dismissed Wallis as a struggling amateur, and discarded his scraps of wood and cardboard as childish. Undeniably, Wallis had the directness of childhood, though I doubt if a child could paint with such control or know so exactly what he was aiming for. It is an odd feature of 'primitive' painting that it should seem so entertaining, almost humorous, yet be wholly serious in contrast to a child's gleeful eye. Douanier Rousseau, the French customs officer whose *naifs* are probably the best ever painted, had such self-importance that he told the young Picasso, 'We are the two greatest painters of our time, you in the Egyptian style, and I in the modern style.'

When Ben Nicholson supplied him with pots of paint, Wallis specified the colours exactly. 'You don't want to use too many,' he told Nicholson, holding up a glass of sea water to the light to prove that the sea was not necessarily blue. His fish may have been as big as his boats, but this was his intention, 'Each boat of that fleet had a soul, a beautiful soul shaped like a fish: so they fish I've painted they aren't fish at all – you wouldn't be much good without a soul, would 'ee? They boats weren't neither, see? That's why I've painted them complete – souls and all.'

True simplicity is one of the hardest qualities to achieve without contrivance. Another reason why his work appeals is nostalgia: 'I do most what used to be, what we shall see no more.'

To the advantage of his work he was never taken up by the dealers nor by the media, who would have transformed him into a 'character'. Instead, he remained 'deaf and difficult', described more kindly by Nicholson as 'a very fierce and lonely man'.

Bridge and Boats   Alfred Wallis   Kettle's Yard, Cambridge

So little is known of his background that there is doubt over his claim that he went to sea as a sailor and fisherman as a young man. But you do not have to go to sea to understand it, and his pale sweeps of paint are truer than the usual ripples of bluest blue. His sea is cold and his harsh greens are instantly recognisable as Cornish. Rumour had it that he was insane, which is not altogether surprising when you learn that he believed his dead wife was indulging in a vendetta against him from a cupboard upstairs which he covered with a life-size portrait of her dressed in black. She was twenty years older, a widow with seventeen children. Their own two children died at birth. She belonged to the Salvation Army and Wallis was equally religious, reading the Bible with some difficulty throughout the Sabbath.

Part of the simplicity which appeals today was forced on him by poverty, using cardboard and the backs of boxes instead of the canvases which he could not afford. And in spite of the encouragement from Nicholson and Wood he enjoyed scant success or recognition in his lifetime.

Alfred Wallis died in the Madron Poorhouse at the age of eighty-seven. And that, of course, is the stuff of the legend he's become.

When Wallis was compared to Grandma Moses on *Gallery*, he was praised by comparison: 'His pictures have a passion which hers lack,' said Maggi Hambling. 'You could look at a Wallis far longer.' I know that is true for I possessed two of his pictures once and they linger in my mind's eye.

Ipswich

MUSEUM

Also at Christchurch Mansion. I refer to the paintings as the 'Ipswich Collection'.

The Exhibition Gallery is distinguished by three of the finest Constables including the famous *Mill Stream*, bought for a mere £1,400 in 1941 with help from the National Art Collections Fund. Exemplifying the serenity of the English countryside, this was a poignant gesture at the very moment when the battle for Britain was being fought overhead. The scene suffers from over-familiarity today, though the picture with Willy Lott's cottage beside the stream has an unexpected freshness.

Another painting depicts the garden of his son, *Golding Constable's Flower Garden*, and is a pure landscape without a stream in sight. It is paired with *Golding Constable's Kitchen Garden*, an oil of the same size (13 x 20 ins).

It is interesting to compare Constable's Mill Stream with Gainsborough's treatment of a similar subject, *A Country Cart Crossing a Ford*, bought by the Friends of the Ipswich Museum in 1982 for £209,000. It is another remarkable bargain, for it shows Gainsborough at his most spontaneous, inspired by the landscape which he preferred to his wealthy sitters. His technique is halfway between the formality of Constable's *Haywain* in the National and the looser sketch in the V & A, meticulous yet exuberant. Also revealing is the contrast between Gainsborough's portrait of Mrs Kilderbee and Constable's freer treatment of his portly son, Golding.

The town or port of Ipswich, as it was in the eighteenth century, is seen through the different eyes of John Clevely, with an elongated, curved, panoramic view with fields and gardens in the foreground.

After this feast, come the unexpected delicacies: the striking Picasso print of the *Drinking Minotaur and Sculptor with two models* (1933); a Bridget Riley and a Roger Hilton; a characteristic Wilson Steer; and an outstanding print by Robert Bevan of *Horse Dealers* (1919). Bevan (1865–1925) studied in Paris, becoming friends with Gauguin in Brittany, joining Sickert on his return to England in the New English Art Club. Later he became an original member of the Camden Town Group, which broke up in the First War. This lithograph, also known as *The Horse Mart, Barbican*, is in black and white, which strengthens the simple composition of the four figures around a horse. Lurking on the fringes in galleries, Bevan evades a greater recognition.

JOHN CONSTABLE

1776–1837

Painting is with me but another word for feeling.

Constable

Constable aimed to 'preserve God's almighty daylight' and did so with such accuracy that you can guess the time when his landscapes were painted. The original title for *The Haywain* was: *Landscape: Noon* and you can tell that it is.

In this pursuit he made fifty studies of the skies, which are rarely the same in Britain, with notes of the time of day, the direction of the wind, the speed and colour of the clouds and their height. He explained, 'The sky is the source of light in nature and governs everything.' A simple reason for this obsession was the flat landscape where he was born in 1776 on the border of Suffolk and Essex, with the limitless sky stretching above.

Constable's father, a prosperous miller, discouraged his son's ambition until he allowed him to join the Royal Academy Schools in London at the age of twenty-three. Influenced by Gainsborough, without the dominating figures in the foreground, and Turner, who was a year older but preferred the cataclysm to the tranquillity of nature, Constable exhibited at the Academy in his late twenties until he rejected 'truth at second hand' and turned to nature herself. It was the natural reality which delighted him rather than the contrived composition and he declared, 'When I sit down to make a sketch from nature the first thing I try to do is to forget

I have seen a picture.' In this respect he was the antithesis of such academic contemporaries as Benjamin Haydon, and he was subsequently defeated in the Royal Academy election in 1828 by William Etty, commenting bitterly on the preference for 'the shaggy posteriors of a satyr' rather than a landscape. In his late twenties he explored the mountainous Lake District in search of Romantic scenery, but returned thankfully to the quiet countryside of Suffolk in 1810, where he developed his love affair with his birthplace with a series of drawings and oils painted in the open air.

This passion for nature in the raw might seem obvious today when such landscapes are familiar, but they were almost revolutionary to those accustomed to the academic prettiness of Claude.

Writing to his patron the Reverend John Fisher in 1821, he expressed his affection passionately: 'How much I can imagine myself with you on your excursion . . . old rotten banks, slimy posts, and brickwork. I love such things . . . They have always been my delight – and I should indeed have delighted in seeing what you describe . . . but I should paint my own places best; painting is but another word for feeling. I associate my "careless boyhood" to all that lies on the banks of the Stour. They made me a painter (and I am grateful), that is I had often thought of pictures of them before I had ever touched pencil . . .' He carried a tiny sketchbook in which to make his pencil studies. When Blake saw it, he exclaimed, 'This is inspiration!' Constable replied, 'I took it for drawing.'

Constable was unfashionable in England during his lifetime and, in spite of his father's mills, was so poor that when he fell in love with an heiress her family did not consider him suitable. Finally he married her in 1816 and this enabled him to travel across Europe and tackle the 'six footer' canvases, which included *A Scene on the Stour*, bought by the Reverend Fisher and shown at the Academy in 1819, and the famous *Haywain*, the title chosen by Fisher, shown two years later. A harvest wagon crosses the shallow stream near Flatford Mill, with Willy Lott's cottage on the left, which belonged to Constable's father, and which was constantly in view when the artist was growing up.

The full-size sketch for *The Haywain*, now in the V & A, was painted the year before the final work and there is argument today as to which is the better. Kenneth Clark stated, 'When we look at it we have no doubt that this is the picture his demon wanted to paint.'

Though an icon today, the final painting had to cross the channel to receive its recognition from Delacroix, who wrote in his journal: 'Constable says that the superiority of the green in his meadows comes from its being composed of a multitude of different greens. The lack of intensity and life in the foliage of most landscape painters arises because they usually paint them in a uniform tone.' Constable was noted also for exploiting highlights of white on his trees and water, which added 'life'.

In 1828 his father-in-law died and Constable was rich, but his wife died a few months later and though he was elected to the Royal Academy by one vote, the zest of life had gone. 'Hourly do I feel the loss of my departed angel,' he wrote. 'I

shall never feel again as I have felt, the face of the World is totally changed to me.'
They had seven children and two of his sons became painters, creating confusion
after his death when a number of paintings were wrongly identified as his.

Following his wife's death he devoted himself to his work, and it assumed a new
strength with the oil of *Salisbury Cathedral* (1831) and the delightful *Dog Watching a*

An Ash Tree in Hampstead   John Constable   Victoria & Albert Museum

Rat in the Water at Dedham, which proves that he was capable of humour too.

The V & A has evidence which suggests that he was a thoroughly decent man. In spite of the unlovely building and the harsh light, the Constable collection has to be seen to appreciate the marvellous freshness of his work. It may sound self-defeating to admit it, but no reproduction can compare with the original and this applies to Constable in particular. I can think of few seascapes more perfect than *Weymouth Bay* and *Beach with Fishing Boats* – as invigorating as sea air itself. His particular affection for trees is evident, and for one in particular: *An Ash Tree in Hampstead*, which he referred to as 'this young lady'. This was not a flight of whimsy but an expression of sympathy – 'It is scarcely too much to say that she died of a broken heart for a billboard had been nailed ALL VAGRANTS AND BEGGARS WILL BE DEALT WITH ACCORDING TO THE LAW. The tree seemed to have felt the disgrace, for even then some of the top branches had withered. Two long spike nails had been driven far into her side. In another year one half became paralysed, and not long after the other shared the same fate and this beautiful creature was cut down to a stump, just high enough to hold the board.' His studies of the tree, ending with the stump and the billboard, record the sad demise caused by the thoughtless vandalism, and reveal his own distress.

There is also a study of clouds, with the information: 'looking S.E. Noon. Wind very brisk – clouds moving very fast.'

Though his seascapes in the V & A are pure exhilaration, it is the Suffolk scenes that we return to: *Flatford Mill*, one of those owned by his father and where he worked as a young man; *Dedham Lock and Mill*; and *The Leaping Horse*, with the barge horse jumping the lock and the steeple of Dedham church rising in the distance. Above all we remember that stretch of placid water near Willy Lott's cottage, immortalised in the *Mill Stream* and *The Haywain*, the dog on the bank, a man fishing, the horses that have drunk and are now about to turn the cart under a Constable sky – the personification of England.

Oxford

Visiting Oxford, I mentioned to the President of the Arts Society that I was going to the art gallery in Christ Church.

'I didn't realise there was one!' he exclaimed. Yet he was at Oxford and concerned with art. Paradoxically, because of their immediate accessibility, we tend to take our own galleries for granted, and before we compliment ourselves on flattering attendance figures – more people go to galleries than they do to football, or some such statistic – it is salutary to learn that a substantial percentage is due to tourists who go everywhere and see everything.

When I visited Christ Church that afternoon I was pleased to see the President of the Arts Society there as well, making amends. Furthermore, he was suitably astonished at what he found.

CHRIST CHURCH PICTURE GALLERY

Opened in 1968, winning awards for its design, this modern gallery is situated at the back of the college's Canterbury quadrangle – a setting which, by contrast, is steeped in history. The collection is noted for quality rather than quantity (though it includes 2,000 drawings), with the discerning selection of old masters that a venerable seat of learning *should* have. The main benefactor, and a former member of the college, was General John Guise, who fought with Marlborough in the Netherlands and died in 1765 – his portrait by Joshua Reynolds is part of the collection. While known for his bravery in battle he was endowed with taste as well and his bequest included works by Tintoretto, Veronese, Van Dyck, and Annibale Carracci's large and impressive *The Butcher's Shop*, which was once owned by Charles I.

One of the earliest works is *Calvary* or *The Crucifixion* by the fifteenth-century artist from Siena, Giovanni di Paolo. It was acquired by Walter Savage Landor and bequeathed by his great-nieces Miss Landor and Miss Duke in 1897. *Scullion* by John Riley (1646–91) portrays a surly looking menial and hung previously in the Christ Church Buttery, where the man might well have worked.

The gallery also includes the striking *Wounded Centaur* by Fra Filippo Lippi, and Van Dyck's *Soldier on Horseback*, a loose sketch with a swift, spontaneous sense of movement, which is one of the most popular exhibits. The favourite work of the Assistant Curator, Miss Lucy Whitaker, is the delicate, moving *Lamentation* by Hugo van der Goes, a fragment of a larger picture.

Altogether, this is a modern gallery which is not as well known as it deserves to be, and whose staff are exceptionally helpful. There are talks on the collection every Thursday at 2.15, lasting forty-five minutes. They are included in the entrance charge of 40p for adults, with reductions for students and children. Guided tours for a party can be arranged in advance by ringing 0865 276172.

ASHMOLEAN MUSEUM OF ART AND ARCHAEOLOGY

The Ashmolean has the distinction of being the oldest public museum in the country. Now part of the university, it started life in 1602 when Sir Thomas Bodley provided a gallery for antiquities in his famous Library. In his turn, Elias Ashmole gave his collection of 'rarities' to Oxford in 1675 on condition that a suitable museum was built to house it, but it was not until 1908 that the galleries in their present neoclassical setting were given the name Ashmolean in his honour.

I had the bad luck to arrive on a Monday morning to find the museum closed, but the good fortune to be given a guided tour by Dr Nicholas Penny, the Keeper of the Department of Western Art, and an authority on Piranesi, Raphael, and Ruskin. Walking through the beautiful rooms with their polished parquet floors, unlocking the myriad security doors, Dr Penny drew my attention to two remarkable paintings whose existence I was unaware of: Paolo Uccello's (1396–1475) *A Hunt in a Forest* and Piero di Cosimo's (1462–1521) *A Forest Fire*.

Uccello's is a joyful celebration of the hunt with a mélange of horses, dogs and huntsmen among the trees. It is marvellously fluid for such an early date, with a perspective and a youthful spirit that are surprising, particularly when one learns that this is the work of an elderly man who complained in a tax return in 1467 (it is reassuring to know that they had them even then), 'I am old, infirm and unemployed, and my wife is ill.'

Although Cosimo's painting came later, it reflects the old belief that primitive animals existed with human heads. This myth was surprisingly widespread; as late as the sixteenth century Andre Thévet illustrated a leopard-like creature with back claws, front human hands and a human head in *La Cosmographie universelle*, with the claim that such a creature could still be seen on the banks of the Red Sea. In 1607 a similar animal, a 'quadruped with a human face', was included in the first English edition of Conrad Gesner's *Historie of the Four-footed Beastes*. It was described as a breed of hyena known as the mantichora, the Persian for man-eater, and was endowed with the body of a tiger, the tail of a scorpion, and the face of a human.

Cosimo's extraordinary painting shows a deer-like animal with a bearded human face, and another sheep-like creature with the face of a woman. It is probably one of a series illustrating the history of primeval man, along with *The Hunt* and *The Return from the Hunt*, both of which hang in the Metropolitan Museum in New York. *The Hunt* depicts centaur-like humans with clubs, not far removed from the copulating animals which they kill – a brutal concept. Fire rages in the background but remains unused for man has yet to discover its advantages, either for warmth or forging weapons.

It is claimed that *The Forest Fire* shows the later development of man's discovery of fire. The art historian Erwin Panofsky states that the painting is concerned with the middle stage in man's evolution – 'a transition from the unmitigated bestiality to a comparatively human life' – and it is suggested that Cosimo may have been inspired by the account of the discovery of fire by Vitruvius in *De Architectura*, quoted in Boccaccio's *Della Genealogia Decorum*, a popular source for Renaissance artists: 'In the olden days men were born like wild beasts in woods and caves and groves, and kept alive by eating raw food. Somewhere, meanwhile, the close-grown trees tossed by storms and winds rubbing their branches together caught fire. Terrified by the flames, those near the spot fled. When the fire subsided, they drew near, and since they noticed how pleasant to their bodies was the warmth of the fire, they laid on wood; and thus keeping it alive, they brought up some of their fellows and, indicating the fire with gestures, they showed them the use they might make of it.'

Although *The Forest Fire* shows animals in flight, and man – a peasant returning to his hut – apparently indifferent, the fire rages just as uncontrollably as it does in *The Hunt*. That is part of the picture's appeal – that it is open to interpretation.

An early *Life of Piero di Cosimo* reveals a glorious eccentric as strange as some of the animals he depicted, living 'the life of a wild beast rather than that of a man. He would never suffer his rooms to be swept, and would eat just at such moments as he felt hungry, he would not have the soil of his garden cultivated, or the fruit trees pruned, but suffered the vines to grow wild . . . and he used to say that everything of that kind was better left to Nature to be tended by herself alone . . .

'While seeking to penetrate the secrets of his art, no effort was too severe; he would endure any hardship for the mere love which he bore to the pursuit . . . totally regardless of himself and his personal convenience, insomuch that he would allow himself no better food than eggs, and to save firing, he cooked these only when he had prepared a fire to boil his glues, varnishes etc; nor would he cook them even thus by six or eight at a time, but boiled them by fifties; he would set them apart in a basket, and ate them at any moment when he felt the necessity for food . . .'

Yet this wild man of art was such good company that 'his hearers would be ready to die with laughing', until he neared the age of eighty when he became so strange and capricious that no one could bear to be with him.

A Forest Fire   Piero di Cosimo   Ashmolean Museum, Oxford

The Ashmolean catalogue, with absorbing illustrations relevant to Cosimo's masterpiece, claims that 'His style of painting forms a link between the Early and the High Renaissance and in this respect Piero di Cosimo's contribution to Florentine painting runs parallel to that of his contemporaries Botticelli, Fra Filippo Lippi (whose *Wounded Centaur* can be seen at Christ Church), Signorelli and Leonardo da Vinci, whose works are often echoed in Piero di Cosimo's own.'

After the impact of *The Forest Fire*, it is a relief to turn to the gentler landscape of Philips de Koninck's massive *A View over Flat Country*, a painting of the Dutch School in the mid-seventeenth century; and the last painting by Claude, *Landscape with Ascanius Shooting the Stag of Sylvia*.

Other paintings to look for are Tiepolo's famous *A Young Woman with a Macaw*, featured on the cover of the Ashmolean catalogue; Poussin's *The Exposition of Moses* and Guardi's *Pius VI Blessing the Multitude* (a similar work hangs in Upton House, Banbury). *Saint Jerome* in the desert surrounded by lions, a subject which inspired artists such as Dürer (Fitzwilliam, Cambridge) is represented here in a small and vivid painting attributed to Bellini by Bernard Berenson. It is close to perfection. A handsome and often winsome selection of Pre-Raphaelites includes

Rest on the Flight to Egypt   Samuel Palmer   Ashmolean Museum, Oxford

Holman Hunt's literary *A converted British Family sheltering a Christian Priest from the Persecution of the Druids*, which is hugely popular and captures everything I dislike in art, for it is as ponderous as its title. Equally popular are Millais's *The Return of the Dove to the Ark* and Arthur Hughes' *Home from the Sea*, also known as *The Sailor Boy* or *Mother's Grave*. While I admire the Pre-Raphaelites, I find these particularly cloying. The eye-openers for me were the Samuel Palmer drawings of Shoreham, kept under glass; the Turner watercolours of the rivers of France; and Ruskin's drawings, which have been compiled in a delightful small book by Nicholas Penny and are on sale at the Ashmolean. The delicacy yet confidence of Ruskin's draughtsmanship make these drawings comparable to Turner, the artist he revered and championed, and whose watercolours he donated to the university.

When you learn that the Ashmolean also contains the largest collection in existence of drawings by Raphael, originally formed by Sir Thomas Lawrence and bought for the university by public subscription in 1846, while a section was acquired by the Prince of Orange; a series of drawings by Michelangelo; and the work of such modern artists as Corot, Boudin, Van Gogh, Toulouse-Lautrec, Pissarro and Picasso, with a lesser-known version of Sickert's famous *Ennui*, painted in Fitzroy Street in 1918, you can only hope to return to do the collection justice.

Study of Gneiss Rock   John Ruskin   Ashmolean Museum, Oxford

Southampton

ART GALLERY

Considering that it opened in 1939, closing that same year for the duration of the war, the Southampton Gallery is surprisingly rich in its possessions. Apart from such old masters as the *Madonna and Child* by Bellini; *Portrait of a Woman* by Van Dyck; and the triptych on wood of *The Coronation of the Virgin* by Allegretto Nuzi, there is work by Blake, Wright of Derby, an important Constable, and *The*

Shipwreck by de Loutherbourg, whose seascapes are so impressive in the Maritime Museum at Greenwich. There is also a seascape by Turner: *The Wave*.

The list is impressive: John Martin; William Etty; Holman Hunt and Ford Madox Brown, but Southampton excels in the equally distinguished collection of twentieth-century art, including work by many of the artists referred to in this book.

Edward Burra has a typical *Café* watercolour, and Mark Gertler a fleshy, dusky nude, one of four works. There are seven by Gaudier-Brzeska, and two contrasting examples of Augustus and Gwen John: his robust *Brigit* (one of six works) and her more reticent *Girl in a Mulberry Dress*. Matthew Smith has five pictures; Stanley Spencer four, including a striking portrait of *Patricia Preece* his second wife; while Walter Sickert has five pictures, with the delightful portrait of himself as *The Juvenile Lead*.

Having known the artists, I have a special sympathy for John Minton's (1917–57) view of *Rotherhithe from Wapping*, having known that view as well; and Nina Hamnet's portrait of Horace Brodsky.

It is curious that Belgium, of all countries, should have produced two of the leading surrealists: Magritte and Paul Delvaux, though this could be a reaction to the flatness of their surroundings. Here is a typical Delvaux, instantly recognisable, of a bare-breasted mermaid on a plinth with a line of classical temples behind her reaching to the sea, *A Siren in Full Moonlight*. Born in 1897, Delvaux came under the influence of Chirico, and subsequently he went to Rome where he was impressed by the architecture. The fusion of these interests, classical and surrealist, created the Delvaux style which you either admire or detest as sickly-sweet exoticism, far removed from true surrealism.

It is difficult and rather pointless to nominate an outstanding picture in this varied collection – or any collection for that matter. Tastes will vary: some people might choose the striking oil by William Roberts, *Revolt in the Desert*; others the Turner of *The Fisherman upon a Lee-Shore in Squally Weather*, instantly recognisable; or Sisley's *Avenue of Chestnut Trees*.

I would suggest the Gainsborough of *George Venables Vernon*, virtually a double portrait of the second Lord Vernon and his brown and white dog, which is leaping up affectionately, stroked by his master. Without the obligatory fussiness of costume of the Gainsborough girls there is a pleasing simplicity and nothing is extraneous. The painting was bought by the Chipperfield Fund with a grant from the National Art-Collections Fund in 1957.

Robert Chipperfield was a local councillor and JP whose bequest to the City provided for an art school and gallery with a fund for further works of art which were bought on the shrewd advice of the late Lord Clark. The other benefactor was a wealthy American called Arthur Tilden Jeffress who ran an art gallery in London and left his pictures to Southampton. (See Collectors, p. 227).

AUGUSTUS JOHN

1878–1961

As the archetypal, bearded, bohemian artist, Augustus John was lionised at the start of the century when the famous were eager to sit for him, including Dylan Thomas, Bernard Shaw and Madame Suggia with her cello.

The most brilliant student of his day, he joined the New English Club in 1903 and became the popular rebel in British art, creating an image of romantic beauty with the gipsy-like models in his paintings, inspired by the real women in his life, who were frequently the same.

This period of his work is memorable, though his bravura personality enhanced it at the time. His promiscuity was so notorious that when he patted the heads of children as he walked through the streets of London, he explained that he did so in case some of them were his. He blazed the way like a privileged hippy by setting up his family in a gipsy commune complete with caravans – delightfully scandalous at the time. His second wife, Dorelia, known as Dodo, had such faith in her husband's genius that she forgave his infidelity and only put her foot down when his girlfriends descended on their country home when he was away, sending young devotees packing. At a later stage, she expressed a doubt to the novelist Richard Hughes as they were walking with a boy of four, believed to be John's youngest illegitimate son:

'There's one thing about John I've never got used to, not after all these years,' she confided. Hughes glanced at the child apprehensively, and she continued.

'I don't know what to do about it. Time after time *he's late for lunch.*'

This revealing story, which sums up marriage in a sentence, is told by Michael Holroyd in his splendid biography of Augustus John published by Heinemann in 1975.

John fell out of favour because he was too proficient, too understandable. Today it is hard to realise how important he was in the first half of this century – an ARA in 1921; RA in 1929; awarded the Order of Merit in 1942. Perhaps his standing has diminished even further because his reputation was so theatrical that it needed the man himself to sustain it, and it became slightly ridiculous after his death. He lived too long, for that can tarnish as well as confirm and in his case he became outdated compared to the shock of the new.

When I travelled to his home at Fordingbridge on the edge of the New Forest, to take his photograph for *Picture Post*, he had turned to sculpture in the hope of finding new inspiration, after the formidable Italian sculptress, Fiore de Henriques, had done his bust. He claimed this was 'a new phase in my history' and that he took to it 'like a duck to water', but Epstein gave the thumbs down, calling it 'the sculpture of a painter; it's sensitive, but you could stick your finger through it. It's interesting, but it's not real sculpture.' After eighteen months the phase was over.

I am not sure if the disconcerting glare in my photograph is due to his new-found confidence or the sickening realisation that he was not going to succeed in his new interest. Perhaps it was simply the last huff and puff bravado which he indulged in when guests arrived expecting an explosion, but by now the fires were damped.

While his sister's reputation soars, Augustus John is underrated by comparison, even excluded from the Royal Academy's exhibition of British art this century, which was an absurd omission considering some of the abstract rubbish it contained. The best of his oils have vigour and such line portraits as that of T.E. Lawrence in the National Portrait Gallery, or that of Yeats in Walsall, confirm that John was an outstanding draughtsman whose reputation will rise again.

Work by Augustus John can be seen in:
Aberdeen, City Art Gallery
Bedford, The Cecil Higgins Museum
Birmingham, City Art Gallery
Cambridge, Fitzwilliam Museum
Leeds, City Art Gallery
London, The Tate Gallery
Newcastle, The Laing Gallery
Preston, The Harris Museum
Southampton, Art Gallery
Walsall, Art Gallery

Sudbury

GAINSBOROUGH'S HOUSE

This is the house where Thomas Gainsborough was born in 1727. With no example of the Newlyn School at Newlyn, nor a single oil by Hogarth in Hogarth House, it comes as a relief to report that sixteen or more Gainsboroughs hang in the house which bears his name, even though only two of these are owned while the rest are on loan.

Gainsborough's house was opened to the public in 1961, started by the Gainsborough House Society which claims that this is the only birthplace of a great British artist where that artist's pictures can be seen.

There was controversy in 1984 when an early work was bought for £68,000 with grants from the National Heritage Fund, the Purchase Grant Fund, which is administered by the V & A, and the Gainsborough's House Society Development Trust. Although the painting of the costume and the landscape indicated his later mastery, there was doubt about the composition, particularly the position of the hat, which might have been moved while the painting was in progress, and a red tulip, which could have been added afterwards to indicate that the boy had died.

These doubts were expressed most forcibly by the fiery, red-haired actress Adrienne Corri, who declared that the work, described as a portrait of Master

Portrait of a Boy   Thomas Gainsborough   Gainsborough's House, Sudbury, Suffolk

William Mackinnon, due to the similarity to a painting by Hogarth with the same title, was 'quite uncharacteristic of Gainsborough. It has none of the quality. It is very sad and very terrible that it has happened.'

Miss Corri spoke with some authority, having rediscovered a genuine Gainsborough, a sooty portrait of the actor David Garrick, lurking in the corner of a theatre in Birmingham. For seven years she defied the experts until she was vindicated when she found her evidence in a Bank of England vault in the form of a receipt for the picture and payment to Mr Gainsborough.

Needless to say her doubts over Master Mackinnon were unwelcome at Gainsborough's House. The Curator, Hugh Belsey, reaffirmed his faith in the picture, pointing out that some of the questions raised could be answered when the heavy varnish had been removed, itself a costly business. The cleaning revealed a large bit of skirt on the left-hand side. Telling me to forget all about Mackinnon,

Hugh Belsey says there is little doubt that this is a fragment of a larger picture of a brother and sister, for 'sibling portraits' were commonplace at the time. He claims that the cleaning has confirmed the picture as a genuine Gainsborough, dismisses the suspicions of Miss Corri, and there the matter simmers.

Less controversial, indeed undisputed, is the impressive late Gainsborough landscape painted in 1782, only six years before the artist's death, purchased for Gainsborough's House in 1988.

THOMAS GAINSBOROUGH

1727–88

Gainsborough was born in Sudbury and moved to London when he was thirteen. He is remembered for his striking portraits of society ladies who were dressed so elegantly that the label of a 'Gainsborough Girl' is synonymous with style. Unlike most of his rivals he did not rely on assistants, painting the dresses and draperies himself with such attention to detail that the eye tends to drift away from the sitter until the outraged haughtiness of the Countess of Howe in Kenwood, or the Hon Mrs Graham in Edinburgh, draws it back. Yet he prided himself on a good likeness, writing to Lord Dartmouth, 'I am vastly out in my notion of the thing if the Face does not look like.'

In spite of such mastery, a few of his portraits seem slightly vapid – such as the Pink Boy, the lesser-known companion to the Blue Boy. His rival, Sir Joshua Reynolds, has been described as 'cool', yet his portrait of Miss Bowles with her dog in the Wallace is positively gleeful compared to Gainsborough's portrait of Miss Haverfield, in which the girl is adjusting her cape as if she is going for a walk, but one feels that no speck of mud would dare to fall on someone so immaculate. Of course that contrast could be due to the different natures of the two girls, yet the same applies to the portraits of Mrs Siddons: Gainsborough's is sedate, another fashion plate, while the Reynolds is a Muse full of fire and passion. Like anyone else artists have to sell their work to earn their keep, and the suspicion that Gainsborough was frequently cursed by this necessity is confirmed when one sees his portrait, *Robert Andrews and his Wife*, for it is set in their own landscape which unfolds behind them. It is a bold concept which works so successfully that it is surprising he did not combine portrait and landscape painting more, as Stubbs did after him. Gainsborough painted this portrait in his early twenties and it reveals his love of landscape painting which gradually took second place as his popularity grew, until his final years.

Fortunately there are numerous landscapes in our galleries to prove his excellence: *Sunset: Carthorses Drinking at a Stream* and *The Market Cart*, both in the Tate; and *Going to Market* at Kenwood are three supreme examples.

Wales

and the

West Country

Diving Woman Paul Cézanne National Museum of Wales, Cardiff

Compared to the abundance of galleries in the north, they are sparse in the West – to put it generously. Some areas are virtually bereft. There is one glorious exception, The National Museum of Wales in Cardiff, which contains the bequest of the Misses Davies (see p. 165).

The Grahan Sutherland Foundation, Haverfordwest, is an honourable exception, too, on a smaller and more personal scale. The Foundation was established by Sutherland himself without support from any public fund, and it contains the largest collection of his work normally available to the public. He loved this part of Britain, which inspired many of his finest and most characteristic paintings – a twisted landscape of boulders, spikes and hawthorn trees, rocks, roots, and a bird flying over Sandy Haven at low tide. As Peter Fuller wrote in his controversial article on the respective merits of Sutherland and Bacon, *Nature and Raw Flesh*, (*Modern Painters*) Sutherland had a 'Ruskinian capacity to see in a pebble the grandeur and scale of a mountain range'.

Sutherland returned to Pembrokeshire in 1967 for a television film and fell in love with that landscape once more, returning on his own the following year and frequently from then on until his death, relating to it more closely than he could to the harsher colours of the south of France at Menton where he had settled. Consequently this gallery is a fitting tribute to this fine and gentle artist, however unfashionable he may be now. Should you go near Haverfordwest, a visit to this gallery will confirm his importance to twentieth-century British art.

The National Portrait Gallery at Bodelwyddan Castle has been described as a Victorian out-station of the main gallery in London, and justifies this with a formidable collection of Victorian portraits. As the so-called 'castle' had been a girls' school since 1920, the recent conversion was a bold project since rewarded by numerous awards including 'Winner of the National Heritage Museum of the Year' in 1989. Deservedly so, for the architect Roderick Gradidge has re-created a sumptuous country house with Victorian furniture, wallpaper and statuary – a brilliantly imaginative concept which attracted 60,000 visitors in the first year. It is so well done that the gallery is worth visiting for the setting alone, quite apart from the paintings it contains.

Possibly due to the lack of local support, compared to those benevolent industrialists in the north, Devon and Cornwall lack the galleries they deserve.

This does not mean that there is no interest in art, simply that it is harder to find an outlet in spite of the fame of such distinguished local artists as Patrick Heron and Roger Hilton, and of course the Cornish primitive Alfred Wallis.

Then there is the Newlyn School, which is becoming increasingly fashionable, many of whose artists were influenced by Bastien-Lepage, who painted Sir Henry Irving but is better known for his scenes of Brittany. The most famous member of the Newlyn School is Stanhope Forbes, who depicted such scenes as *Off to the*

Graham Sutherland, Cap Ferrat, circa 1954

Fishing Ground, now in the Walker Gallery, Liverpool.

Another artist, little known during his lifetime and virtually forgotten now, is Walter Langley, one of the aberrations in British art who painted scenes of grieving families waiting for fishermen to return from the stormy sea, with endless sentimental titles like *Never Morning Wore to Evening but Some Heart Did Break*. Of all the Newlyn School he received the highest praise from the unlikely source of Leo Tolstoy.

In his essay *What is Art?* Tolstoy referred to a picture exhibited in the English Academy of 1897 (presumably the Royal Academy) which was reproduced in a book and showed a stray beggar boy befriended by a woman who is giving him something to eat, while a girl of seven looks on and 'realised for the first time what poverty is, and what inequality is, and asking herself why she has everything provided for her while the boy goes barefoot and hungry? She feels sorry and yet pleased. And she loves the boy and goodness . . . And one feels that the artist loved this girl, and that she too loves. And this picture, by an artist who, I think, is not very widely known, is an admirable and true work of art.' Indeed, Tolstoy was so moved that he went further: 'If I were asked to give modern examples of the highest art, flowing from love of God and man in literature I should name *The Robbers* by Schiller; Victor Hugo's *Les Misérables*; the novels and stories of Dickens . . .; *Uncle Tom's Cabin*; Dostoevsky's works; and *Adam Bede* by George Eliot. In modern painting, strange to say, works of this kind, directly transmitting the Christian feeling of love of God and one's neighbours, are hardly to be found.' Then he quotes the exception: the painting by Walter Langley.

I hope the forgotten Langley knew that he was Tolstoy's favourite British artist. Disconcertingly, there is not a single painting of the Newlyn School in the Newlyn Orion Gallery, but this is a beautiful building right on the waterfront, worth seeing for temporary exhibitions and local work.

The Falmouth Art Gallery has a wide selection including engravings by Dürer and Blake, and paintings by Sir Alfred Munnings and Dame Laura Knight. Probably the best-known picture was *The Lady of Shalott* by John Williams Waterhouse, a full-size study of which was the artist's Royal Academy exhibit of 1894, and now hangs in Leeds.

There are also six paintings by one of the leading members of the Newlyn School, Henry Scott Tuke, with scenes of Genoa and St Tropez in addition to the inevitable subject which obsessed him, naked *Boys Bathing*. Apparently this was an innocent passion, even if a deep desire was sublimated on to canvas.

The Plymouth Museum and Art Gallery has a richer collection than most people appreciate, a neglect that may be due to its position in the same institutional building as the museum. In the gallery you can find a wide representation of the Newlyn School, with work by Norman Garston and his daughter Alathea, Samuel Lamorna Birch, and Scott Tuke's painting of a boy on the deck of a fishing boat, *Taking a Spell*. Here, too, is one of the most famous works by Stanhope Forbes, *A Fish Sale on a Cornish Beach* (1885). And, as a special bonus, be sure to see the work by Tolstoy's favourite British painter – *When One is Old*, by Walter Langley.

There are examples of the Camden School; Wilson Steer; and Christopher Wood, himself a Cornish artist, along with work by Roger Hilton and Patrick Heron.

A Fish Sale on a Cornish Beach   Stanhope Forbes   Plymouth City Museum & Art Gallery

If the Newlyn School has captivated, continue to Penzance, where the Penlea House Museum has work by Elizabeth Forbes, the wife of Stanhope, and, in particular, the celebrated picture by Norman Garston, *It Raineth Every Day*.

Exeter

ROYAL ALBERT MEMORIAL MUSEUM

Returning north, you could stop at Exeter to visit the Royal Albert Memorial Museum in Queen Street, which was founded in 1868 after Albert's death by Sir Stafford Northcote, a leading Exeter personality who acted as secretary to the Prince in the Great Exhibition of 1851. Northcote founded a complex – college, library, school of art – similar to that at South Kensington, as a tribute to Albert's memory, though it has dispersed over the years.

The entrance hall is magnificent and has been recently restored in the Victorian colours which the original designers intended – marine blue, cherry, gold and black – though they ran out of funds and resorted to the Ruskinian theme of cream and maroon. Even more startling is the natural history collection of North American and Indian artefacts, with immense stuffed animals.

After this, the pictures seem an anticlimax, though the museum possesses a valuable album of drawings by Constable, discovered in Exeter's library in 1976 and transferred to the gallery two years later. It also contains a similar volume of drawings by Benjamin Robert Haydon, an extraordinary artist whom Plymouth and Exeter have in common.

Haydon was born in Plymouth where his self-portrait, painted at the age of sixty, hangs alongside two of his gigantic canvases. While painting the *Maid of Saragossa*, Haydon had a mishap, dropping a bayonet on to his left foot: 'It bled copiously. As I wanted blood, I painted away on the ground of my Saragossa whilst the surgeon was coming. Never lose an opportunity!' The episode epitomises Haydon's life.

Exeter contains the largest collection of Haydon's work in Britain, including his famous *Marcus Curtius Plunging Into the Gulf*, which caused a sensation in its day and was widely parodied. This is so large that it is frequently hidden behind a screen to make way for other work – a characteristic fate. But several Haydons are on display, and Exeter contains another self-portrait, the *Spirit of the Vine*, as well as the volume of drawings.

Sometimes, especially in the case of such eccentric artists as Walter Greaves, Richard Dadd and Haydon, it helps to know what the man is like. If you wish to see more of his work at Exeter after reading the ensuing chapter, it would be advisable to check beforehand with the curator, Miss Jane Baker, in order to make an appointment to see the work not normally on display. As always with Haydon, a warning is wise.

BENJAMIN ROBERT HAYDON

1786–1846

> Let us do honour to his perennial worth
>
> Holman Hunt

Haydon was one of the sublime failures in British art. He would have been dismayed by such a description, for he regarded his work with desperate solemnity as he veered from triumph to disasters of his own making. He tilted at every artistic windmill, upset the very patrons prepared to help him and antagonised the Royal Academicians whose support was crucial. He exasperated his friends by airing his grievances in public, provoking David Wilkie to implore him, 'Don't be violent, flying in their faces is not the way,' but it was Haydon's way. Yet there

Marcus Curtius Leaping Into the Gulf   Benjamin Robert Haydon
Royal Albert Memorial Museum, Exeter

was enough basic decency in the man to retain the loyalty of his friends even when he drove it to breaking point. His tolerant landlord allowed him to eat on credit, and his family adored him. Some of the most distinguished figures of his time – Sir Robert Peel, Sir Walter Scott, and the powerful patron Sir George Beaumont – were prepared to stand by him when he landed in trouble, though he exasperated Beaumont by disclosing their correspondence after a dispute concerning the size of a commissioned canvas: 'I have a great aversion to people showing letters,' protested Sir George, 'nothing, you know, is so indelicate.'

Another patron was so enraged that he punished a painting he bought from Haydon by hanging it in his stables. Today it is back in the stately home, though the descendants of the Marquis admits it is not in the best condition.

Keats admired Haydon and Wordsworth composed a sonnet in his honour, though the words are as turgid as Haydon's worst excesses in paint:

> Haydon! let worthier judges praise the skill
> Here by thy pencil shown in truth of lines,
> And charm of colours; I applaud those signs
> Of thought that give the true poetic thrill . . . and so on.

These lines were inspired by Haydon's 'Picture of Buonaparte', a subject he painted incessantly, with thirteen 'Musings at St Helena'. He was equally obsessed by the Duke of Wellington.

It was a close-run thing that he became a painter at all, for his eyesight was so poor that he had to wear concave glasses and place his models at a considerable distance in order to gain the right perspective. Then he charged at the canvas as he did at life.

How simple it would have been if Haydon had not been so obstinate, but when he came to London at the age of eighteen, against the wishes of his doting parents in Plymouth, he did so 'breathing aspirations of "High Art" and defiance to all opposition'.

Throughout his life he was determined to paint on the grand scale with immense historical and biblical themes. He believed this was his destiny, ignoring the harsh reality that such paintings had gone out of fashion and were hard to sell. 'Why did you have to paint it so large?' asked Hazlitt of *The Judgement of Solomon*. 'A small canvas might have concealed your faults.' Cruel, because it was so true.

I Smell a Stink   Benjamin Robert Haydon   Royal Albert Memorial Museum, Exeter

Haydon could not be dissuaded from his lofty purpose and when he was obliged to paint portraits in order to support his family, he took his revenge on the sitters: 'Finished one cursed portrait,' he wrote in 1829. 'I have an exquisite gratification in painting portraits wretchedly. I love to see the sitters look as if they thought, Can this be Haydon's painting? I chuckle. I am rascal enough to take their money and chuckle more. When a man says "Paint me a historical picture" my heart swells towards him.' Inevitably the demand for his 'wretched' portraits decreased, while few people asked for historical paintings. Yet Aldous Huxley insisted, in a surprising defence of Haydon's scope, 'Reduce him within narrow limits, and you cut off half his resources. His genius is gigantic.'

Describing his 'national triumph' at the age of thirty-four when he exhibited *Christ's Entry into Jerusalem* at the Egyptian Hall in Leicester Square, Haydon exulted, 'I had proved that the people cared about High Art, and that an Englishman could execute it. I had defied the Academy; I had kept my position against its incessant obloquy. The rush was so great and went on increasing; the success so palpable, so decided that the Academicians got into a fury and crept in to see it one at a time, each holding forth to their friends and damning it by saying it had good parts. Notwithstanding the feeling displayed in its favour, the abuse was so great that it was the subject of a positive battle.'

In those days the artist paid all the expenses, sometimes with a lottery for the picture itself, so it was vital to attract the crowds, and such controversy helped.

A year later, in 1821, Haydon wrote about another 'remarkable day' in his life: 'I am arrested. After having passed through every species of want and difficulty, often without a shilling, and without ever being trusted; now when I am flourishing, I am become a beacon; and a tradesman, who, if I had been on a level with himself, would have pitied my situation, is proud of the opportunity to show me he is as good a man.'

Haydon cheered up when he found the arresting officer staring with amazement at his painting of 'Lazarus'. 'Oh my God, Sir!' the man exclaimed with awe, 'I won't take you.' Delighted, Haydon surrendered voluntarily.

Haydon was sent to prison with surprising regularity, although debt was not the disgrace it would be today. 'I am in prison,' he declared with the nonchalance of Mr Toad, 'so were Bacon, Raleigh and Cervantes. Vanity! Vanity! Here's a consolation!'

Two years later he wrote to his creditors, 'gentlemen, after nine years' intense devotion to historical painting, known and respected by many of the most celebrated men in Europe, and acknowledged in my own country to deserve encouragement, the Bench is my refuge! That I have not failed in the execution of my pictures the thousands who have seen them in Scotland and England, and paid for seeing them, give proof.' He failed to realise that he was caught in a vicious circle with his paintings scattered among his creditors as a form of security.

'Where is your *Solomon?*' asked a friend. 'Hung up in a grocer's shop.' 'Where's your *Jerusalem?*' 'In a ware-house in Holborn.' 'Where's your *Lazarus?*' 'In an upholsterer's in Mount Street.' 'And your *Macbeth?*' 'In Chancery.' 'Your *Pharaoh?*'

'In an attic, pledged.' 'My God! And your *Crucifixion*?' 'In a hayloft.' '*Silenus*?' 'Sold for half-price.' The friend expressed astonishment that Haydon had not gone mad.

His faith in himself takes on the dimension of blind courage. Turning his experience of prison to his advantage, he wrote, 'In the midst of this dreadful scene of affliction up sprang the masquerade election – a scene which, contrasted as it was with sorrow and prison walls, beggars all description. Distracted as I was, I was perpetually drawn to the windows by the boisterous merriment of the unfortunate happy beneath me. Rabelais or Cervantes alone could do it justice with their pens. Never was such an exquisite burlesque.'

The Mock Election was shown at the Egyptian Hall the following year and bought by King George IV – 'Today has been a bright day in the annals of my life. The King has purchased my picture and paid me money.' It remains in the royal collection. The royal patronage strengthened his belief that the government should act as a patron of the arts, which was a novel idea for the time, and gave him renewed confidence. Armour-plated in the cause of High Art, without a chink of self-doubt showing, he acknowledged his personal indebtedness to God in an annual report: 'The moment I touch a great canvas I think I see my Creator smiling on all my efforts.'

In 1841 he assessed the profit and the loss: 'I have loved Art always better than myself. I dissected and drew two years before I painted. My pictures of Solomon, Jerusalem and Lazarus are indisputable evidences of genius. I stood forth and defended the Elgin Marbles [Haydon was instrumental in saving them for England]. I have lost all my property; have been refused the honours of my country . . . [etcetera] . . . for my invincible devotion to the great object now about to be carried.'

At this low moment, fame and fortune came within his grasp. The great 'object' was the fulfilment of his campaign during the previous twenty years to persuade parliament to subsidise historical painters on the grand scale – like himself – pestering anyone in authority to commission him to paint a series of murals for the new House of Lords, which he saw as the fruition of his genius. In Parliament, at least, there was sufficient *space*.

Perhaps he wore them down, or his friends spoke out in sympathy, for they decided that Haydon was indeed the right man for this massive task. At this critical point, he blustered into print with an attack on the 'vicious influence of German art' on the Royal Commission. As this was headed by the Hanoverian prince consort, the aghast commission awarded the murals for the Houses of Parliament to his younger rival, G.F. Watts.

Outraged at seeing his rightful prize offered to someone else, Haydon determined to prove himself the better man and started work on two of the murals he had in mind, a rash undertaking with no guarantee of a sale. When the work was finished he hired the Egyptian Hall as usual, sent tickets to everyone listed in the court guide, looked after the printing of the catalogue and posters, and sat back and waited expectantly. 'Admit Noodle, Doodle and their numerous friends,' he

Waiting for the Times Benjamin Robert Haydon
by kind permission of the Managing Editor of The Times

scribbled merrily on the invitation cards to his closest friends, certain that the crowds would flock to see the two masterpieces '*The Banishment of Aristedes* and *The Burning of Rome*, but neither Noodle, Doodle nor their friends appeared. It rained all day. 'Nobody came,' he confided to his journal. 'Twenty-six years ago the rain would not have prevented them. However, I do not despair.' After two weeks he counted his receipts which came to £1 2s. Three catalogues added an extra 1s 6d.

Haydon was the victim of a cruel joke played by fate: the crowds who avoided him flocked to another part of the Egyptian Hall to see a lesser attraction, the midget General Tom Thumb, exhibited by the greater showman Phineas T. Barnum.

On 21 April, Haydon made the bitter observation in a newspaper, 'Tom Thumb had 12,000 people last week; B.R. Haydon, 133½ (the ½ a little girl). Exquisite taste of the English people!'

Haydon was sixty and the first terrible doubt began to dawn, with his admissions which are poignant in view of his former bravado, 'It is the agony of ungratified ambition . . . The solitary grandeur of historical painting is gone.'

On 2 June he made a will, assessing his existing work so highly that his wife would never have to worry financially. Concluding his journals with a line from King Lear – 'Stretch me no longer on this rough world' (adding 'God forgive me. Finis of B.R. Haydon') – he placed an early portrait of his wife on an easel beside the picture he was working on, *Alfred and the first British Jury*, then he cut his throat.

Even in suicide, he botched the job and needed to shoot himself with a small revolver. A letter to his wife contained the explanation: 'Had I been encouraged nothing but good would have come from me, because when encouraged I paid everybody.'

As for that will, it proved a final act of self-delusion. Sir Robert Peel assisted the widow generously and a public subscription was raised for her in a sudden belated surge of sympathy for the artist who had lost faith in himself only at the end.

The tragi-comedy of Benjamin Robert Haydon has a happier postscript: his journals are his greater legacy to posterity. Recorded in copious detail, they give a revelatory glimpse of the life and people surrounding him, and fulfilled his vow to write the EXACT TRUTH, even to seeing the other person's side in an argument. He put them in a trunk, entrusting them to Miss Elizabeth Barrett in Wimpole Street, who was appalled by the imposition, until she read them after his death. Published in 1853 they proved a huge success and then went out of fashion like the paintings. Revived in a Macdonald illustrated classic in 1950, the editor, Malcolm Elwin, compared the journals to Pepys: 'All is here . . . among the liveliest documents in literature.'

Haydon touches the heart because of his *artlessness*. Sometimes this comes across in his painting, and certainly in the journals. Lord Oxford and Asquith paid a fitting tribute which recognised the innocence of the man: 'Haydon discloses to us his own personality with a freedom of reticence not unworthy of Rousseau – but one will look in vain to Rousseau for Haydon's simplicity and sincerity.'

Ultimately, Haydon's vaulting belief in himself was justified.

Benjamin Robert Haydon's work can be seen in:
Exeter, Royal Albert Memorial Museum
London, The Tate Gallery (*Punch or May Day* – probably his best-known painting)

Bristol

MUSEUM AND ART GALLERY

A worthy, stolid gallery in the best old-fashioned tradition, and if there is not much excitement it is blessedly free from the designer-cleverness which attracts or irritates at the Arnolfini at Bristol's Narrow Quay.

Foreign artists are represented by the excellence of Vuillard, Courbet and Boudin, and by an astonishing Giovanni Bellini of *Christ descending into Limbo*, which retains the power to shock.

British artists include many of the artists featured in this book: Matthew Smith, Sickert, Nash, Gertler, Leighton, and Stanhope Forbes, with a study of clouds by Constable, and Tissot's *Les Adieux*.

Contemporary British art is represented by the delightful artist Peter Blake, whose technique is compared to Warhol and Hockney, and who suffers from the label of a 'pop-artist' due to his affection for that scene, which he has celebrated with his famous sleeve for the Beatles' LP 'Sergeant Pepper's Lonely Hearts Club Band'. When Ken Russell featured Blake on the BBC programme Monitor in 1961, he called the film *Pop goes the Easel*. Yet Blake stands apart, less camp and more cosy. Because he is jolly and easy to understand, his versatility is underrated, though he was appointed a full member of the Royal Academy in 1981 and he has the distinction of having founded his own movement, The Brotherhood of Ruralists, when he moved from London in 1975 to live in the country. In his introduction to the Tate exhibition in 1983, Michael Compton concluded: 'finally he cannot be thought of as a Pop artist. His work has remained too personal, it has roots in other traditions, especially those of historic fine art, graphic art and illustration; "pop" imagery has only been a part of it.'

When Peter Blake appeared on *Gallery* I asked him which picture he would like to see in this book and he chose *The Owl and the Pussycat* (oil on hardboard) which was made to fit an embossed copper frame from which the shape of the boat is derived (much in the tradition of the Pre-Raphaelites), inspired by the poem of Edward Lear:

> The Owl and the Pussycat went to sea
> In a beautiful Pea-green boat.
> They took some money
> And plenty of honey
> Wrapped up in a five-pound note.

JAMES TISSOT

1836–1902

It is easy to dismiss Tissot as 'sweet'. Ruskin compared his work to 'coloured photographs of a vaguely vulgar society', and when I saw the exhibition at the Barbican I was overwhelmed by the similarity, as if I had devoured a meal composed of nothing but dessert.

Yet when I stumble on one of his pictures in a gallery, I am enchanted by the observation and wit. Two that spring to mind are *The Convalescent* in Manchester – an angry military figure in a wheel chair – and *Les Adieux* in the Bristol Art Gallery, which is painted with such sensitivity that the sentimentality is redeemed. As always with Tissot, the more you look the more you will find.

Tissot is an odd man out in British art, though one of the few expatriates who adapted instantly to England, as did Whistler. He was born in Nantes and moved to London in 1871 after the Franco-Prussian war. Unlike Monet and Pissaro, he stayed. This was partly due to Whistler who had known him in Paris and persuaded him to change his name from Jacques to James.

Though he had enjoyed success at the Paris Salon, he proved even more popular in London, selling *The Concert* to Agnew's for 1,200 guineas, a sensational sum a hundred years ago. When Degas asked him to join the first Impressionist exhibition in 1874, he refused, which is hardly surprising, for by then Tissot was no longer an Impressionist. His skill lay in the meticulous detail of his puzzle-pictures in which the title held a clue, and this appealed to the Victorians who enjoyed the element of mystery surrounding the elegant women in their elaborate dresses: a costume drama. In the *Portsmouth Dockyard* we wonder if the kilted soldier has forsaken the glum looking girl in the tartan shawl for her friend in the black and white dress. In *The Last Evening* the young mate stares wistfully at the girl who reclines in the long deck chair – lovers, perhaps? Are they being parted forever by her father and the captain who look on disapprovingly? *Les Adieux* (1871) conveys the agony of farewell, but why is it *adieux* rather than *au revoir*? And why do a pair of scissors dangle from a string against the maid's dress, indicating severance, while the ivy at their feet suggests togetherness? One can only guess, and that was the charm of it. Possibly this element of fun, always so alien to High Art, explains the dismissive attitude towards Tissot, but the picture is more than guesswork. Painted in the year he moved to London, Tissot has caught the flavour – almost the smell – of Cheyne Walk on an autumn day, and the particular class distinction of the English. One can imagine the enjoyment of the Victorians as they identified the details and read the thoughts of the girl whose face lacks the refinement of the upper classes while the contemplative groom, with his horse behind him ready for departure, takes her hand in his for the last time.

From 1876 to 1882 Tissot lived with an Irish divorcée called Kathleen Newton, beautiful and wholly delightful judging by the photograph of the two of them on a garden bench, his hand enclosing hers. His painting *The Artist with Kathleen Newton and her Daughter on a Riverbank* shows his scratching out the letters I LOVE

YOU with his stick. Eighteen years younger, she died of consumption when she was only twenty-eight, leaving him bereft. He returned to France and then spent years in the Holy Land working on religious paintings and a series on the life of Christ which was never completed, his former, gentle sense of fun eradicated. Tissot died in 1902 and for the next thirty years his work was virtually forgotten.

Tissot's work can be seen in galleries and museums throughout the country, including:
Bristol, Museum and Art Gallery
Manchester, City Art Gallery

Cardiff
NATIONAL MUSEUM OF WALES

This is the glorious exception to the comparative indifference to art in the West Country, even though the place seems frequently closed for 'refurbishment' with the French Impressionists on loan. The gallery remains surprisingly unknown to the public, even, I suspect, to the Welsh themselves.

The French Impressionists are the priceless asset, bequeathed by the Misses Davies referred to in the chapter on *Collectors* (see p. 227). Not only is the range extensive, the artists are seen at their best. Cézanne's *Montagnes, L'Estaque*, originally bought by Gauguin and sold by his wife, was praised by Roger Fry as one of the greatest of all his landscapes. Monet is represented by a study of Rouen Cathedral, three of the *Waterlilies*, which obsessed him at the end of his life, and *The Pool of London*.

Renoir's joyful *Parisian Girl*, dressed in blue, was shown at the first Impressionist exhibition in 1874, and was bought by Miss Gwendoline Davies at the National Portrait Society's exhibition in 1913. The girl was an actress, Madame Henriette Henriot, one of Renoir's favourite models at the time, and although the picture was criticised for a lack of finish, it seems close to perfection now. *The Head of a Girl*, a later oil of around 1882, was bought by Margaret Davies in Paris in 1914. The *Seated Couple*, from the later 'red period' (1912), exudes the wellbeing of a hot day, with two people who could not be described as young lovers but who share the understanding of a long affection. It was painted in Renoir's garden at Essoyes near the wine-growing district of Burgundy, an old apple tree with a leaning trunk appearing on the right. A fine example of Renoir's old age, Gwendoline Davies bought it in Paris in 1917. What acumen those sisters possessed!

Probably the most famous, and certainly the most valuable of their Impressionists is *La Pluie*, or *Rain at Auvers*, painted by Van Gogh in 1890 shortly before his suicide. The timing lends an added poignancy: the radiance of the *Flowering Garden at Arles*, painted two years earlier, had passed. *La Pluie* is one of the ninety works completed at Auvers within sixty-nine days, indicating that his creative tension was undiminished, indeed heightened. The influence of Japanese prints is evident in the rain, which falls like stairrods.

Van Gogh arrived at Auvers on 21 May and his life seemed to acquire a new impetus due to the encouragement of Dr Gachet, a local specialist to whose care he was committed. Gachet was an art collector who had known Cézanne and was wholly understanding of his patient, a sympathy reflected in Van Gogh's portrait of the doctor.

Vincent wrote to his brother Theo at the end of May, 'This is an almost lush country, just at the moment when a new society is developing in the old, it is not at all unpleasing; there is much well-being in the air.' Early in June he wrote less cheerfully, 'Once back here I set to work again – though the brush almost slipped from my fingers . . . I have since painted three big canvases already [one was almost certainly *La Pluie*]. They are vast stretches of corn under troubled skies, and I did not need to go out of my way to try to express sadness and the extreme of loneliness.'

On 27 July Van Gogh shot himself and Theo hurried to his bedside, writing to his wife, 'He was glad that I came and we are together all the time . . . poor fellow, very little happiness fell to his share and no illusions are left him. The burden grows too heavy for him, at times he feels so alone. He often asks for you and the baby, and said that you would not imagine there was so much sorrow in life.'

Van Gogh died two days later. The wreaths included a large bunch of sunflowers from Dr Gachet, and Theo wrote to his mother, 'He rests in a sunny spot in the cornfields . . . One cannot write how grieved one is nor find any comfort. It is a grief that will last and which I shall certainly never forget as long as I live; the only thing one might say is that he himself has the rest he was longing for . . . now, as so often happens, everybody is full of praise for his talents . . . Oh! mother, he was so my own, own brother.'

The faithful Theo, who was four years younger, was left bereft and died six months later. Fittingly, they are buried side by side in the small cemetery at Auvers where the picture was painted.

Cardiff is rich in British painters too, especially in the works of Richard Wilson, Joshua Reynolds and Gainsborough. Later work includes Augustus John's fine and famous portrait of Dylan Thomas, painted in 1936.

London

Lion Rembrandt Courtauld Institute Galleries

Crisis and Renaissance in the London Art World

The 1980s in the London art world ended with complaints and a whimper. Many of the whines and warnings were justified, with galleries in desperate need of repair – cracks in the walls of the Tate, water stains concealed by plastic sheeting, and a lack of air conditioning, which buckled paintings or caused their removal. Donors started to withhold their pictures because of the risk of a roof which leaked so badly that Matisse's *L'Escargot* (The Snail) narrowly escaped a catastrophe. As a member of the staff explained, 'Paintings at the Tate are being hospitalised by the building.'

Even more serious was the under-funding which prevented the galleries from making such repairs, discouraging expansion and prompting the V & A to make the disastrous 'voluntary' admittance charge, followed by the purge of the veteran staff, and the trendy advertising campaign which referred so rashly to 'an ace caff with quite a nice museum attached'.

The Royal Academy suffered a lean time after the failure of the two successive exhibitions in 1989 of Italian and Swedish art which lost £350,000 and £150,000 respectively, and in the opinion of certain critics deserved to do so.

Ironically 1989 was Museums' Year and Mrs Thatcher gave a stirring endorsement:

> Museums make an outstanding overall contribution to our national life and to the local community. They bring educational, cultural and economic benefits to the nation. They bring enormous prestige and a very real boost to the economy. To the inner cities they bring much-needed inspiration.

Well said. Yet somewhat hollow without the realistic backup of money. In the 1980s museum funding was virtually frozen, with the British Government spending £400 million a year compared to France's *£1 billion*. Cuts in university funding have created severe problems for the Fitzwilliam and Ashmolean and explain why the former is so deplorably understaffed. Perhaps a *compulsory* entrance fee *is* the answer (with suitable concessions) to cope with the crisis, unless the Government can astonish us by giving our galleries a sympathetic and imaginative response in return for such 'a very real boost to the economy'.

Considering the buoyant state of the art market and the belated recognition of contemporary British art, the animosity towards the Government is surprisingly vociferous, ranging from the Director of the National Gallery, who compared the dilapidation of our museums to the dissolution of the monasteries, to the artists who attacked the Government in an exhibition at the Flowers East Gallery in Hackney in the summer of 1989, entitled *The Thatcher Years: An Artistic Retrospective*. As fine an artist as Peter Howson was involved but reactions were mixed, with the implication that such a protest was more of a stance than a thought-out argument.

After all these alarums and whimpers, it is a relief that the 1990s have opened with a bang. They herald a renaissance of the London art scene with the long-awaited transfer of the Courtauld Institute to the sumptuous setting of Somerset House on the banks of the Thames, and the transformation of the Tate Gallery under the new director, Nicholas Serota, who has rescued a number of British artists from the basement and let them breathe again. And we have the *new* Imperial War Museum. The extension of the National Gallery opens in 1991.

Cracks may remain or be papered over, but there is cause for celebration too, and, if I dare be so old-fashioned, for renewed pride in British art. In 1989, approximately 100 million visitors went to our museums and galleries compared to 65 million four years earlier. Our interest in art has rarely been so keen, or so necessary, in view of today's cynical materialism.

THE COURTAULD INSTITUTE

One of the greatest of the British collectors, Samuel Courtauld was a vigorous man with numerous interests, ranging from literature and music as well as art, contrasted by a zest for fast cars and hunting. Yet he was not an innovative collector as Dr Dennis Farr, the Director of the Courtauld Institute Gallery, has pointed out: 'even within a British context, Sir Hugh Lane and Gwendoline Davies had started their collections of Impressionist painting long before. Where Courtauld surpassed his British predecessors was in scale and sheer quality.' In 1922 at the age of forty-six, Samuel Courtauld started to form his collection and the following year he gave £50,000 to the Tate, as part of the Courtauld Foundation, to buy Impressionist and Post-Impressionist paintings, having realised how poorly these were represented in Britain.

It was Hugh Lane's exhibition at the Tate five years earlier which was his second 'eye-opener' – the first was in Italy after his marriage – when he was particularly impressed by Renoir, Manet and Degas. When he saw Cézanne's *Provençal Landscape*, lent by Gwendoline Davies for an exhibition, he realised that 'magic' also. A late starter, he made up for lost time by acquiring numerous paintings over the next ten years, confirming Dennis Farr's emphasis on 'quality': Renoir's *La Loge*; Monet's vibrant *Antibes*; Gauguin's *Haymaking*; and Manet's masterpiece, *A Bar at the Folies-Bergère*; also, Seurat's affectionate yet humorous portrait of his mistress Madeleine Knoblock, *Young Woman Powdering Herself*, in which his self-portrait in the background was replaced by a still life of flowers for the sake of discretion.

The death of Courtauld's wife in 1931 led to the offer of his Adam house in Portman Square to London University and the Institute accepted the first art students later that year. Not only did Courtauld form his collection but he also encouraged the Institute to be a place of learning: Vincent Price was one of the early students and Anita Brookner, more recently, one of the distinguished teachers. Subsequently, the art collection was housed in Woburn Square.

Writing to Christabel, the Dowager Lady Aberconway, who became his close companion, he said, 'I shall shortly leave this house – to come here and find it *still* empty is too painful.' He provided £70,000 to house his collection and his Trust declared the high objectives:

a. to be dedicated to some object calculated to increase the enlightenment of mankind . . .

b. to promote for the benefit of the nation the preservation and exhibition of a building of beauty and historic interest.

Outwardly an autocratic, remote figure, the cotton millionaire loved his paintings so deeply that when he parted with *La Loge* (on loan to the National Gallery) he wrote to Lady Aberconway that he had not dared to tell her because 'I thought it would make you sad, and at moments I felt like weeping myself. However, it fulfils a scheme which I have been working for from the beginning, so I must not repine now.' In 1941 he wrote to her explaining his philosophy:

> Beauty to me of course is spiritual as well as physical and the most complete beauty must be both. I feel too that bodily beauty is closely and subtly linked with beauty of spirit. This feeling about beauty, and the need for it, are essential parts of me: unless women have beauty they are antipathetic to me in life as well as art, it is an ingrained prejudice . . . What interests me most in writing – in any other art – is to try to get into touch with the mind of the artist, for this revelation of his own mind is the most interesting thing in his art . . .'

When he died he bequeathed a number of paintings to Lady Aberconway in addition to the splendid house in North Audley Street and I remember my surprise when I went there for the first time and thought it curiously inappropriate that the walls should be hung with reproductions of such famous paintings as Picasso's *Child with Dove* until I realised these were the originals. Many of them hang in the National Gallery today.

Since Courtauld's death, his collection has been enhanced by the collection bequeathed by Count Antoine Seilern in 1978, though at the time of the bequest he preferred to remain anonymous. They include three hundred drawings ranging from Mantegna, Rembrandt and Rubens to Delacroix and Picasso. Another bequest came from Anthony Blunt, once the Courtauld's Director and later the self-confessed traitor.

When I was younger I considered the Courtauld Collection as the one I should wish to possess more than any. Even now it raises the spirits just to look at the catalogue: *The Tête-a-Tête Supper* by Lautrec, a joyful, sensual portrait of the smiling and rather blowsy demi-mondaine, smiling at her table in the Rat Mort, with a gentleman friend at her elbow; contrasting with the gaunt figure of Jane Avril arriving at the Moulin Rouge. Gauguin's Tahitian nude *Nevermore*;

Cézanne's *Card Players*; Degas's *Dancers*; and Seurat's high-kicking chorus girls – all in celebration of life. Could one ask for anything more? As I grow older I love those paintings no less, yet can equally love work that is less immediately easy to appreciate, and the same applies to literature and music.

This extra dimension is provided in the Courtauld Collection by the bequest by Count Seilern, which spans six hundred years from Bernardo Daddi's triptych (1338) and includes work by Bellini, as well as the six sheets by Michelangelo. *The Madonna Standing with the Child and Angels* by Quentin Massys (1466–1530) is another astonishing work. Once the centre panel of a silver-gilt jewelled altar with twelve small oval pictures set in the wings, it stands in total contrast to the brutal caricature of his *Grotesque Old Woman* in the National. There are thirty works by Rubens, and the modern painting includes the best of Kokoschka and Cézanne's *An Armchair*.

As Helen Braham claims in her introduction to the catalogue for the Princess Gate Collection: 'The breadth . . . reflects a considerable catholicity of taste, but there is also a discernible pattern to its formation. The high quality and good condition of the majority of works of art of all types are evidence of Count Seilern's connoisseurship . . . It is a collection of outstanding taste and the product of a love of fine works of art for their own sake. It is also a scholarly collection *par excellence*, and much of its interest derives from the relationship of works brought together here, often for the first time since the artist's death.'

The move to Somerset House in 1990 is a greater achievement than most visitors will realise. First there was the cost, an estimated £3 million which rose to ten. The University of London, to which the Institute belongs, contributed £4 million, but the Government considerably less, around £150,000, half of it from the Office of Arts and Libraries. The greatest share has come from the public appeal which raised £5 million, an extraordinary gesture of generosity considering that the galleries in Woburn Square are little known, even if the collection attracts 90,000 paying visitors a year.

Costs seem to spiral inevitably, and were aggravated in this case by the disrepair of Somerset House – even though it is a listed, governmental building – which was so severe that the Tate had declared it unsuitable for the Turner bequest. Partly occupied until 1972 as the registry for the nation's births, marriages and deaths, it had been neglected until the Courtauld's architects moved in and discovered to their horror, as they dug an ever deeper hole in search of foundations, that there were no foundations. This meant that the property had to be underpinned throughout and the floors strengthened with tons of steel to meet the new safety requirements, apart from being equipped with sophisticated lighting, smoke controls, humidity regulators, and all the precautions needed to protect the collection.

Now the future looks secure. If so many visitors made their way to Woburn Square, how many more will head for Somerset House? 'It is true to say it will be the first time that almost the entire collection has been displayed together under the same roof,' Dr Farr told me, explaining that this consists of seven major collections altogether: the Courtauld; Roger Fry; Lee of Fareham; Gambier-Parry; Witt (drawings); Hunter; Lillian Browse; plus the Blunt collection of architectural drawings, and thirteen Turner watercolours given in memory of Sir Stephen Courtauld by his family.

There will be the excitement of work rarely seen before: Bernardo Dadd's 1348 altarpiece brought out of store, Botticelli's *Holy Trinity*, Goya's *Don Francisco de Saavedra* and the huge triptych of *Prometheus*, which is probably Kokoschka's masterpiece.

Until now, 35 per cent of the Courtauld Collection has been displayed at Woburn Square. This will rise to 80 per cent at Somerset House, with the opportunity to appreciate such familiar work as Manet's *Bar at the Folies-Bergère*, and to make discovery of work hitherto concealed for lack of space.

THE NATIONAL GALLERY

In a book which hopes to prove the richness of our galleries north of Trafalgar Square, the National Gallery needs no recommendation from myself. Yet, for reasons I find inexplicable, the National Gallery is the constant target for complaint: gloomy, badly lit, and unworthy of the title of our foremost gallery. I should say in contradiction that every time I go there I leave elated, as if I had just enjoyed an unforgettable meal.

Sometimes I enter from the back in order to be surprised by unfamiliar work, as I was when confronted by Titian's *Allegory of Prudence*, with three heads of animals, and three ages of man. I included this in *Gallery* and it was used subsequently by Alan Bennett in *Single Spies* as part of a lecture by Anthony Blunt, with the implication that there's more to art than meets the eye, and more to art historians too. On my last visit, with the particular purpose of seeing Holbein's *Ambassadors*, I entered a back gallery and this was the first picture I saw and recognised instantly, though I had no idea what it looked like. It was as if it had been waiting for me. With the curiously elongated skull in the foreground (and once you make it out this becomes apparent) at the feet of the two courtiers surrounded by their riches – a reminder of mortality – this alone is a painting which is worth a visit to the gallery.

Far from finding the galleries sombre, I welcome the dark backgrounds which show the paintings to advantage. There are too many in this formidable collection to indicate here, so I shall list a few in particular, with an Author's Eye.

St George and the Dragon by Paolo Uccello (circa 1460) – a semi-surrealist concept with a sort of air-force insignia on the snarling dragon's wings, and a very pert princess. A rare example of a painting on canvas when most Italian pictures of that period were executed on wood.

St Jerome in a Rocky Landscape by Joachim Patenier (active 1515) – yet another image inspired by the legend of the patron saint and his lion, which always stretches the artist's imagination.

Portrait of a Man by Titian (died 1576) – a perfectly simple concept with his consummate use of colour.

The Shrimp Girl by William Hogarth (1697–1764) – a radiant, almost slapdash glance at a cockney fisher girl with a flat basket of shrimps on her head, embodying the humour and zest of youth. Hogarth's widow called it *The Market Wench*: 'They say he could not paint flesh. There's flesh and blood for you!' Compared to the meticulous detail in his *Rake's Progress*, this has all the virtues of spontaneity.

The list could stretch indefinitely – Bellini's *The Madonna of the Meadow*; Leonardo's cartoon of the *Virgin and Child*, recently restored after it was shot at; Caravaggio's *Supper at Emmaus* . . . this must be a case of finding out for yourself, though there is one painting in particular I urge you to look for – *The Baptism of Christ* by Piero della Francesca (active 1439–92), full of serenity, with the dove stretched vertically above the central figure of Christ in a landscape of hills and trees. As Sir David Attenborough confirmed on Gallery, when faced with such a work as this one actually feels '*blessed*'.

THE NATIONAL PORTRAIT GALLERY

When I have an hour to kill on a morning in London I head for this gallery, which never disappoints. Care is taken to entertain the visitor with constant change and new displays, providing a welcome antidote to the more traditional National Gallery around the corner in Trafalgar Square.

The National Portrait Gallery started as a visual record of the nation's famous men, and a few women if they happened to be royal, and was founded in 1856 before photography provided the greater realism. By 1896, when it finally opened, its purpose was virtually redundant, though there is more joy in a painted portrait than you can find in a photograph, and I speak as a photographer whose work is on permanent display in the NPG.

Upstairs you will find the heavyweights: the finest copy of Holbein's portrait of *Sir Thomas More*; numerous depictions of Elizabeth I; above all, Henry VIII towering in the fragment of a cartoon intended for Whitehall Palace but largely destroyed by fire. A later study shows the king on his deathbed, handing the succession to his son Edward VI.

From a historical point of view, the National Portrait Gallery is educational, with the fascination of seeing how these leaders of men appeared to their contemporaries. It is usually in a flattering light: Richard III, mean-mouthed with no indication of his physical deformity; Shakespeare resembling Shylock; Nell Gwyn, buxom and sedate in the eyes of Sir Peter Lely; many so heavily shrouded by wigs so that Hogarth's baldness in his self-portrait comes as a welcome relief. The static solemnity of such portraiture is seldom broken, with a few striking exceptions: Joshua Reynolds shielding his eyes as he stares at the canvas; the famous portrait of Charles James Fox by Karl Hickel, which has a semblance of spontaneity; Sickert's Churchill in a cloud of smoke, one of the artist's 'snapshots' and an interesting contrast to Sutherland's sketch for the ill-fated portrait.

Occasionally, very occasionally, the painting has a beauty which makes a likeness irrelevant, as in the portrait of Ellen Terry by George Frederic Watts (1864), who married the actress when she was sixteen and he was forty-six. Obviously the picture (properly entitled *Choosing*) was painted with passion, though the marriage lasted for scarcely a year. As a curiosity, the *Brontë Sisters* painted by their brother Branwell, is astonishing.

Field marshals, admirals of the fleet, prime ministers and national heroes, all are honoured here in this visual graveyard. Kitchener's vaulting ambition shows in the portrait by Hubert von Herkomer (1890), while the loose yet splendidly controlled drawing of T.E. Lawrence by Augustus John reveals an inner doubt.

Photographs of today's celebrities compete, yet it is the early photographic portrait which makes the greater impact: Isambard Kingdom Brunel, photographed by Robert Hewlett in 1857 in front of the giant chains of the *Great Eastern*; Julia Margaret Cameron's Thomas Carlyle (1867), a slightly blurred impression; and the historic scene of Captain Scott in his hut at the base camp in the Antarctic.

The greatest pleasure for me lies in the sidelong look at people I thought I knew, or had no idea what they looked like: a rare portrait of E.M. Forster by Dora Carrington, painted surreptitiously when he visited the home she shared with Lytton Strachey and her husband; Claire Ewald's dashing Rupert Brooke in a hat and emerald-green background; Michael Ayrton's William Walton, and a delightfully arrogant portrayal of Delius. Henry Lamb, whose elongated Lytton Strachey is a masterpiece in its own right, has a surprisingly formal full-length of Neville Chamberlain clutching a top hat; and there is a heart-breakingly beautiful self-portrait by Gertler, who killed himself in 1939 due to poverty, depression and unrequited love. There are also, striking self-portraits by Dame Laura Knight, Gaudier-Brzeska, and John Minton.

The area of failure lies in the royal portraiture, which gets steadily worse the more crowd-pulling it becomes, starting with the grand simplicity of Holbein, to the staged conversations by Lavery, deteriorating to the 'sloppy-jeans' approach of Bryan Organ, with the assurance that the royals are 'just like us', to even worse today, though John Wood's portrait of Prince Charles is an honourable exception. Yet I admit to a sneaking affection for such set pieces as *Queen Victoria Presenting a Bible* to a coloured visitor from her far-flung Empire; and a massive scene near the entrance – *The Landing of HRH Princess Alexandra at Gravesend* in 1863 – a genre which is totally out of favour today, with a crowd of fifty figures including a 'bevy of pretty maids with dainty little baskets of spring flowers to scatter at her feet'. It

Max with Onde   Maggi Hambling   National Portrait Gallery

Maggi Hambling explains: The source of this painting was a moment in the kitchen
when Onde was being rather fussy about her tea, causing Max to serenade her
with a verse or two of 'Poor Little Rich Girl' in encouragement.

is easy to say that a colour photograph would do as well, but the artist went to
great pains to make his details accurate while retaining a freshness. I find it a
charming document.

Unfortunately, the lack of space is now becoming apparent, to the detriment of
the gallery. The organisers have tried to solve it by hanging pictures on several
levels, with revolving displays for photographs. The wish to show as much work
as possible is understandable, but has led to congestion. It would be better to show
fewer works to greater advantage. Going to the gallery for the launch of Maggi
Hambling's portrait of A.J.P Taylor, I joined the painter Fred Ingrams, and his

father Richard (the founder of *Private Eye*), who expressed his dismay at seeing pictures hung above eye-level, including the excellent portrait of Constant Lambert by Christopher Wood, virtually eclipsed by lesser work jostling around it. Since then, Richard Ingrams has suggested (*Modern Painters*, autumn 1989) that the gallery needs a 'face-lift', condemning the relegation of James Gunn's *Delius* to the basement, and the hanging of *Beatrix Potter* by Delmar Banner, and Sir William Nicholson's *Gertrude Jekyll* in the postcard shop, where they could be mistaken for reproductions. Ingrams is particularly critical of the prominence given to photographs, asking 'If a photograph is as valid, i.e. can be displayed alongside a painting as something of equal worth, why should an artist go to all the bother of painting a portrait?' He is right in rejecting photographs that are not even portraits, included simply as art, but sometimes a photograph can serve as a complement to a painting. One example is the shot of Mrs Thatcher, which reveals that there *is* a slight cast in one of her eyes, as caught by Rodrigo Moynihan, though his portrait was returned by Downing Street to have it corrected. Occasionally a photograph is so distinguished that it deserves inclusion, especially if it has an historical interest too, like Karsh's *Winston Churchill*.

Ingrams is harsh in his recommendation that the present 'mess' can be corrected 'quite easily by removing most of the junk and all the photographs', but he writes as an admirer of the gallery, 'For some reason the English have always been and are still (despite the photographs) very good at painting portraits. No other country could provide an exhibition half as good as this one which would, within the scope of a small gallery – and all the best galleries are small – give a feel of the national character and the national history. Going to the National Portrait Gallery is like revisiting a number of old friends: Doctor Johnson, John Bunyan, Delius . . .' Undeniably, there needs to be a more discerning selection instead of the attempt to be comprehensive by showing *everyone* of any merit.

At their best, the paintings are both an indication of the sitter and a work of art in their own right. These should be given pride of place, with the photographs yielding gracefully. The directors have a difficult task: I am sure they will succeed.

THE TATE GALLERY

The Tate Gallery opened in 1897 as the showcase for British painting. The birth was painful, conceived by Sir Francis Chantrey in 1841 with a generous bequest for the purchase of paintings, though not a place to house them. This situation was aggravated when Turner left a mass of paintings to the nation with the stipulation that a special gallery should be built in order to display them (a condition finally fulfilled in the 1980s with the opening of the Clore extension). The Tate came into being due to the sugar manufacturer Henry Tate, who offered both his collection and the money for a new gallery provided the Treasury maintained it. After

Pegwell Bay   William Dyce   The Tate Gallery

various unsatisfactory sites were offered him, Henry Tate withdrew his offer until the present site became available.

One could make a comparison between London and Paris: the National Gallery and the Louvre for the older masters; the Tate and the Musée d'Orsay for the lighter contemporaries. However, this worthy comparision has yet to be fulfilled. British art faded away after 1900 and was either given an inferior space or hung in the basement. Even Stanley Spencer was neglected, hidden below or simply not displayed at all.

A visit to the Tate in 1987 proved a bitter disappointment, with British artists relegated as if they were inferior instead of meriting a pride of place. Taking some friends from abroad who were eager to see the best of comtemporary British art, I felt ashamed. All that is changing.

Under the new directorship of Nicholas Serota the Tate's transformation began in January 1990, with a total re-hanging on the main floor with the connecting theme of galleries devoted to modern art by British painters, interspersed with rooms of foreign artists, in a chronological sequence. Like a Russian dissident, Spencer has been reinstated, reflecting a personal enthusiasm of Serota himself. His personal enthusiasm is invaluable.

Another welcome act of favouritism is the belated recognition of the Neo-Romantics: Sutherland, Piper, Minton, and particularly Robert Colquhoun. Colquhoun may be closer to such sources as Picasso and Jankel Adler than the Neo-Romantics, a suspect label, but he deserves to be reassessed.

Each room in the redesigned gallery will be an entity in its own right, changing every nine or twelve months. Bacon, Freud, and the alleged School of London will be featured at the outset; Gilbert & George in the second phase.

The Pre-Raphaelites will be honoured with a larger room, along with the painters who came after them, and the Sickerts, shown in the new Tate Gallery in Liverpool in 1989, will be granted an entire room.

'It doesn't mean we'll put our Picassos in store,' Mr Serota told me, reluctant to beat his own drum to the detriment of his predecessors, though he has every right to do so. The revival of the Tate is overdue and I believe that visitors from abroad will be shocked, in the best sense, by the strength and variety of British art. Nicholas Serota will have his critics, but the public will be grateful.

Many, if not most of the artists featured in this book are represented in the Tate. Works of particular note include:

Horse Attacked by a Lion – George Stubbs

Elohim Creating Adam – and numerous work by William Blake

Hampstead Heath with a Rainbow – Constable

On a grander scale, the uninhabited romanticism of Francis Danby's *Deluge* and John Martin's *The Great Day of his Wrath* which toured America as well as England and could well have inspired the extravaganza of Cecil B. de Mille.

Old Battersea Bridge – Whistler

The Resurrection: Cookham – Stanley Spencer

Three Studies for Figures at the Base of a Crucifixion – Francis Bacon

The So-called School of London

However misleading, labels tend to stick. That of 'The Angry Young Men' was attached to as genial a group as you could hope to meet, and 'The Beautiful People' to those who were anything but. Of all such labels, 'The School of London' is one of the most fatuous, though it is now accepted and a book called *The School of London: the Resurgence of Contemporary Painting* was published in 1989.

'School' is too ponderous a term for the lively talents involved, but if they have to be grouped together, 'The Colony Room Mob' would be more apt.

The Colony was also known as Muriel's, after the redoubtable Muriel Belcher who ruled her tiny kingdom with the imperious cry of 'Members Only!' On the first afternoon that I was taken there, I was introduced to Francis Bacon, who has always been the club's most distinguished member. He had been taken there, in his turn, the day before it opened on 15 December 1948 by an infamous dandy called Brian Howard and he liked the look of it – it was smarter then, with a bamboo bar and stools upholstered in fake leopard skin. Miss Belcher took to Bacon on sight

Frank Auerbach, circa 1949

and offered him £10 a week and free drinks if he brought his wealthier friends to her club, and he agreed. I have no idea how long this strange arrangement lasted. I suspect that at first Bacon enjoyed the unexpected role until his innate generosity got the better of him. Afterwards, if he was desperately broke, which was frequently the case, he could always 'chalk up' the champagne, which he poured generously with the Edwardian cry of 'Real pain for your sham friends; champagne for your real friends!'

I have described Muriel Belcher in my book on Soho in the 1950s, and her disconcerting habit of referring to her gentlemen members, however respectable, as 'she', with such nicknames as Kate or Clara. A charming old man who had fought in the First War and came there every evening was called 'a plucky little woman in the Somme'; Hitler was 'Miss Hitler'; and when I introduced John

The Colony Room   Michael Andrews   Collection: Colin St. John Wilson,
courtesy of the Anthony d'Offay Gallery

Braine to her, the best-selling author of *Room at the Top* and a man to whom she took an instant, irrational dislike, she mouthed at the other members, 'There's plenty of room at *her* top!' Francis Bacon received the accolade of 'daughter' and she became someone for whom he had an infinite respect, even love. He was desolate when we met in Wheeler's restaurant in Old Compton Street before her Memorial Service on 29 November 1979 where I had to give an Address. It is hard to avoid both length and platitudes on such occasions, but at least I started by saying what I felt: 'I cannot imagine a finer opportunity than a service like this to give thanks, as we do now, for our great good luck in knowing Muriel Belcher, who turned life into a marvellous party.' When I asked Francis Bacon to define the qualities which made her small, uncomfortable club exceptional, he said it was a place to go where we could lose our inhibitions; and he painted her portrait because he found her 'beautiful'.

   The point is that she knew nothing about painting – nor did he want her to – but she assembled a powerhouse of talent around her. She was far too wise to indulge in pretence of knowledge, yet she possessed a rare instinct which enabled her to judge people astutely and she recognised that artists are fun, especially when they lose their inhibitions, and generous too, which appealed to her also, for she was as

Lucian Freud and Francis Bacon in Bacon's studio, circa 1952

happy at the till as a master-mariner at the tiller. The so-called School of London is due to her.

On any afternoon in the 1950s I could enter the Colony in the expectation of finding Francis Bacon, Lucian Freud (then one of his closest friends), Michael Andrews, and Frank Auerbach, who went there for the company rather than the drink, though we all liked that too. The late John Minton was another regular, and Rodrigo Moynihan, both popular teachers at the Royal College of Art, where a group portrait of the staff provided the inspiration for one of the latter's most famous paintings.

It was, however, Bacon, Freud, Andrews and Auerbach who formed the nucleus of the group, and Andrews' painting of *The Colony* was included in the Royal Academy exhibition of twentieth-century British art in 1987.

So why the ludicrous label of 'London' when all they had in common was friendship under the nicotine-stained ceiling of Miss Belcher's room? Of course the label has been applied with the benefit of hindsight, for none of these artists were famous outside their circle, even if Bacon was revered within it.

Bacon was unique; Freud was already recognised by the discerning few as a draughtsman of outstanding originality whose portraits featured many mutual friends such as the painter Eleanor Bellingham Smith, the wife of Rodrigo Moynihan; the photographer John Deakin; John Minton, whose haunting image hangs in the Royal College of Art today; and the small, astonishing portrait of Bacon himself, bought by the Tate Gallery and stolen from the Freud retrospective when it was transferred from the Hayward to Berlin.

Michael Andrews was admired for the imaginative interior crowded with people, called *The Deer Park* (after the novel by Norman Mailer) and his portrait of Muriel Belcher executed in her club, for which he contributed a greenish mural to cover up the stains.

Frank Auerbach, also painted by Freud, was starting to establish his reputation, encouraged by Helen Lassore at the Beaux-Arts Gallery, where I bought two of his paintings, and where Andrews held his first one-man show.

This sounds suitably incestuous, but why 'London'? Confusingly, the title came from the painter R.B. Kitaj, the American-born artist who rarely, if ever, set foot in the Colony. In 1976, in a Hayward Gallery catalogue, Kitaj wrote: 'There are artistic personalities in this small island more unique and strong and I think numerous than anywhere in the world outside America's jolting vigour. There are ten or more people in this town, or not far away, of world class, including my friends of abstract persuasion. In fact I think there is a substantial School of London . . .' Eleven years later, the label was sufficiently secure for *Art International* to run a series of articles on the 'School'.

I appreciate that Kitaj drew attention to the formidable and largely figurative artists in England who were neglected in favour of the trendier American abstract painters like Rothko and de Kooning, and this is admirable, but Kitaj scrambles too many eggs for his omelette, including Howard Hodgkin, the young artist William MacIlraith, still in his twenties, presumably Kitaj himself, four painters who did not even live in London. As the acerbic critic Brian Sewell has commented – 'twaddle'.

Yet it is true that in the 1950s the influence of Francis Bacon was overwhelming. Sometimes it was disastrous, as with Graham Sutherland who found the Colony too frightening, and with John Minton, who is now becoming fashionable as one of the Romantics (another label) yet who felt his inadequacy in comparison to the genius of Picasso and Bacon to such an extent that it may well have contributed to his suicide.

Lucian Freud patronised the Colony largely due to his admiration for Bacon, and for a brief and not wholly successful period started to experiment with a looser style until he recovered his aim and returned to those intensely realistic representations that created a sensation at the Hayward Gallery in 1988. Invariably short of money due to his gambling, a compulsion shared by Bacon, Freud sold most of his paintings before they were dry and his work was largely known through reproduction. Faced by the power of the originals, visitors to the Hayward were awed by the massive output which reflected his capacity for hard work over the years. He paints slowly but remorselessly. The expression of despair on the faces of so many of his sitters is frequently literally that, reflecting the ordeal which continues day after day, week after week . . .

On one occasion, when a young man sat holding Freud's pet rat alarmingly close to his genitals, though the animal had been sedated, the model was so bored that he asked

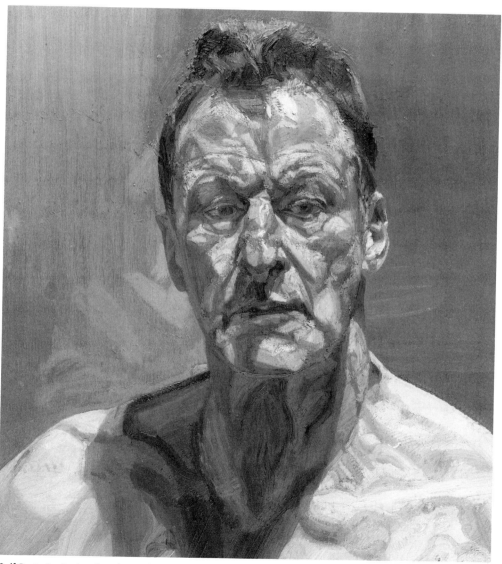

Self-Portrait Lucian Freud Kind permission of James Kirkman

Freud if he could be joined by his friend for the next portrait, and Lucian allowed the older man the dignity of doing so in his pyjamas. Both men recline on a couch, the younger resting a hand on his friend's ankle; both appear asleep, and might have been for it took the artist six months to complete the painting over a period of two years. When I commented that it looks spontaneous, he gave one of his sly smiles and replied, 'That's where the art comes in.' The result is a picture of rare tenderness, for Freud is kinder to men because he loves them less, whereas his women are rendered defenceless in their nakedness, sprawling in 'the milieu of the unmade bed', to quote the memorable phrase of Sir Lawrence Gowing.

Today each artist is acclaimed but Muriel Belcher would have the last laugh, and I hope she has: 'School of London! Get you, Lottie. I knew them when they didn't have a pot to piss in!

GILBERT & GEORGE

1943/1942–

They live in a sedate street in Spitalfields overshadowed by Hawksmoor's splendid Christ Church, where the Huguenots settled after the revocation of the Edict of Nantes in 1685. In the heart of the East End, surrounded later by Polish and Russian Jews, this was an elegant oasis, with the street closed at either end to spare the residents from the common touch. The rooftops have identical chimneys inscribed with the name of William IV and the eighteenth-century house below has been restored with evident devotion. The wooden floors are highly polished and though one of the rooms is filled with their startling collection of vast, glazed pottery vases made in Barnstaple, and the furniture is English Neo-Gothic, the house is welcoming – like themselves – a blend of museum and home and a suitable setting for these two courteous men in their respectable suits made by the tailor next door.

Another man opens the door and asks if I drink coffee as if this is a rare ritual. Showing me upstairs, Gilbert & George await me, carefully posed like their Barnstaple vases and I retain the impression that one was standing and the other seated like a Victorian photograph, though I am not sure if this was the case. Certainly there is an air of Madame Tussaud's and the conversation is equally stiff to begin with as they assess me, with George resembling a youthful Dr Crippen or Christie, bald with staring eyes behind the spectacles, and Gilbert looking bemused, almost nonplussed, as well he might. I have a feeling that I am placed on trial – 'And when did you last see your father?' – and this was probably the case.

George (surnames are not mentioned) was born in Devon in 1942, and Gilbert in the Dolomites a year later. A slight Italian accent enhances his perfect English. George studied at the Dartington Hall College of Art in Devon, and then the Oxford School of Art ('nothing to do with the colleges'), while Gilbert went from various schools to the Academy of Art in Munich, until they met at St Martin's in London in 1967, where they were students of sculpture. They say that they left

Gilbert & George, 1989

with no knowledge of art and no technical proficiency – 'empty and drained of meaning' – but it led to their collaboration and a close friendship which has lasted for twenty years.

Their rapport is extraordinary. They are not identical but complementary; united. As Gilbert & George they are a one-man show. At first this disconcerts, then it is entertaining, especially when they relax and you realise they are terribly funny, and all the more so because their critics take them so seriously. 'We are the most miserable sods in the world,' George assures me, and looks reprovingly when I laugh. 'We think everyone is chasing pleasure, but you are more alive if you're miserable.' Warming to my theme of humour in art, they are reluctant to apply this to themselves – 'Not more than there is in life' – and when I refer to the celebration of life as painted by Renoir, George makes the shrewd observation: 'perhaps he *avoided* life.'

Life is the yardstick and with a show of indignation they protest that if their pictures are provocative they are no more so than life itself. 'We don't set out to shock but to unshock. We want people to behave differently after they've seen them, that's what we live for.'

As if to nurture this objective, they channel their lives into a narrow rut, wearing 'exactly the same every day to save our energy for art', eating at the same corner caff where they have dined for the last ten years – 'boring food,' boasts George, 'We don't like fussy restaurants where every meal's a celebration. We like food as it used to be.' Inwardly I cringe from the thought of greasy chips and ask what is wrong with celebration: 'That would be selfish,' says George, 'we wish to be left free for our art.' They never go to the theatre – 'We don't like soothing art forms' – and proclaim that they have few friends – 'We are completely free.' And when I ask if they entertain, Gilbert reproves me with a devastating '*NEVER*!' Evidently content in this cocoon, George insists that 'Two hundred yards from the house is quite far enough.'

Yet, as I discovered when we moved into Soho for lunch, they enjoyed the outing as much as children let out of school, and they proved the best of company, witty, generous and fun. George even likes a drink. 'Oh yes,' said Gilbert with his Stan Laurel glumness, 'George drinks a lot,' but this was said as a statement of fact without a hint of censure. Lunch took place in the Groucho Club, which should be everything they disapprove of, though they appeared to enjoy the 'fussy' food immensely after their diet of chips and pud. We were joined by James Birch of the Birch & Conran Gallery next door in Dean Street, the modest young man who charmed the Russians into staging the historic exhibition of Francis Bacon and who had now achieved the same for Gilbert & George. The three of them were off to Moscow in a few weeks' time on a preliminary visit.

Gilbert & George outside the Kremlin is hard to envisage until the suspicion dawns that the Russians may accept them at their face value – polite, respectable men, the very model of English aristocrats. Presumably the titles will need to be modified, for I doubt if 'glasnost' is ready for *Cock*; *Bent*; *Fuck*; *Cunt*; *Scum*; or *Bollocks We're all Angry*.

This is one explanation for the resentment felt towards them: 'The critics are 100 per cent against us,' they say with a hint of satisfaction, and when I point out that Richard Dorment has written that they will be remembered in a hundred years time, they counter this quickly with the qualification that he is American.

Few modern artists have been so reviled yet so popular. They were included in the Royal Academy's exhibition British art of the twentieth century, with several gigantic 'photo-pieces' with such titles as *Wanker*, *Bummed* and *Prick Ass*, which prompted Peter Fuller; the editor of *Modern Painters*, to condemn the organiser, Norman Rosenthal, for doing so, and to describe the artists as 'inconsequential'.

Obsessed by the subject matter of the penis, narcissistic young men, and themselves, they ask for trouble, attracting the labels of 'fascist' – 'a cliché applied to every person who doesn't fit' – and 'homoerotic'. Their work is restricted to male sexuality with women excluded, and this is deliberate: 'The female form is used up in art,' Gilbert explains. 'If there were a poster for an exhibition called *Nudes* people would assume they were female nudes. The male nude is still shocking.' George adds: 'The nudes have always been women because men have the money. Look at advertising.' They stress the point that if a woman artist painted women, her work would not be described as 'lesbian'.

Leafage   Gilbert & George   Courtesy Anthony d'Offay Gallery

'We know we're turning over stones, but we don't seek to shock,' they insist ingenuously, and Gilbert points out that blatantly homoerotic pornography can be found in any dirty bookshop, 'but if you want to show the new possibilities of life, people are intolerant towards the form we use. We accept this. We believe in truth.' To a certain extent they alienate themselves from art itself, refusing to go to art galleries: 'We don't *like* art,' says Gilbert impassively. 'We *do* it, they look.' And George, inevitably, agrees: 'Art has to come from life, not from art, and we appeal to young people who don't necessarily go to galleries. When students come to us we say their work is brilliant. "But you haven't seen it!" they explain. "It's not necessary," we tell them. Support is the most important thing. Teachers always criticise.'

However sincere, their alienation fans the controversy which surrounds them. This started with their 'living sculptures', when they 'metallized' their hands and faces with gold paint and stood motionless for five hours on end. As a boy I was entranced by a dapper little man with a waxed moustache who was paid by department stores to stand in their windows like a tailor's dummy, baffling the passers-by, who are uncertain if he was alive until he gave a sudden wink, creating a sensation which attracted the crowds. Gilbert & George turned this trick into an art form. Their most famous 'living sculpture' was titled *Underneath the Arches*, and 'posed' to a tape of the popular song by Flanagan and Allan. They performed this in numerous countries, appearing in Tokyo in 1975 with *The Red Sculpture*, their faces covered with red pigment, but after a further performance in Amsterdam they abandoned living sculpture. Yet the influence persists in their everyday life – they pose for the camera rigidly.

Photographs of the period, around 1970, show two extremely jolly young men. The titles of the grinning artists are 'George the Cunt' and 'Gilbert the Shit', which smacks of puerility, though they explain, 'All is invalidated and value-free: even rude words lose their force.' I prefer the wittier message in their *Postal Sculpture* (1969), 'All my life I give you nothing and still you ask for more', signed 'from the sculptors George and Gilbert.'

After a brief experiment with the convention of oils, they turned to the massive photo-pieces or photographic collages for which they are known today. The impact is undeniable, coloured with vivid reds, blues, yellows and greens, and when I enter a gallery where they are exhibited, like the D'Offay off Bond Street, their size and strength are overwhelming. Including themselves in virtually every picture, their work is a form of graffiti with a hint of menace in the background, drifting young men and urban decay, the relationship between contemporary sex, violence and politics, and the occasional intrusion of the Christian cross. Significantly, in the bulky, handsome books which they subsidise, many of the illustrations show these pictures in the context of an exhibition where the scale dominates the gallery. Predictably, their work is hugely popular in Germany and America, where they received the accolade of a retrospective at the Guggenheim Museum in New York. They have been treated similarly at the Pompidou in Paris. Their work is composed of panels which they develop in the studio behind their home, working round the clock when the mood is right. They say they enter the workshop with 'empty heads' and because of the way they work, 'it's too late to change once we've started.'

'We know exactly what we want to say, like visual letters.' George gives a triumphant smile. 'We're not *foggies*, like a lot of artists.'

The technique is clever to the point of sterility: a brilliant use of colour and a skilful combination of photographic blow-up and drawing so the two are indistinguishable, with a finish which could hardly be improved. Yet critics who might applaud such technique when practised by Warhol condemn it in Gilbert & George because of the apparent smut. 'English art critics have been Marxist,' they reply, 'and so narrow minded. Art is there to bring out the prejudice. Our work brings out the bigot.' Devoting all the proceeds of their 1989 exhibition at the D'Offay to AIDS, they remark that the *Guardian* is 'anti-gay only in our case, while the *Sun* has never gay-bashed us.'

The charmless landlord of the odious pub devoted to Jack the Ripper at the corner of the street referred to them dismissively when I asked the way as 'the gay couple', yet I doubt if their relationship can be labelled so neatly, even if it is true. Though little about them can be described as 'straight', they are the most straightforward of men and I suspect that in their open hatred of Gilbert & George the critics miss the point. To say they have perpetrated a tremendous practical joke is tempting, and Gilbert & George would deny it, yet anyone who could perform the Living Sculpture *Gordon's Makes Us Drunk* (1972) in which they became increasingly blotto on Gordon's gin, must have a highly developed sense of the absurd. It is one of their strengths that people see what they wish to see in Gilbert & George and the reaction reveals as much about the viewer as it does of the artists. With my own fondness for eccentricity, I believe they have the last laugh.

I had been told that one of their pictures showed underpants floating down from the sky. It is called *Coming* and when I mentioned this to George as an instance of their humour he deflected me by finding it in one of their books, which he thrust towards me.

'And do you know,' he glowered, 'a critic said the underpants were *soiled*!'

Yet, when I laughed, they stared at me surprised.

Work by Gilbert & George can be seen in:
Leeds, City Art Gallery
Southampton, Art Gallery

Untold Pleasures

One of the treats of looking at art in London is the search for the lesser-known galleries. Dulwich, Kenwood, Leighton House and Sir John Soane's are particularly rewarding. If you need to entertain friends from abroad, take them to one of these. They can go to the National Gallery on their own.

DULWICH COLLEGE PICTURE GALLERY

On every level, the Dulwich gallery is distinguished. Probably the earliest public art gallery in Britain, it is housed in the elegant buildings designed by Sir John Soane (see p. 204) which were completed in 1813 and are set in attractive grounds surrounded by Dulwich village which, dating back to 967, remains one of the most complete of London's surviving villages. The gallery's staff are helpful and the enthusiastic Director, Giles Waterfield, has charted the development of the gallery in detail in his booklet, *Rich Summer of Art*, published in 1988.

Children are encouraged to enjoy the gallery due to the perseverance of Gillian Wolfe, Dulwich's education officer, who is fully aware of the importance of first impressions: 'If the children don't like it at once, they'll never come back. Above all, we must get away from the idea that art is for nice, middle-class people and not relevant to the other lot.' To this end she helps to bring the pictures to life with music, stories and 'mix-your-own painting sessions' adapted to the particular local schools. She has been rewarded by letters of thanks – 'It was one of my favourite days I've had in my life,' wrote one girl poignantly – and by the satisfaction of seeing children return with their parents, eager to show off their new interest. Restrained by working on a financial shoe-string, Gillian Wolfe and her volunteer teachers blaze the way for other galleries, never lecturing *at* or *down* to the children but helping them to have a go themselves at mixing pigments and stretching canvases.

In this she fulfils one of the original intentions of Dulwich, which was founded to enable young artists to study the old masters – a policy that proved so popular that the copyists had to be restrained because they were distracting the public.

Today, visitors are warned to watch their step in case there's a child on the floor copying a picture which has captured their imagination, a marvellous achievement at a time when television has reduced the attention of a child to a couple of minutes.

Gillian Wolfe teaches with love: 'Whatever their age, we give all of them lots of cuddles. We make every group feel they're the most marvellous lot we've ever had and they go away glowing. It's important to us and to them because so many of them have such a poor image of themselves.'

The one drawback is getting there. Taxis are tedious and expensive; buses are slow; so the best way is probably to take a train from Victoria to West Dulwich and to walk from there.

The Paintings

The collection is one of the most interesting in the country, and includes Rembrandt's famous *A Girl at a Window*, also known as *Girl leaning on a Window-sill*, which is probably my favourite picture in the world. I saw it first on loan at Agnew's and as I went inside a woman who was coming out guessed the reason for my visit and told me, 'Hurry up, it's caught the natural light from the

A Girl at a Window Rembrandt Dulwich Picture Gallery

skylight,' and I was able to see the picture much as Rembrandt painted it, glowing and sensual and beautiful. To say more would be pointless. It is hung in a similar light at Dulwich, near the smaller Rembrandt of a young man, which has the added distinction of having been stolen four times from the gallery, though it is currently in its rightful place.

The history of the collection is startling. A London dealer, a Frenchman called Noël Desenfans (1745–1807), was commissioned by the King of Poland to assemble a collection for a national gallery in Warsaw, a project which came to grief with the suppression of the Polish monarchy. Desenfans sold some of the pictures but kept the rest in the hope of establishing a national gallery in England. On his death they were left to his close friend Sir Francis Bourgeois, who fulfilled the dream by presenting them to Dulwich College, which already possessed a modest gallery. Founded in 1810, students from the Royal Academy were admitted five years later, taking precedence over the public, who were allowed in in 1817. Altogether, 650 works were acquired, mainly of the seventeenth and eighteenth centuries.

In Charles Kingsley's novel *Alton Locke*, set in the 1820s, the hero proposes a visit to the National Gallery but his worldly cousin insists on going to Dulwich instead – 'much better ones in Dulwich – that's the place to go.' In spite of Benjamin Haydon's (see p. 156) criticism in 1832 of the fellows of the College, who 'get worse and worse, snarling at each other, and sneering at the world, from their eternal allusion to women and their restlessness under the consciousness of not being able to marry', he admired the collection and Dulwich became a painters' gallery, praised by Ruskin, who remarked that he had never gone there over fourteen years 'without seeing at least three copyists before the Murillos'. At that time Murillo was so popular that Hazlitt described the *Spanish Beggar Boys* as the 'triumph of this collection, and almost of painting – so truthful to Nature, so evocative of common life and of arch roguery, of animal spirits, of vigorous elastic

Queen Victoria, aged Four   S. P. Denning   Dulwich Picture Gallery

health.' Writers flocked there too including Tennyson, Thackeray and Dickens, who spoke of 'a charming gallery of interesting pictures . . . seen with an unusual absence of glare and bustle, with pleasant gardens outside . . .' When Mr Pickwick moved to the area, he became a regular gallery goer.

After 1857, when the Dulwich College Foundation was given a new constitution by an Act of Parliament, it became more liberal in opening hours though less appealing to students due to the competition from the old masters acquired for the National Gallery.

Today, Dulwich deserves a wider recognition. Giles Waterfield lists the paintings which he considers are the major attributes and they prove a formidable group: the two Rembrandts; Rubens' *Hagar in the Desert*; two Poussins; Watteau's *Bal Champêtre*, which is one of his own favourites; Murillo's *Flower Girl*; Canaletto's *Old Walton Bridge*, which makes a welcome change from the grander reaches of the Thames; Guido Reni's *St John the Baptist*; Cuyp's *A Road Near a River*; a fine and typical Gainsborough of *The Linley Sisters*; and Reynolds' *Mrs Siddons as the Tragic Muse*.

I include S.P. Denning's *Queen Victoria, aged Four*, not as a major work, but as a pleasingly comic portrait tinged with the knowledge that the overdressed little girl will become the most powerful, and equally overdressed, woman in the world.

THOMAS CORAM FOUNDATION FOR CHILDREN

The Thomas Coram Foundation is open to the public, though it is wise to phone beforehand if you wish to visit the Courtroom in case it is being used for the benefit of another charity.

Captain Coram was a blunt, bluff mariner who went to sea at the age of eleven and made his fortune in Boston as a shipwright. Originally a Dorset man, he settled in Rotherhithe on his return and was shocked by the sight of children murdered or abandoned by their parents, their discarded corpses frequently flung on the local dung heaps. After a lengthy campaign in which his own morals were questioned, with the suggestion that this was a means of procuring young girls for his own enjoyment, he succeeded in obtaining a Royal Charter for a Foundation. Throughout, Coram was supported by Handel and William Hogarth, who was one of the first trustees. At that time (1739) there was no public gallery where artists could exhibit and Hogarth blazed the way by encouraging his friends to hang their pictures at the Coram Foundling Hospital, repeating the exhibition at the Turk's Head in St Martin's Lane. This in turn led to the formation of the Royal Academy, whose president is automatically an honorary Vice President of the Coram Foundation today.

An old print of The Foundling Hospital – L'Hôpital des Enfants Trouvés – indicates the palatial scale of the buildings set in comparative countryside, and can

Thomas Coram   William Hogarth   courtesy of The Thomas Coram Foundation

be gauged by the model in Brunswick Square today where the premises were transferred on a smaller scale in 1935 after the original hospital was demolished in 1926.

Former walls and ceilings were sliced off and *relocated* rather than reconstructed, with the happy consequence that the Courtroom upstairs is one of the loveliest settings in London. It contains the fair copy of the *Messiah* bequeathed by Handel; a study for a cartoon by Raphael, now in the V & A; and several pleasing roundels (decorative medallions in the form of a disc) of London scenes, one of them by Gainsborough.

Above all, there are the works by Thomas Coram's friend, William Hogarth. Ironically, the latter's own house in Hogarth Lane, Chiswick, usually comes last on the Tourist Board's list of places of popular interest and was due to be closed until the left-wing Hounslow Council came to the rescue, claiming that as Hogarth was a 'socialist painter' he was politically acceptable and should be supported. Yet Hogarth House does not contain a single Hogarth oil painting.

In contrast to the abundance of his work at the Sir John Soane's Museum, there are only two works at the Coram Foundation, but they are of exceptional interest. *The March of the Guards to Finchley* (1746) records the licentiousness of the drunken soldiers and the prostitutes leaning out of the windows trying to tempt them inside. In the fashion of the time, this painting was raffled by lottery and when 167 of the 2,000 tickets remained unsold, Hogarth gave them to the hospital of which he was a governor. The lottery was drawn on 7 April 1750 and the hospital won.

In contrast to the scenes of London revelry, Hogarth's finest work in Brunswick Square is his massive portrait of his old friend Captain Coram resplendent in a red coat. This confirms the description by Horace Walpole to his brother, the Prime Minister, when Coram was appointed a trustee of the new Crown Colony of Georgia – 'the honestest, the most disinterested, and the most knowing person about the plantations I ever talked with.' Yet there is a hint of irascibility in Coram's expression too, a shortness of temper which led to Coram's expulsion from his own Foundation after he meddled in gossip concerning the staff. However, this is a portrait painted with admiration for a fearless man and Coram looks splendidly upright with his flowing white hair, which was natural, in contrast to the usual stiffly moulded wig, his right hand holding the royal seal with a globe at his feet and an open book nearby, just as Hogarth placed the work of Shakespeare and Milton in his self-portrait.

Combining his personal affection with the distinction of an official record, Hogarth's Coram ranks with the greatest European portraiture and alone is worth a visit to Brunswick Square.

IMPERIAL WAR MUSEUM

Until the triumphant transformation – with the opening of the *new* Imperial War Museum by the Queen in 1989 – it was little known, and this is understandable. War is scarcely a cause for celebration unless you possess a boyish enthusiasm or are expert in such campaigns as Gallipoli, which was covered in detail in the basement. It could not be described as fun except by the obsessive few. The paintings were hard to find, directions confused, and the knowledge that this was once the Bethlem Hospital for the insane, better known as Bedlam, made macabre sense. War and madness were linked, the lunacy exemplified by the last fifteen-inch British naval guns on the lawn outside, from the battleships *Ramillies* and *Resolution*. Cast in 1915, they weigh 200 tons and were capable of firing a 17.5 cwt shell over a distance of sixteen miles.

The inevitable emphasis on battle tended to obscure the finest collection of twentieth-century British art outside the Tate.

In the summer of 1989 all that changed. The *new* museum is a cause for celebration, with the realisation that far from being dedicated to war, the paintings (at least) provide as great an indictment as the poems by Siegfried Sassoon and Wilfred Owen in the First War. Re-hung in brand new galleries upstairs, the paintings can be assessed as never before.

Admittedly, as you pass those massive naval guns the first impression as you enter is that of a boy's games room on a gigantic scale, complete with a life-size (or death-size) Sopwith Camel and other war planes, tanks, a submarine and Polaris Missile. Downstairs is a re-creation of the London air raids with the Blitz Experience – a tableau of a bombed street complete with shelter, bombing, and the all-clear siren. For children it must be a treat, though it saddened me to see a line shuffling forward at the entrance, hand in hand, with the poignancy of realising they were blind. They looked so glum – what would they gain? Then it dawned on me that the Blitz Experience, with all the sounds and smells and commentaries, would enchant them.

Dr Alan Borg, the Director General, claims that 'human behaviour' is the objective. 'We deal with controversial and often unpleasant topics, but we also reflect the exceptional qualities of courage and self-sacrifice that are brought out by war.' These are exemplified by the paintings in the new galleries upstairs which are anti-war, inspired by an anger rare in art. They are works not merely by observers, but by participants too, steeped in the immediacy of war:

Paul Nash (1889–1946) enlisted in the Artists' Rifles in 1914 and two years later received his commission in the Hampshire Regiment. He saw active service at Ypres in 1917 where he dislocated a rib, which spared him from the attack on Hill 60 where most of his fellow officers were killed. In October of that year he returned to the front as an official war artist.

Christopher Nevinson (1889–1946) whose life span was the same as that of Nash, volunteered in 1914 as a Red Cross ambulance driver. In 1915 he joined the Royal Army Medical Corps, and married. His first war paintings were exhibited in 1917, when he also took part as a futurist in the Vorticist Exhibition, though he retained his individuality. That same year he was appointed an official war artist, the first to draw from the air.

Stanley Spencer (1891–1959) Though less familiar as a war artist, Spencer served as an orderly in the Medical Corps and later as an infantryman in Macedonia, a searing experience which gave him the inspiration for the murals at Burghclere, and the moving *Resurrection of Soldiers*.

Battle of Britain, August–October 1940   Paul Nash   The Imperial War Museum

Percy Wyndham Lewis (1882–1957) enlisted in 1916 and served in France with the Sixth Howitzer Battery before he was seconded to the Canadian Army as an official war artist. The Imperial War Museum commissioned him to paint *A Battery Shelled*.

Of the First War artists, those I have mentioned are outstanding and the title of Nash's most famous painting *We are Making a New World* – with a devastation of trees – has a damning irony. Nash is becoming recognised as one of the leading British artists of the twentieth century, and of all the War artists is remarkable in covering both World Wars – *Totes Meer* (1940–41), a dump or 'Dead Sea' of crashed German aircraft at Cowley, echoes the desolation of his *New World*: 'The thing looked to me suddenly like a great inundating sea ... hundreds of flying creatures which invaded these shores ... by moonlight, this waning moon, one could swear they began to move and twist and turn as they did in the air. A sort of rigor mortis? No, they are quite dead and still.' Paintings to look for are the watercolour *Ruined Country* and the air bombardment of the *Battle of Britain* (1940) exuberant in open space compared to the trench confinement in 1914, which lingers longer in the memory. The sketch for *Over the Top* (First War) is by Paul's brother, John Nash.

To compare the war artists as if they were competing in a race is pointless for each was individual, but Nevinson, who was the same age as Paul Nash, comes closest to his peer with the memorable flow of *Marching Men* (1916). Each of the

Gassed   J. S. Sargent   The Imperial War Museum

artists stretched and manipulated their artistic power in the process of recording war, with an element of cubism in Nevinson and the vorticism of Wyndham Lewis, also represented by the watercolour *A Battery Position in a Wood* (1918). Spencer's *Travoys Arriving with Wounded at a Dressing Station at Smol* (Macedonia 1916) shows the horse-drawn stretchers arriving at the operating table with their casualties. They are seen from *above* – an extraordinary concept, completely fulfilled.

The Second World War produced fine work by Graham Sutherland, recording the steel mills of Wales and the London Blitz, also immortalised by Henry Moore, who had taken part in the First War, was gassed at Cambrai in 1917, and gave up sculpture in the second to take up drawing. His reaction to the air raids, and the Cockney cheerfulness in the face of them, reveals the contrast to the sombre quality of the trenches: 'Then the air raids began – and the war from being an awful worry became a real experience. Quite against what I expected I found myself strangely excited by the bombed buildings, but more still by the unbelievable scenes and life of the underground shelters . . . like a huge city in the bowels of the earth . . . I saw hundreds of Henry Moore reclining figures stretched along the platforms. I was fascinated visually, I went back again and again.' His sketchbook led to his commission from the War Artists' Committee for finished drawings, with pencil, pen, ink, crayon and watercolour.

It is hardly surprising that the subject of war should have inspired arists from Goya's *Firing Squad* to Picasso's *Guernica*. The excitement lies in the way it stretched their talent. For sheer realism you need go no further than the evocative photographs of life in the trenches, and probably the artists knew of these and such harrowing newsreels as the blind soldiers leading the blind in single file, which is why they did not attempt to record the war realistically.

The Imperial War Museum includes a photograph of *Third Ypres* (1917), of Australian soldiers walking along a duckboard track through a devastated château wood. The trees in the background are as shorn as those of Nash, but there is a crucial difference: it seems as if one soldier, at least, is grinning, thrilled to bits at being photographed. The camaraderie in the First World War is an aspect that the camera has recorded more than the artist, though the artist endowed it with nobility.

This great collection, with the promise of more space and more paintings to come, is protected by the latest light controls so that the most sensitive watercolours can be shown without risk. The *new* Imperial War Museum is a place to visit if you have any pride or interest in twentieth-century British art. It proves that war can enhance as well as destroy it.

LEIGHTON HOUSE

In a country of follies, this is one of the most exotic. Within a few yards of the roar of Kensington High Street, you enter the serenity of an Arabian palace with marble halls and the finest Iznik tiles I have seen outside Turkey – and a spacious garden with statuary to enhance the oasis. Alhambra in London – extraordinary!

In an area beloved by Victorian artists, this was the home of the highest of them all: Frederick, Lord Leighton of Stretton (1830–96), President of the Royal Academy, and the first and only artist to be ennobled with a peerage. He embodied the Victorian values.

Leighton designed the house in 1866 with the architect George Aitchison, a fellow Royal Academician, and lived here as a bachelor for the last thirty years of his life. The exterior is dull, red brick but like the Victorians themselves the façade is misleading. Inside, he fulfilled a fantasy which is so extravagant that it verges on the absurd except that Leighton's innate good taste prevails. With mock modesty he described it as his 'mews house'; his friends called it 'quite the eighth wonder of the world.'

In the staircase hall a Persian chest lies between two columns, topped by a stuffed peacock with pottery by De Morgan below. Beyond is the wooden staircase where Simeon Solomon slid naked down the banister, as befitted the outrageous Pre-Raphaelite who ended up as a pavement artist after his behaviour caused a scandal.

The Arab hall is the centrepiece and masterpiece, based by Aitchison on the banqueting room of a Moorish palace in Palermo, with a fountain trickling gently in a pool cut from a single block of black marble. The screens on the windows came from Cairo and the dome from Damascus, and the house abounds in ebony, the hard black wood.

It was not vanity which possessed Leighton to conceive such extravagance but a genuine passion for the East, prevalent at the time, and a practical need to house the tiles he had collected, which dated from the thirteenth century, as well as those brought back by his friend Richard Burton. Other friends were invited to enhance the opulence: Edgar Boehm designed the capitals on top of the alabaster columns in the Arab hall, while Walter Crane provided the gilt frieze.

For anyone unfamiliar with the ostentation of the East, the effect from the tiled walls could be overwhelming. The Iznik craftsmanship belongs to the past with the source of the colours long since secret; and there is the unusual depiction of birds in one panel in contravention of the Islamic law under the Ottomans which prevented the representation of any living creature. The explanation is curious, if only because the birds are such a rarity: their throats are 'cut' by a line in the glaze to render them 'dead'.

In today's jargon, Leighton House is frequently described as 'a bachelor pad' and it is true that sleeping arrangements were sparse with only one bedroom, Leighton's own, apart from the servants' quarters. Overnight visitors were unwelcome because they interfered with his work, which was the purpose of the place, apart from the sheer delight of exhibiting his friends' paintings in such surroundings. The studio upstairs – sixty foot long – was so expansive that musical evenings were held on the day before the 'Sending-In' to the Royal Academy's summer show, and they must have been magnificent, with the walls banked with flowers, the floors draped with Turkish carpets, and such performers as Clara Schumann. Tall windows overlooked the garden.

Old photographs confirm that Leighton liked to live in cluttered chaos with the walls crowded with prints and paintings by his friends and himself. As a collector he showed surprising discernment, with two Corots; a sketch by Delacroix; and particularly Constable's sketch for *The Haywain*, often considered superior to the finished painting, and much admired in France. The rooms were decorated richly, with furniture designed especially by Aitchison.

Sadly, everything was sold on his death with the irony that this sum was needed to pay for his endowment of £10,000 to the students of the Royal Academy. This makes the gradual acquisition of the present collection a form of recompense, a careful choice of work by such friends as Alma-Tadema and Burne-Jones, with paintings by Leighton himself. Even the walls reproduce his colour scheme for showing pictures to their best advantage. This is dedication rewarded.

Yet the question remains: what made Leighton so special that Queen Victoria ennobled him and Princess Alexandra gave him an armchair embroidered in silk by herself? Leighton's Olympian status in comparison to the other Pre-Raphaelites seems excessive, and in spite of such fame he appears remote.

He had every advantage from the start, with a wealthy grandfather who amassed a fortune from his unlikely post as doctor to the Russian Czarina. His father was also a doctor. Treatment for his mother's illness necessitated travel and when he was sixteen he studied in Frankfurt under a German 'Nazarene', whose cloying touch can be seen in such early work as *The Death of Brunelleschi*, painted in 1852 when Leighton moved to Italy. Meeting him in Rome, Thackeray warned Millais that this handsome young artist would become his rival for the Presidency of the Royal Academy.

Although the Nazarenes may be cloying to me, they appealed to the Victorians and influenced the painting *Cimabue's Madonna*, which Queen Victoria herself bought three years later in 1855 from the Royal Academy exhibition when Leighton was only twenty-five, establishing his reputation by doing so.

Moving to Paris on the grand artistic tour, Leighton also moved towards the more traditional influence of academic painting, though he fell briefly out of fashion with the critics who regarded his success with understandable suspicion.

By the time he was thirty he was through with Europe and returned to England where he became the darling of London society and a favourite with the Prince and Princess of Wales at Marlborough House. Selling a picture to the famous dealer Gambert for a thousand guineas, he was able to consolidate his position with the purchase of the house in Holland Park.

The clever caricature by Tissot is revealing: still the 'young' dandy, slightly dissolute and world-weary, yet this was drawn for *Vanity Fair* when Leighton was forty-two.

This image was typical of many Victorians who grew increasingly raffish with age. Yet his status as a bachelor – 'lavishing money and gifts on beautiful young protégés', to quote an article in the *Observer* in 1988 – and his Pre-Raphaelite embrace of sensuality in the cause of historical allegory, makes his peerage all the odder. That, I suspect, is the point: they were an odd lot altogether. Awesomely attractive on the outside, as upright as their buildings, they seethed with neuroses. The protégés may have been young men and the dinner parties exclusively male, but that was their way. The garden contains an 'erotic' sculpture by Leighton of an *Athlete Struggling with a Python* which does not mean that Leighton wanted to take athletes to his single bedroom. Until Wilde spoilt it, Victorian men embraced their friendship even if they were unaware of the implications. Sir Henry Irving, the first actor to be honoured, for all his private life was reproachable, scribbled a note to his lifelong friend and manager, Bram Stoker, declaring 'You above all men whom I hold dear ...' but that was the way they expressed themselves. Stoker, incidentally, accompanied Irving to Dublin in 1892, where Trinity College conferred degrees on Leighton and Alma-Tadema, and was outraged that Leighton tried to hog the stage artistically without a reference to the actor or the theatre in his acceptance speech.

As for the imputation of homosexuality, it only matters if this reveals his work in a new light and it does not. Apart from his devotion to his favourite model, Dorothy Dene, whom he helped to become an actress, his paintings were true to the Pre-Raphaelite obsession with female flesh at a time when it was considered risqué if a woman showed a turn of ankle – hence the popularity of such performers as the male-impersonator Vesta Tilly in her tight-fitting uniforms. Nudity on stage was unthinkable yet respectable on canvas, if tastefully presented in classical scenes – another example of Victorian hypocrisy. Albert Moore's *A Summer Night* is a famous example of the genre, and *In the Tepidarium* by Lawrence Alma-Tadema another. Alma-Tadema's bath scene, *A Favourite Custom*, is so sickly that even Vern G. Swanson in his book *The Painter of the Victorian Vision of the Ancient World* admits that 'the subject matter veers toward coyly risqué

Lord Leighton　Tissot　Leighton House Museum

Edwardian humour', yet the artist received his knighthood and the odious picture can be found in the Tate.

The Victorians and Edwardians did not regard this as an aberration but a convenient form of classical peepshow, a trick exploited by Cecil B. de Mille in the years to come. Leighton's contribution to the genre reveals that he was essentially a man of the time when he tackled such themes as *Perseus and Andromeda*. The bare-breasted woman in the serpent's embrace, with Perseus riding to the rescue in

Tepidarium   Alma-Tadema   Lady Lever Art Gallery, Port Sunlight

the sky above, may be magnificent but is slightly ridiculous by our standards today.

A visit to Leighton House, however, reveals that Leighton was not so simple as that. *Elisha Raising the Son of the Shunamite* is finely painted in a splendid frame, yet predictable compared to *Clytie*, the dark, mysterious picture of which he painted two versions towards the end of his life, taking the theme of a mortal who fell in love with the god of the sun. The immortals, taking pity on her, turned her into a sunflower so she could always gaze at that which she loved best – the mortal yearning for the immortal, appealing to Leighton's pursuit of artistic perfection. Does it also reflect an artist trapped by the conventions of his time?

Broken by devastating attacks of angina in January 1896, his final words were, 'give my love to the Royal Academy'. Thousands of cards bearing his portrait and embossed with these words were sold outside St Paul's on the day of his funeral, when Millais dropped the Queen's wreath into his coffin.

Galleries and museums with Leighton's work include:
Sudley
Manchester, City Art Gallery
Wightwick Manor

SIR JOHN SOANE'S MUSEUM

Should you have friends, then drag them here. It is worth the effort for your own satisfaction, and they will bless you for showing them one of the most surprising art galleries in Britain.

The Soane's is a folly, the home of Sir John Soane who designed the Bank of England and other palatial buildings, which would have transformed London into Ancient Rome had they been fulfilled.

Born in 1753, the son of a country builder, Soane spent the last twenty-four years of his life in this house in Lincoln's Inn Fields, which he designed like those on either side. If you happen to be a Soane enthusiast, he designed the Dulwich College Picture Gallery, while his country villa at Ealing, the ornate Pitzhanger Manor, has been restored and is now open to the public as the Pitzhanger Museum.

The interior at Lincoln's Inn Fields is redeemed by his infallible though eccentric taste as a collector. The proportions of the rooms are so fine that they exert a sense of restful tranquillity, yet the corridors and alcoves are crowded with marble busts. There is a crypt, a monk's parlour, catacombs with Roman urns, and a sepulchral chamber containing the sarcophagus discovered in the tomb of Seti I (1303–1290 BC), which was offered for £2,000 to the British Museum, and snapped up by Soane when they refused. Perfect of its kind, it is considered the gem of his collection.

In 1883 a private act of Parliament allowed Soane to turn his house into a museum, endowing it with the bulk of his fortune, though it is maintained today by parliamentary grants. Few galleries are run so well; there is no charge and you are welcome from the moment the front door is opened by one of the attendants, who are among the kindest in a profession which must be infinitely tedious. They are so involved with the paintings that one of them took pleasure in pointing out the white, fluffy dog in Canaletto's *Venetian Scene* which was his hallmark, like Whistler's butterfly. Telling me that he was about to go on his annual holiday, the attendant confided that he was going to Venice in order to see the scene which faced him every day. There's devotion for you.

Apart from the Canalettos and Turner's *Admiral Tromp's Barge*, the real surprise awaits you in the picture room, built in 1824 when Soane was seventy-one, with the oil paintings of Hogarth's depiction of London life: *A Rake's Progress* and *An Election*, the latter bought at the sale of Mrs David Garrick's possessions in 1823 for 1,650 guineas. As he knocked down the lot, the auctioneer remarked: 'As returning officer I have the honour of declaring that John Soane Esquire is the successful candidate in this warmly contested election.' The series consists of eight pictures charting the Rake's Progress and includes *Heir*, *Arrest* for debt, *Imprisonment* and incarceration in *The Madhouse*. The *Election* is no less cynical, with the triumphal procession of the successful candidate in *Chairing the Member* through a scene of cheerful chaos: a sow and her litter let loose among the mob; a man with his head in a beer barrel; a fainting woman and half-naked sailor.

There are more surprises to come as the attendant steps forward and peels back the walls revealing them as panels – or 'movable planes' – with architectural designs behind, many by Soane with his vaulting triumphal arches and royal residences which were never realised. As I wondered if the museum was compensation for his disappointment in seeing so few of his fantasies reach fruition, the attendant performed another sleight of hand as he folded back the walls to disclose the crypt below, surrounded by sculpture and antiquities. An American couple beside me *gasped* with delight.

Sir John hoped that his house and museum would be kept in the state in which he left them on his death in 1837. This objective is reaching fulfilment with the restorations supervised by the new Director, Peter Thornton.

THE IVEAGH BEQUEST, KENWOOD

Kenwood is the doyen of art galleries. The house was restored by Robert Adam with panels painted by Antonio Zucchi, the husband of Angelica Kauffmann, and is set in wooded parkland where you might be in the countryside instead of London, close to Hampstead Heath.

Appropriately, this is a gallery to savour. Instead of a headlong dash through endless rooms with hundred of pictures to absorb, the few paintings in this distinguished setting are the finest of their kind: Gainsborough's masterpiece, the epitome of haughtiness, *Mary, Countess Howe*; Rembrandt's poignant self-portrait as an old, self-knowing man; and Vermeer's *The Guitar Player*. Three paintings to which one dares apply the word, *perfection*.

THE WALLACE COLLECTION

Another formidable though broader collection in an elegant setting, at the heart of London. Originally, the mansion was built as Manchester House between 1776 and 1788 for the fourth Duke of Manchester, and was acquired only ten years later by the second Marquess of Hertford. After his death it became the French Embassy until it reverted to the fourth Marquess of Hertford, who used it to store his pictures. He acquired his collection from London and Paris between 1841 and 1870, adding to his father's, with the notable purchase of Titian's *Perseus and Andromeda*.

The Marquess had an illegitimate son, Richard Jackson, who changed his name to Wallace and became a Baronet in 1871, moving from Paris to make his permanent home in the building in Manchester Square, which he renamed Hertford House. His widow, Lady Wallace, a Frenchwoman, bequeathed his collection to the nation in 1897, and it was opened as a national museum by the Prince of Wales in 1900.

Again, you find the finest examples of the artist's work: *The Lady with the Fan* by Velasquez; the joyful, mischievous *Swing* by Fragonard – one of the most delicious scenes ever painted, which tells a story too; and *The Laughing Cavalier* by Frans Hals, of a twenty-six-year-old cavalier, an icon of art used for pub signs and beer mats. Yet if he is laughing at all, his sardonic expression suggests that he is doing so at our expense.

The

National Trust

Lady Churchill at the Launching of H.M.S. Indomitable Winston Churchill
by kind permission of Winston S. Churchill

Upton House Apart from protecting our countryside, the National Trust acts as guardian to numerous art collections when it assumes the maintenance of stately homes.

The scope of these collections is startling: who would have thought that Upton House in Banbury, a forty-minute drive from Oxford, contained a priceless grisaille by Pieter Bruegel the Elder of *The Death of the Virgin*, an interior setting thronged with people around the bed while the rest of the room is deserted apart from a cat and a sleeping figure by the fireside? Praising the lighting effects as 'a major technical feat', the art historian Bruce Bernard claims that it 'anticipates Rembrandt'.

The Bruegel masterpiece is not the only surprise at Upton. Other work includes an El Greco; Francesco Guardi's *Pope Pius VI Blessing the People of Venice*; Stubbs' *Reapers* and *Haymakers*; two works by Hogarth; and Raeburn's cheerful trio, *The Macdonald Children*. There is also an unusually restrained triptych by Hieronymus Bosch of *The Adoration of the Magi*. The personal favourite of the administrator, Simon Murray, is *St Jerome* by the Master of the St Lucy Legend.

This formidable collection was assembled between the two World Wars by Lord Bearsted and while he bought mainly from dealers the selection reflects his personal taste, for nearly all the paintings deal with people rather than places. Originally the picture gallery was built as a squash court, but his collection grew so quickly that it had to be converted.

Cragside, Rothbury is one of the most extraordinary private houses in Britain, designed by Norman Shaw to adjoin an existing building. It stands high up like a Victorian Castle Dracula, a monument to the first Lord Armstrong (1810–1900), a scientific genius and inventor who was also an armament magnate, though apparently a shy and genial man in spite of this. He planted several million trees, which protected Cragside from the fierce winds and changed the area's climate; he diverted streams to form the waterfalls and lakes in the park's 9,000 acres, which made Cragside the first house in the world to be lit by electricity derived from water power.

After such excess, the paintings are secondary, but include a portrait by H.H. Emerson showing Armstrong as a benign old gentleman sitting in an inglenook in the dining room in the company of two of his dogs. Plainly a dog lover, another Emerson is a classic of the canine genre, *Faithful Unto Death*, a winter landscape with a dead shepherd lying in the snow guarded by his sheepdog.

The artistic glory of Cragside lies in the late Pre-Raphaelite decor and elaborate furnishings, with numerous oils by Evelyn de Morgan with such titles as *Demeter Mourning for Persephone*; a sunset by Danby; and another portrait of Armstrong, this time by George Frederic Watts, painted after the industrialist had been raised to the peerage in Queen Victoria's Golden Jubilee Honours List in 1887.

Wightwick (pronounced Witick) **Manor**, Wolverhampton is another Pre-Raphaelite stronghold. The old manor house was bought by a Wolverhampton businessman in 1887, who commissioned a new house from an architect who specialised in half-timbered buildings. He turned to Morris & Company for the interior design and this is the attraction of the house today. Most of the Morris fabrics and wallpapers are intact, displayed alongside Jacobean furniture, Chinese porcelain and Persian rugs, a combination based on the principle that furniture of different periods can work together when the craftsmanship is good.

As you enter, you are greeted by a Burne-Jones embroidery, *Love and the Pilgrim*, which hangs by the front door, and the presence of William Morris is immediately evident in the drawing room, with his *Dove and Rose* wall-covering of silk and wool. The walnut panelling above the chimneypiece has a motto from Ruskin's *Modern Painters* and the furniture includes a rosewood piano made for the Crystal Palace Exhibition in 1851.

Pictures include the work of Ford Madox Brown, Lord Leighton, Holman Hunt, G.F. Watts and Ruskin himself. Probably the most famous, at the far end of the room underneath the gallery, is *Love Among the Ruins* by Sir Edwin Burne-Jones, a later version of a watercolour which was damaged when he sent it to Paris in 1890.

With tiles by William de Morgan, and the Wild Tulip wallpaper designs by William Morris, Wightwick Manor provides a feast for anyone who admires Pre-Raphaelite romanticism.

Ickworth House, Horringer is the family home of the Earls of Bristol. Its main feature is the magnificent circular rotunda built for the fourth Earl (1703–1803) to house his unique collection of paintings which he acquired during his years in Europe, and which was particularly large because of his longevity. Unfortunately, it was diminished when the French invaded Italy in 1797 and most of his paintings were seized. A few were returned and added to by later members of the family, with works by Gainsborough, Hogarth, Lawrence and Joshua Reynolds. There is also a version of the famous *Death of Wolfe* by Benjamin West.

The most impressive of the family portraits is that of the third Earl of Bristol, a full-length, slightly sardonic painting by Gainsborough showing the Earl leaning against an anchor in his capacity of Vice Admiral of the Blue, his telescope raised like a rifle.

Other work includes *Lady Elizabeth Foster* by Angelica Kauffmann; *Portrait of an Unknown Man* by Titian; *Don Bathasar Carlos* by Velasquez; and a *Classical Landscape* by Poussin.

There are two further National Trust properties with particular appeal: Plas Newydd, Llanfairpwll, with the mural by Rex Whistler; and Chartwell, Westerham, where the portrait of *Sir Winston Churchill* by Birley complements the work of Churchill himself.

Plas Newydd has belonged to the Anglesey family for the last 200 years. In 1784, after inheriting the estate, Lord Paget was created Earl of Uxbridge. His eldest son fought with Wellington at Waterloo as his second in command. As they rode off the battlefield, Uxbridge's right leg was smashed by grapeshot, which prompted a classic exchange of military sang-froid:

'By God, sir,' Uxbridge exclaimed, 'I've lost my leg.'

'By God, sir, so you have,' replied the Duke, replacing his eyeglass to observe the retreating French. Rewarded by the Prince Regent, who made him the Marquess of Anglesey, he was presented with the recent invention of an 'articulated wooden leg'. This became known as the Anglesey leg, and an example is included in the Cavalry Museum at Plas Newydd, along with the blood bespattered hussar trousers worn on that memorable day.

Artistically, Plas Newydd has a particular treasure: the long mural by Rex Whistler in the dining room, commissioned by the Sixth Marquess in 1936. The last and most extensive of Whistler's murals, it is considered the best, superior even to his early work for the Tate Gallery restaurant.

The trompe l'oeil is so convincing that Rose Paget tried to climb the steps when she was a child in order to pat her sister's dog, and was startled when she bumped her head. Her brother Henry, the present Marquess, takes up the story:

> Rex was wonderful with children. We loved his sense of humour. We also loved being allowed to paint in bits on the wall painting, under his instruction. These were later discreetly removed!
>
> The island in the centre appeared between 10.00 p.m. and 7.00 a.m. after a longish period of idleness. During that night he had removed a

Mural   Rex Whistler   Plas Newydd, by kind permission of the Marquess of Anglesey

large sailing boat, having declared at dinner that there were too many vessels on the canvas, and painted the island in its place.

The statue of my father, as patron of the whole enterprise, shows him crushing an enemy under the legs of the horse. My father suggested, rightly, that this was not typical of his behaviour. Rex said there had to be something to hold up the animal's front legs!

The wall painting is not technically a mural, being painted on canvas. This single piece of canvas which stretches from one fireplace to the other (fifty-eight feet) was woven in France, no loom in Great Britain being large enough. It was set up on rollers in a scene-painter's studio in London, where most of the painting was done, and brought up here by rail and road, fixed in position by being glued to the plaster direct. It is, of course, too heavy for stretchers. Although it was believed that the plaster had dried out, it in fact had not. For about six months after it was put up bubbles occurred. A little man came from somewhere with a syringe to burst the bubbles. The task took many months!

The Marquess continued with such personal details, as Whistler's 'hopelessness' concerning money:

Originally, when my father asked him what the thing would cost, he said £600. Certainly his assistant's wages exceeded this, as also did the gold leaf. Dollops of money had to be periodically doled out (not at all reluctantly!) by my father to keep Rex in bread and paint.

Rex Whistler took pleasure in entertaining his friends and inserted details to delight the family. The French bulldog on the cushion, called 'Cheeky', belonged to Henry's sister, Elizabeth; and Rose's bulldog, 'Zinia', looks as if she is rash enough to poach Cheeky's meal. The cigarette belonged to the Marchioness, and so did the book. The tower to the right of centre was added as an afterthought and the sailing ship it replaced was not fully painted out, its masts looming increasingly like a ghost ship. One evening, when Whistler ran out of white paint, he borrowed some of the 'coarsest possible white paint' from the local boatman, which explains the perpetual shine on the tower.

His concept is rich in pastiche. While he was inspired originally by the view of the Straits from the window of the dining room, he imposed a fantasy landscape with romantic mountains, Welsh farmhouses, a sunlit renaissance city, and the steeple of St Martin-in-the-Fields, taller than the actual masterpiece by Gibbs, while the Trajan's Column is an exact replica. It is a work of art created with humour and love.

REX WHISTLER
1905–44

It is no exaggeration to say that the English aristocracy doted on Rex Whistler, and he became their trusted confidant. Peter Quennell wrote of him, 'Lovable, lively, graceful and intelligent, Rex Whistler should have been born in the late seventeenth or eighteenth century. In the twentieth, his extraordinary gifts as illustrator and decorator won him much uncritical adulation but little understanding.' Yet without the chance to paint on the grand scale in their country houses, 'there would have been far fewer opportunities in this poorer and drabber age for the particular form of art in which he incomparably excelled.' (Christopher Hussey) If he courted the aristocracy, they rewarded him with space.

Without knowing him, I can only guess the nature of his charm, but it is undeniable that he possessed it. When Christabel Aberconway showed me his sketches for the two wooden urns designed for Samuel Courtauld's house in North Audley Street (which she inherited, with a number of Courtauld's French Impressionists) she told me, 'He was more imaginative, inventive, and more to be loved than almost anyone I have known.'

Although he might have astonished us had he survived the last war, I suspect that he belonged to the 1930s like that other 'charmer', Denys Finch Hatton, so adored by Baroness Blixen. There is almost a sense of that impending war, as if he was playing for time, posing affectedly for one of Cecil Beaton's *fêtes champêtres*, enchanting everyone he met. In her introduction to *Mr Korah*, a children's story illustrated by Whistler, Christabel Aberconway wrote that, 'Children as well as grown up people loved Rex Whistler, and my family and I had no greater treat than when Rex came to see us. Often, after luncheon or dinner, he would tell us a story, an impromptu, fantastic story which he illustrated, even while he was talking, with lightning sketches made on the little note-book lying beside my plate.'

His humour was appreciated on many levels: his famous work *The Spirit of Brighton*, for instance, showing a winged caricature of a portly George IV, was designed to amuse his fellow officers. It is claimed that he was the model for Charles Ryder in *Brideshead Revisited*, the artist whose avoidance of reality is bitterly chastised by Anthony Blanche. He seized on the war as a reason for breaking free from this image. Shortly before he was killed, he told Henry Anglesey that he was becoming 'fed up with doing what he too cruelly called eighteenth-century pastiches', and was longing to continue the process which he had already started of 'becoming a free-brush man'. His wish was to become a portrait painter and his last portraits show how brilliant he had become.

After the stylish confectionery of the murals, it comes as a shock to stumble on the hardness of a drawing like that of William Walton the composer, another member of that enchanted circle between the wars.

Rex Whistler was killed in 1944. His brother Laurence, the eminent glass engraver who has written his biography, *The Laughter and the Urn*, wrote to me: 'Few artists have been so versatile, working equally well in murals, easel paintings, portraits, book illustrations, theatrical scenery and costumes, advertisements, drawings for children, jeux d'esprit . . .' He added, 'I hope you won't say he was "the darling of the aristocracy" or anything like it. The fact is that he was beloved, quite as much, by the forgotten and uncelebrated work people in theatres and elsewhere, fellow officers in the war, and especially by his own troop.'

Work by Rex Whistler can be seen in:
London, The Restaurant of the Tate Gallery (which he completed at the age of twenty-two).
The National Portrait Gallery (with portraits of Lord Berners and Edith Sitwell) and the ten illustrations to A.E.W. Mason's *Konigsmark.*
The Rex Whistler Exhibition at Plas Newydd, with designs and illustrations.

SIR WINSTON CHURCHILL

1874–1965

Winston Churchill wrote about the joy of painting, comparing it in characteristic prose to 'a companion with whom one may hope to walk a great part of life's journey'.

The question remains – was he any good? Undeniably he was a gifted amateur and gained pleasure from the act of painting, which helped to distract him from the pressures of political life. Indeed, he started in 1915 at the age of forty when he was desperately in need of solace after the débâcle of the Dardanelles. He began tentatively until Lady Lavery encouraged him to be bold: 'the canvas grinned in helplessness before me . . .' he growled. 'I seized the largest brush and fell upon my victim with berserk fury. I have never felt any awe of a canvas since.'

Whereas Hitler, in many ways the superior artist, was meticulous, Churchill endowed his paintings with typical bravura and childish passion: 'Just to paint is great fun, the colours are lovely to look at and delicious to squeeze out . . . I cannot pretend to be impartial about colours. I rejoice with the brilliant ones and am genuinely sorry for the poor browns.' Whatever anyone might say against him, Churchill could never be accused of being 'a poor brown' himself.

It is claimed that he could have become a professional painter if politics had not tempted him instead, and this is not merely a case of sycophancy with the benefit of hindsight. When Sir Oswald Birley and Lord Duveen judged an exhibition they gave the first prize to 'a picture of a red house in sunlight with snow on the roof, painted with great vigour', though Duveen protested that it must be the work of a professional and therefore disqualified. The painter was Churchill. Even so, it is Churchill's amateurism that makes his work appealing, and when he was made the first Honorary Academician Extraordinary it was more for his services to politics than art.

At his best, his work is highly enjoyable and no one enjoyed it more than he did: 'When I get to heaven, I mean to spend a considerable portion of my first million years in painting and so get to the bottom of the subject. But then I shall need a still gayer palette than I can get here below. I expect orange and vermilion will be the darkest, dullest colours upon it, and beyond them will be a whole range of wonderful new colours which will delight the celestial eye.' This endearing side of Churchill makes his vulgar abuse of Picasso, egged on by Alfred Munnings, and the desecration of Sutherland's magnificent portrait, destroyed by Lady Churchill after her husband's death, all the more regrettable.

Stately Homes
and Castles

Oliver Cromwell   (actual size: half that of a postcard)   Samuel Cooper
Duke of Buccleuch Collection, Bowhill, Selkirk, Scotland,
by kind permission of His Grace the Duke of Buccleuch

For most of the twentieth century the greatest works of art that have appeared on the world market have come from English stately homes. The great collections, formed in the eighteenth and nineteenth centuries, have been gradually dismembered under the pressure of taxation.

Geraldine Norman, the *Independent*

The British aristocracy – and royalty too – have always enjoyed the role of patron of the arts. Moreover, many have assumed it as their responsibility. Sir George Beaumont, an amateur artist himself, encouraged Constable, providing support at a crucial moment; and Lord Egremont invited Turner to Petworth House where the artist spent some of the happiest periods of his life, providing him with a studio with a strong north-east light.

Petworth House today has a Turner Room with nineteen Turners on permanent display, including the untypical portrait of *Jessica* in *The Merchant of Venice*, which Turner painted after his second visit to Venice and which was bought by his patron. *The Times*, however, called it a 'trumpery' when it was shown at the Royal Academy in 1830, the *Morning Chronicle* compared it to 'a lady getting out of a large mustard pot', and Wordsworth thought that Turner must have 'indulged in raw liver until he was very unwell'.

I chose it for Gallery, finding it spontaneous and delightful.

Unlike the Americans, the British patrons held on to the loot they brought back from Europe. While Guggenheim, Frick, Melon and Getty built museums to share their collections with the public, British aristocrats were more selfish until recently, when changing conditions have forced them to make the occasional sale in order to maintain their stately homes, or open their houses to the public. The revelation of the treasures they contain has been astounding.

Bowhill, Selkirk, is the Border home of the Duke of Buccleuch, the owner of one of the finest collections in Britain, only rivalled by the Duke of Sutherland, who is noted for his generosity in lending his Titians, Rembrandts and Raphaels to the National Gallery of Scotland.

Drumlanrig Castle to the south-west, another stately home owned by the Duke of Buccleuch, has Rembrandt's *Old Woman Reading* (1655), generally claimed as a 'masterpiece', while Bowhill has the greater surprise of a painting by Leonardo da Vinci, *The Madonna with the Yarn-winder*, depicting the Madonna and the naked infant Christ.

Apart from a small work at Chatsworth and the mysterious *Mona Lisa* at Belton House (allegedly one of three, painted on board and comparable to the version in the Louvre, which used to hang in the Red Room but now seems to have disappeared), this is believed to be the only painting by Leonardo in a private collection in the world.

There is something odd about the composition and the size of the Madonna's hand, and though it sounds blasphemous from a layman like myself, I would be tempted to think that it was not *wholly* the work of Leonardo himself if it had not been authenticated by the late Sir Kenneth Clark. This is another reason for going to Bowhill, to judge for yourself, but I should warn you to check beforehand, for the house is frequently closed to the public.

Next to the Leonardo, the most important possession at Bowhill is the unique collection of a hundred miniature portraits, including two rare Holbeins, several Hilliards and Isaac Olivers, and a dozen by the later artist, Samuel Cooper, including his simple yet powerful unfinished portrait of Oliver Cromwell.

The Miniaturists

NICHOLAS HILLIARD
1547–1619

SAMUEL COOPER
1609–72

Hilliard was the master of the miniature and taught this essentially English craft to Isaac Oliver, who subsequently became his rival. The son of a goldsmith, Hilliard benefited from the apprenticeship and painted his first portrait of the Queen when he was twenty-three. His intimate form of portraiture was encouraged by the Queen as he revealed in his *Arte of Limning*, which recorded her agreement that 'portrait-painting should be done without shadows . . . best in plaine lines'.

Elizabeth's personality was ideal for Hilliard's art and her patronage helped him to achieve greatness. In the avoidance of shadow, she sat 'in an open alley of a goodly garden, where no tree was near' to assist him attain the clarity which was necessary for so meticulous an art. His capacity for detail was exactly what she wanted, presenting an image of splendour enhanced by her abundant jewellery. On a small easel, and a rectangular card stuck with fine vellum, he used liquid gold which he burnished for the jewels, dresses and swords. Even the ermine, one of her favourite pets, has a golden collar.

Until Hilliard, Elizabeth disliked her portraits so intensely that in 1563 her councillors stopped all commissions until 'some special persons . . . shall have first fynished a portraiture thereof, after which fynished, her majesty will be content that all other payntors, or gravers . . . shall and maybe at their plesurs follow the said pattern . . .' This explains the surprising similarity of the subsequent portraits of Elizabeth, which are painted from the same angle. Once she approved of the first miniature, all the other artists copied the pose.

Elizabeth was wise to withhold her approval until she was satisfied. Once

Hilliard appeared she knew she had found her 'special person' and was so captivated that when she saw a miniature of the young Cecil on Lady Derby's neck, 'she snatched it away and tying it upon her shoe, walked along with it . . .' Hilliard's languid youth, *An Unknown Young Man Among Roses* (1588, V & A), leaning against a tree in lovesick ecstasy is rich in humour. The gallant knight takes his plight most seriously, while Hilliard makes us smile, the visual counterparts to an Elizabethan sonnet. His miniature of the *Earl of Cumberland* has the same delicacy as well as a pleasing bravura, almost an exaggeration, but his pupil Isaac Oliver moved from the languid *Lord Herbert of Cherburg* reclining on the ground to the greater realism of his portrait of *Richard Sackville, Earl of Dorset*, in which the full-length figure in a conventional interior might be that of a large-scale painting.

This trend for miniatures reached fulfilment with Samuel Cooper, who was described by Aubrey as 'the prince of limners'. For one thing, he used shadow, regarding the miniature as a painting in its own right rather than a specialised art. Cooper's most famous miniature is the unfinished portrait of Cromwell, warts and all, owned by the Duke of Buccleuch at Bowhill, Selkirk. When I selected it for *Gallery*, His Grace reminded me of Walpole's claim that 'If a glass could expand Cooper's pictures to the size of Van Dyck's they would appear to have been painted for that proportion.' As His Grace pointed out, the television screen provided the perfect 'glass' for suggesting that Cooper's Cromwell and Van Dyck's Charles I appeared on a comparable scale. Walpole added that 'If his portrait of Cromwell could be so enlarged, I do not know but Van Dyck would appear less great by the comparison.'

Masterful though Cooper can be, Hilliard exemplifies the delicate delight of the miniature, his colours retaining a brightness which seems miraculous when performed on such a tiny scale. Though influenced by Holbein who started *limning* (from *illuminate*) and also by the precision of Dürer's engravings, Hilliard has been recognised by Simon Wilson in his book on *British Art* (Bodley Head, 1979) as the 'first native-born genius of English painting'.

Work by Hilliard can be seen in:
Birmingham, Barber Institute
Cambridge, Fitzwilliam Museum
London, National Portrait Gallery
　　　　　National Maritime Museum
Selkirk, Bowhill

A Brief Guide To Other Important Stately Homes And Their Paintings
(In view of erratic opening times, you would be advised to phone beforehand)

Abbotsford House, nr Melrose
This was the home of the novelist Sir Walter Scott, who expanded a farmhouse on the banks of the River Tweed into the imposing mansion you will find today. Understandably, the painting to look for is the portrait by Henry Raeburn of Sir Walter, with his greyhound Percy staring at his master adoringly, with another dog, known as Camp, at his feet. Curiously, in the comparable portrait which dominates the study at Bowhill and is painted with greater delicacy, Camp remains but Percy has vanished.

Alnwick Castle
This is one of those castles which look forbidding from the outside yet reveal a surprising richness inside. Alnwick is the seat of the Duke of Northumberland and the lavish furnishings are due to the fourth Duke, who was the First Lord of the Admiralty in Lord Derby's cabinet in 1852, and who became a leading patron of the arts. Travelling in Italy, he noticed that the Italians left the exteriors of their medieval fortresses untouched while filling them inside with the finest classical decorations of the Renaissance. Finding that the opposing styles were not at all incongruous, he did the same with Alnwick, introducing the best of Italian art, thus enhancing the fine collection which existed already and included two portraits by Anthony Van Dyck. There are two views by Canaletto; one (a copy) of Alnwick Castle before the first Duke's restoration; the other of Northumberland House, the family residence in Trafalgar Square before it was demolished to make way for Northumberland Avenue. Two outstanding works by Titian include *A Conversation*, highly praised by Byron as 'the loveliest to my mind', and a Tintoretto, *Ecce Homo*.

Althorp House, Northampton
In her introduction to the brochure, the Countess Spencer writes that 'Althorp contains one of the finest private art collections in Europe'. This is a loyal exaggeration, exonerated by the Van Dyck in the picture gallery, *War and Peace*, a portrait of the second Earl of Bristol and the first Duke of Bedford, so called because one man wears a breastplate while the other is in mufti. Two other pleasing portraits are by Sir Joshua Reynolds of Viscount Althorp as a small boy and the study of Lavinia Bingham, Countess Spencer, wearing a hat and a quizzical expression.

Arundel Castle
The home of the Dukes of Norfolk contains a fine portrait of the third Duke by Daniel Mytens (1590–1648), who was the official court painter to Charles I until he was eclipsed by the arrival of Van Dyck. Mytens has suffered from the comparison

ever since, but further confirmation of his brilliance as a portrait painter in his own right can be seen in his picture, *The First Duke of Hamilton as a Boy*, in the Tate.

Belvoir Castle, Grantham

The home of the Dukes of Rutland offers numerous activities such as jousting tournaments and possesses a varied art collection apart from the inevitable family portraits.

A work by Murillo hangs above the altar in the chapel, and a series of pink Gobelin tapestries of the Adventures of Don Quixote dominates one side of the Regent's Gallery. The finest picture is the Holbein of Henry VIII, legs akimbo as usual but standing against an unusually sumptuous background.

There is a puzzle picture of *The Proverbs* by David Teniers II (the most famous of the three) in which forty-three proverbs can be identified, and a Jan Steen, *Grace Before Meat*, as well as a series by Poussin which is ranked among his finest work. It was bought in Rome in 1786 by the fourth Duke on the advice of Sir Joshua Reynolds. The Duke expressed the hope that 'they will remain at Belvoir as long as the name of Manners (one of the family titles) and its splendour endures'.

Boughton House, nr Kettering

Another of the houses belonging to the Duke of Buccleuch, which in spite of its rich collection remains comparatively ignored. The paintings to look for are *The Adoration of the Shepherds*, an early work by El Greco, and next to it in the Little Hall is *A Young Man in a Plumed Hat* by Annibale Carracci, the greatest of the three brothers. Take a look, too, at *St John the Baptist* by Murillo and *Rubens* by Van Dyck, one of the set of thirty-seven grisailles.

Because I lived happily on the banks of the Thames at Limehouse, I have a particular affection for the *Thames by Montagu House* by Samuel Scott (1702–72), one of the finest English marine and topographical painters before the arrival of Canaletto. Some scenes by the two are so similar that it seems they influenced each other, but this particular work has a warmth which is sometimes lacking in Canaletto, especially in his later work, however brilliant his topographical representation and scale.

Bowood House, Calne

The home of the Earl of Shelbourne, with an orangery designed by Robert Adam in 1789 and a narrow lake created by Capability Brown.

The pictures include the collection acquired by the third Marquess of Landsdowne in the first half of the last century and have been compared to the Wallace Collection in London. This is a bold, extravagant claim but they include sixty-eight drawings by Richard Bonington, and watercolours by Edward Lear and Turner.

The most popular paintings are *Landscape with Cattle Returning Home*, once owned by Mrs Thrale; portraits by Joshua Reynolds including the exotic Mrs

Baldwin in Turkish costume; and the striking oddity of Lord Byron in Albanian costume in the famous portrait by Thomas Phillips (1814).

Castle Howard, Malton

One of the greatest houses in Britain, which became known to millions when used as the location for *Brideshead Revisited* on television. The first building was designed by Sir John Vanbrugh and if the domes are reminiscent of those at Greenwich Hospital, this is due to the influence of Nicholas Hawksmoor, who assisted in both. Hawksmoor was also responsible for the famous Mausoleum, described by Walpole as tempting one to be buried alive.

The most important painting is probably the famous portrait of King Henry VIII, one of many by Hans Holbein. Few kings are so instantly recognisable – bluff, formidable, his feet striding the earth, with a nasty little mouth that smacks of petulance. This portrait hints at the unflattering truth, that he was ugly not just because he was gross but because of that tight, twisted mouth and the small black eyes, with the overall impression that he was humourless (unlike the portrayal by Charles Laughton in the film) and liable to fly into a groundless rage. He was also sufficiently vain to wear a bell-shaped surcoat of Venetian velvet to hide his bulk. When one learns, however, that this was painted shortly after Queen Catherine Howard's execution, the expression of growing disillusionment becomes more comprehensible. The portrait seems familiar because of the number of copies, but it is assumed to be the work of Holbein alone because it has decorations on the coat which could only have been made by a left-handed painter like himself.

Other paintings to look for are:

Herodias and Salome with the Head of John the Baptist by Rubens; *The Finding of Moses*, Orazio Gentileschi; and the bas-relief of *Madonna and Child* by Andrea Sansovina in the chapel, which has stained glass windows designed by Burne-Jones and executed by William Morris.

Euston Hall, Thetford

The home of the eleventh Duke of Grafton was built by the first Duke's father-in-law, Lord Arlington, in the 1660s, who acquired his art collection at the same time, buying pictures either for his town house in London on the site of Buckingham Palace, or Euston itself. The paintings have been here for nearly three hundred years.

The large portrait of Charles I is by Van Dyck and though the original is in the Louvre it was accepted that an artist might produce replicas of such an important work. On the right of the Outer Hall is the famous portrait of the *Eldest Children of Charles I*, also by Van Dyck, and his portrait of Henrietta Maria hangs in the Dining Room.

The other considerable attraction is *Mares and Foals*. Painted by George Stubbs for the third Duke, it is set beside the riverbank not far from the house itself, the personification of the English countryside.

As the surrounding gardens were laid out by John Evelyn, with a park and temple landscaped by William Kent, Euston Hall offers an enjoyable visit in the summer when it is open to the public, with the added temptation of 'home-made kitchen teas'.

Harewood House, Leeds

This grand Palladian building was designed by John Carr of York, replaced by Robert Adam while it was being built between 1759 and 1771. Adam also designed the interior, commissioning furniture from Thomas Chippendale. With grounds landscaped by Capability Brown, a visit to Harewood is an occasion in itself, apart from the outstanding collection of pictures which include works by Gainsborough, Bellini, Titian and Tintoretto.

Some of the most interesting pictures concern the house itself. Girtin and Turner travelled there in 1797 in their early twenties at the invitation of Edward, Viscount Lascelles who was himself a watercolourist. This gives us a rare opportunity to compare the work of the two young friends. Girtin's view of Harewood House from the south-east is the more dramatic, with a dark foreground and the house illuminated on a distant hill by the sun setting behind swirling rosy-ambered clouds. Turner's view is more traditional, showing the early influence of Poussin. The north front of the house is seen close-to by their teacher, Thomas Malton, a more architectural approach showing the house as it looked before Charles Barry spoiled the simple façade.

The elegant entrance hall with wooden columns, elaborate filigree and a decorated ceiling contrasts strangely with the squat, and some would say hideous, figure of *Ecce Homo*, Epstein's massive Adam, carved from a single piece of alabaster. To include it in such a setting – Epstein's Adam in a hall designed by Robert Adam – is superbly impudent, yet the daring succeeds. How rare it is when the owners have the courage to contrast the old with the shock of the new.

There are two views of Venice by the American artist John Singer Sargent, and several of his portraits, including one of the princess royal which she disliked. *The Wedding Procession*, of the marriage between Viscount Lascelles and Princess Mary in 1922, was painted by Sir John Lavery.

In the Rose Drawing Room, all the pictures are by Italian artists of the fifteenth and sixteenth centuries and were collected by the sixth Earl. The two Madonnas by Giovanni Bellini are outstanding. So is the unusual, almost surrealistic landscape by Cima da Conegliano of *St Jerome and the Lion*, a subject which has always inspired artists to extend their imagination.

The Green Drawing Room is lined with portraits by Venetian artists, with an interesting work by El Greco, *A Man, a Woman and a Monkey*, their faces lit from the glow of a fir cone which the woman is burning. At least that is what is attributed, but after seeing the alternative version recently acquired by the National Gallery of Scotland I wonder if the woman is in fact a boy, based on the artist's early self-portrait – though I admit this is amateur detective work on my part.

The present Earl of Harewood takes an active interest in the arts, organising an exhibition for charity in 1989, 'Visions of Paradise as seen by contemporary artists'.

Holkham Hall, Wells-next-the-sea

This Palladian house was designed by William Kent for Thomas Coke, the first Earl of Leicester and a famous art collector. Of 250 works, more than eighty are on view to the public, with the Landscape Room hung entirely with works by Nicolas Poussin, Claude, and Gaspard Poussin.

The Saloon has paintings by Gainsborough, Van Dyck, and Rubens' *Return of the Holy Family*. With work by Reynolds, Raphael and Reni, this is one of the finest collections in the country.

Hopetoun House, South Queensferry

The greatest Adam mansion in Scotland, and the home of the Marquess of Linlithgow. The rooms, designed by William Adam and decorated for the second Earl by his sons Robert and John, provide a spectacular setting for an art collection of unusual importance.

The *Portrait of an Old Woman* by Rembrandt is a version of the painting which hangs in the National, seen here in the Yellow Drawing Room. Canaletto's *Doge's Palace and Campanile from the Grand Canal of Venice* is in the Red Drawing Room. *The Adoration of the Shepherds* by Rubens, and Gainsborough's portrait of *Jane, Second Countess of Hopetoun* enhance the collection, as does the work of van de Welde, Teniers, Annibale Carraci and Aelbert Cuyp.

A comparison to the work of Rex Whistler (see Plas Newydd, p. 210) can be found in the modern murals above the main staircase, painted by the Scottish artist William McLaren in 1967 as a memorial to Lord Linlithgow's first wife, who died in 1963. The trompe l'oeil harmonises with the pine panelled walls carved with flowers and fruit, and the oak handrail and balusters.

Leeds Castle, Maidstone

This has been described by Lord Conway as 'the loveliest castle in the world'. It is one of the most surprising too. In the first place it is nowhere near Leeds but was named after a man called Led, Chief Minister of Ethelbert IV, King of Kent in 857. It lies four miles east of Maidstone, exactly an hour by train from London.

The castle's attraction is its position on two islands in the middle of a lake, which made it the ideal stronghold in Norman times before Henry VIII turned it into a Palace and a Royal Residence for the next 300 years.

More recently, the owner was a remarkable woman, Olive, Lady Baillie, who bought the house in 1926 and undertook a painstaking restoration, leaving it to the nation in a magnificent state of preservation when she died in 1947. Evidently, she was a woman of unusual dedication. The theme of exotic birds in the interior decorations reflects her interest in the aviaries which are still maintained today. In particular, she was devoted to medical research, assisting the great plastic surgeon, Sir Archibald McIndoe in his treatment of the wounded pilots in the last war. She expressed the hope that the castle would become a centre for medical seminars when she established the Leeds Castle Foundation as a charitable trust.

The arts are an integral part of this extraordinary setting. The tapestries from Brussels are sumptuous – one depicting Hercules struggling with the Cretan Bull – and the paintings include one masterpiece of timeless simplicity, *Adam and Eve* by Lucas Cranach. Van Dyck's portrait of the youngest children of Charles I is another.

The group of hunchbacked figures resembling the crooked Punchinella of the Commedia dell'Arte is impressive, if disconcerting; conversely, the still life by Fantin-Latour of full blown white roses is one of his loveliest, making the still life by Vuillard look stiff by comparison. Surprisingly, Fantin-Latour's popularity as a painter of still life was virtually confined to this country, only realised by the French after his death.

Luton Hoo, Luton

The curious name comes from the Saxon word for the spur of a hill – Hoo – and the first family to live here in the thirteenth century, the de Hoos of Luton, took their name from the location.

The original Adam house has been spoiled by fires and alterations, so the interest lies in the paintings collected by Sir Julius Wernher, and with one in particular. This is the masterpiece by Altdorfer of *Christ taking leave of his Mother before the Passion*. Albrecht Altdorfer (1480–1538) was a Bavarian painter influenced by Cranach and Dürer, who was recognised as one of the first of the landscape painters. The trees in this work are much as we know them today.

The most spectacular treasure in Luton Hoo is the altarpiece of *St Michael* by Bartolomé Bermejo, whose work is rarely seen outside Spain. It was painted around 1470 as the altarpiece of a church near Valencia where it remained until 1864 when it was purchased in Berlin by Julius Wernher. It is allegedly the finest example of Spanish painting of that period to be found in Britain. The dragon is as monstrous as anything in Bosch, horribly macabre in contrast to the serenity of the kneeling, richly cloaked figure of the patron who presented the altarpiece to the church. Towering above them both is the beautiful St Michael with his raised sword, crimson cape with wings, and golden armour. One may not like it, but it is hard to turn away.

Wilton House, Wilton

There are many stately homes which are grander, but who could cope with Blenheim? Few are so perfect as Wilton, for every part is satisfying and the Palladian Bridge built in 1737 which spans the end of the lake, is one of the loveliest in the world.

The home of the Earls of Pembroke who have lived here for 400 years, it is partly the work of Inigo Jones; the cloisters are designed by Wyatt; and the forecourt memorial garden was laid out in 1971 by the seventeenth Earl as a tribute to his father, framed at one end by a triumphal archway topped by a statue of Marcus Aurelius on horseback.

The excellence of the paintings is not surprising considering the taste of the Herberts, but the magnificence is. The contents reads like a catalogue for a major exhibition, with work by Peter Bruegel the Younger; Poussin; Claude; Rubens; van de Velde; and a portrait of Lord Pembroke by Batoni. The group portraits by Van Dyck are predictably fine. The largest is 17ft long and 11ft high and shows the fourth Earl and his family. It dominates the Double Cube Room designed by Inigo Jones. Portraits of Charles I and Henrietta Maria hang on either side.

Disconcertingly, Rembrandt's *Portrait of his Mother* is stiff compared to his best work, though I would not dare to question its authenticity; conversely, I am bowled over by the portrait of *Prince Rupert of the Rhine* by Gerard Van Honthorst (1590–1656), a master of the Utrecht School influenced by Caravaggio. He adopted the style of Van Dyck when he came to England to paint Charles I in a massive portrait which hangs in Hampton Court.

Woburn Abbey

It is fitting to end with Woburn, for this was the first great English country house to open its doors to the public when, in 1955, the Duke of Bedford launched himself and his family into the Stately Home Business, with a flair for showmanship which was considered outrageous at the time, though acceptable now. Today the house is maintained by his son, the Marquess of Tavistock, with wild animals pacing the parks.

The true wealth of Woburn lies inside with the paintings, and they are abundant: the dining room alone contains twenty-four views of Venice by Canaletto, which have hung there ever since they were commissioned by the fourth Duke in 1800. Considering the proliferation of Canalettos in Britain, one wonders how the artist found the time.

The Reynolds Room, sometimes used as a breakfast room, is flanked by portraits of the fourth Duke's family and friends. It contains one of Reynolds' finest paintings, *Lady Elizabeth Keppel*, showing her in the magnificent silver silk, pearl-encrusted dress she wore as a bridesmaid at the wedding of Queen Charlotte, arranging a garland of flowers around the bust of Hymen, the God of marriage.

When she married Francis, the fourth Duke's only son, Walpole commented, 'Lord Tavistock has flung his handkerchief and except for a few jealous sultans who had marketable daughters, everybody is pleased that the lot has fallen on Lady Elizabeth Keppel.' Her husband's portrait hangs nearby and it seems that the couple were ideally suited, a love-match rather than a marriage of convenience. Three years later Francis was killed in a hunting accident, leaving Elizabeth with two boys and another born soon afterwards. Bereft, she carried a miniature of her husband and died herself eighteen months later.

There is no hint of the impending tragedy in this tremendous portrait by Reynolds, which confirms his greatness in spite of the occasional lapse and sentimentality.

The Long Gallery is dominated by the Armada portrait of Queen Elizabeth I by George Gower, showing the Queen in her full regalia as Empress, with one hand on the globe of the world. An appropriately patriotic note to end on.

Collectors

The First Born   Frederick Elwell   Ferens Art Gallery, Hull

To claim I was an art collector is a sad sort of swanking, although I did possess several pictures. Francis Bacon gave me a small painting of a surgeon; Sutherland a splendid sketch of Somerset Maugham; I bought Lucian Freud's portrait of John Deakin, and another which he bought back; and two Auerbachs which I exchanged in a moment of commercial folly for two by Alfred Wallis. I inherited a Henri Gaudier-Brzeska from my grandmother, a drawing of a tiger which was so simple it might have been done in a single line in a few seconds, and probably was.

I must also admit that I was the worst type of collector, buying my Freuds and Auerbachs without a thought of profit. One should collect pictures one loves, yet to do so without the hope of commercial gain loses the vital zest.

Conversely, I cannot warm to the fashionable collector Charles Saatchi, who appears to use art as a mere commodity in the course of power rather than pleasure. His formidable collection (800 works altogether) can be seen at 98a Boundary Road in St John's Wood, London, on Fridays and Saturdays only. The pictures include twenty Warhols and numerous works by Kiefer, Schnabel – the crockery man – and Baselitz, the upside-down German artist. With his undoubted influence and wealth, Saatchi has been instrumental in making these artists internationally successful, and if you wish 'trendiness' in art, you will find it here. Admittedly, he has extended his purchases recently to include Frank Auerbach, Carel Weight, and Lucian Freud.

At the same time it is only fair to point out that London's art dealers, who are claimed to number 400 against eighty-three ten years ago, applaud a man who encourages living artists and has proved to their customers that buying contemporary art is big business. Equally, that is the basic flaw in his collection.

In my ignorance, I was more interested in the artists than their art, though this proved an advantage in understanding it later. I have always enjoyed the company of artists, who have the capacity to relax away from the studio, unlike actors, who are constantly on stage. I sympathise with Alexander Macdonald (1837–84) whose bequest forms the basis for the collection in Aberdeen: 'I desire that no pictures painted more than twenty-five years before the date of purchase shall be eligible,' he instructed, adding, 'I purchased all my pictures direct from the artists, and that doing so was the avenue to much pleasant intercourse and association.'

I like the fact that Macdonald was a 'granite merchant', for this is one of the happiest attributes of British art collectors – that men who have made their pile repay their community with the permanent pleasure of paintings. Take, for instance, Courtauld, the cotton magnate whose collection of French Impressionists forms the basis of the Courtauld Institute; and Sir Henry Tate, who could be described as the first sugar daddy of the arts, devoting part of his profits from cube sugar to a collection of Victorian paintings and a gallery to display them in.

There is another 'attribute' of some collectors which is deeply moving: the love of art by spinster ladies who do not seem to have known such love for themselves. Painting has provided them with a faithful substitute, and they have passed on their appreciation so that we can benefit too.

I am not certain if Miss Haworth at Accrington comes into this category, but the Misses Davies most certainly do. Unless the photographs do them a cruel injustice, the Misses Davies were decidedly plain. They should be among the most celebrated women of the century; instead they are virtually unknown, largely due to their innate shyness, which was one of their endearing traits. Even if they were fortunate with their dealers, advised by the brother of their former governess, their initiative has enriched the Museum of Wales in recompense for the scarring of the Welsh valleys by their mine-owning father.

By 1924, the Misses Davies of Greynog, Montgomeryshire, had assembled the largest collection of Impressionists in England. This is their triumph, that they were the first. Dennis Farr, Director of the Courtauld Institute, acknowledges that Samuel Courtauld was 'by no means a pioneer in this country. If one has to award that title it must go to Miss Gwendoline Davies, who in 1912 began to collect modern French pictures on an appreciable scale. She not only took over from where Sir Hugh Lane had left off at his death in 1915, that is Impressionist art of the 1860s to 1890s, but extended her taste to include artists of the next generation.' The extent of her taste can be seen in Cardiff (p. 165), and the quality of her taste, both adventurous and wise, in such paintings as Renoir's *La Parisienne* and Van Gogh's *La Pluie* which, painted shortly before he committed suicide, must be worth around £20 million today.

The Misses Davies sought no publicity, preferring to be known as 'friends interested in art' (a lovely understatement) who desired to remain anonymous when they lent their paintings. They were sufficiently audacious to hold a salon in their home, encouraging the recital of music and poetry, yet their prudery was such that Joyce Grenfell was rebuked after her performance there because it was too risqué.

Ironically, the best word in their favour comes from abroad. When their collection was exhibited in Paris in 1980, the curator was surprised that the ladies were 'practically unknown in France. A collection is an act of love and a proof of perseverance. In this, the collector is always admirable and one can only praise it when the taste has the quality of the sisters Davies.'

Emma Holt is in the same, felicitous tradition. George Melly, who happens to be her cousin, has described the Liverpool heiress in the admirable reminiscence of his childhood, *Scouse Mouse*: 'She never married although the prospect of such a fortune must have offered a challenge to many an ambitious or mercenary young man. She was in fact remarkably plain with a long face, an incipient moustache, and very small eyes. At the same time she was both shrewd and self-aware. It is possible that she knew it was unlikely she would be loved for herself alone and rejected any suitors, but here I am only speculating. Her character on the other hand was original and her generosity, especially to young people, unstinting.'

He was taken to visit her house near Mossley Hill when he was a child, usually for Sunday lunch. As Emma was a relative of some importance, Mrs Melly implored George and his brother to be on their best behaviour, which had little effect:

'Bill suddenly announced one lunchtime that he had received a Christmas card of a monkey which our nanny had said "looked just like Cousin Emma". Maud turned crimson.

'"No, Bill," she improvised in panic, "I'm sure what she said was that Cousin Emma *sent* you the card of the monkey."

'This was a brave try, if unconvincing. Cousin Emma's cards were inevitably of Beatrix Potter animals, and anyway Bill wasn't going to let her off the hook.

'"No," he said emphatically, "she said it *looked* like Cousin Emma."

'"What lovely plums!" said my mother on the edge of hysteria. I was watching Cousin Emma closely during this exchange. I could see she was not at all angry – if anything, she was almost imperceptibly amused.'

The house, which is known as Sudley, stands at the end of a winding drive and is not particularly attractive, built in the Victorian neoclassical style. Once it was surrounded by fields with grazing sheep and woods with bluebells, which enhanced it. The interior, however, is elegant, with parquet floors and a staircase curving under a glass dome. The various rooms are used to display the collection left by Emmas's father, George Holt, who left a fortune of £600,000 which he acquired through shipping. In the catalogue, Timothy Stevens, the former Director of Liverpool's Walker Gallery, points out that Holt was one of several Liverpool merchants who bought British paintings but his is the only collection that remains intact: 'It shows the quality and variety of these great collections, formed by men who were responsible for Liverpool's mercantile greatness. At this period Turners in the city could be counted by the dozen and works by more academic artists, whom George Holt also admired, by their hundreds.'

Holt was a friend of Holman Hunt and was responsible for the purchase by the Liverpool Corporation of that painter's 'grotesque masterpiece' (to quote George Melly), *The Triumph of the Innocents*. He acquired a smaller version of Hunt's *Christ in the Temple* for himself, a work that was the climax of the tours conducted by Cousin Emma as she led young George round the collection, explaining the history of the paintings now that she had discovered his interest in art. Even at that age, George had realised 'the charm and possibility of a private collection', and became a collector himself.

'"You see, George," explained Cousin Emma, "Mr Hunt went to endless pains to be true to nature." She then picked up the magnifying glass and focused it on the head of one of the Jews listening to the young Lord Jesus. "He even," she continued, "painted in the cataracts on the old man's eyes." At this she drew back the glass so that an eye increased dramatically in size, and I could see the milky translucent skin over the eyeball, a demonstration I never tired of.'

Miss Holt died in 1944, bequeathing the house and grounds, and her father's art collection to the City of Liverpool. Dear, plain Miss Holt, and the plainer Misses Davies, to have left us with such beauty.

ARTHUR JEFFRESS

The life of Arthur Jeffress was devoted to his art collection and his homosexuality. The latter finally destroyed him; the art lives on in the Southampton Art Gallery.

A rich American expatriate who settled in London, he was one of The Bright Young Things who burnt themselves out, the subject of a scandal in 1931 when he held the infamous Red and White Party, when red caviare and lobster were washed down with pink champagne. Guests danced to a Negro band and white nuns cavorted with men dressed as exotic birds, while a man dressed as Queen Elizabeth I in a red wig sat in the hall playing 'Abide with Me' on the organ.

Tom Driberg, subsequently the Chairman of the Labour party and himself a homosexual, betrayed his friendship with Jeffress by condemning the party in the Hickey column which he wrote for the *Daily Express*, and the *Bystander* suggested that the money could have been spent more usefully at a time of unemployment. Unfortunately for Jeffress, he posed for a newspaper photograph wearing 'a modified sailor suit of white angel skin' and a spray of white orchids, which was touched up to make it look as if he was wearing evening dress. When it was published, Jeffress fled the country, returning when his solicitor assured him he could do so without the fear of arrest.

Times have changed, but Jeffress made a worse mistake. The excellent catalogue of the Southampton Gallery refers to 'his much loved Venice' where he owned a palace on one of the canals. Making fun of a family at the Lido where he entertained his friends, Jeffress was unaware that they were the wife and children of the Chief of Police. Later his gondoliers informed on him, yet it seems harsh that Jeffress was ordered to leave the country and told never to return. Continuing to Paris, Jeffress booked himself into a hotel room and killed himself.

There was a rumour at the time that his will left everything to a Sailor's Benevolent Fund on the strict conditions that nothing went towards a female Wren or a naval officer. If this unlikely story is true, the pettiness was redeemed by his generosity towards Southampton. Ninety-nine works were bequeathed, including *Napoleon* by François Gérard; and paintings by Paul Delvaux, Tchelitchew and Lucian Freud.

There are twelve works by Graham Sutherland, who was a personal friend, among which is his portrait of Jeffress painted in Venice in 1954, which catches the brittle nature of the man without making this too obvious. I suspect that Jeffress was unaware of the febrile, feline look, but admired the rather flattering reflection as 'a true likeness'.

THE SAINSBURY CENTRE FOR VISUAL ART

In 1973 Sir Robert and Lady Sainsbury gave their entire private art collection to the University of Anglia. With a further endowment of £3 million from their son David, this enabled the Centre to acquire new works of art as well, an act of generosity on the scale of Paul Getty Junior.

The art collection was assembled by Robert and Lisa Sainsbury over forty years. Describing himself as a 'passionate acquirer' rather than a collector, Sir Robert has defined his approach to art: 'I am not ashamed to say that my personal reaction to any work of art is mainly sensual, intuition largely taking the place of intellect. Jacob Epstein used to speak of his "stomach reaction" to works of art and his phrase perhaps best expresses what I myself seek in the first instance.'

Sir Robert's lack of pretension is refreshingly un-arty: 'I was not subjected to any dictums and so, uninhibited, without any preconceived ideas regarding the reputedly good in art, or the right way to approach a work of art, I was able to make my own discoveries.' He was true to his eye. An admirer of primitive African art, which forms a large part of the Sainsbury collection, he went to a dealer in Paris who put him off from the outset by asking what he was looking for, as if it was a pound of Sainsbury's beef. He produced a carving and named the price unasked. Sainsbury turned away to the surprise of the dealer who wondered whether he knew that it was genuine.

'Yes, as far as I know,' Sir Robert replied.

'And reasonably priced?'

'Yes.'

'Then why don't you buy it?'

'Because I don't want it.'

Sir Robert says the dealer regarded him as if he was a lunatic: 'After all, what more could a customer want – genuine, rare and a reasonable price! I have never been back to his gallery.'

His determination to follow his instinct gives consistency to the Centre which bears his name: 'I realise, of course, the limitation of sensual enjoyment without the application of knowledge and I know what I am missing in not being a scholar. However, I draw a distinction between the ability to appreciate or understand and the capacity to enjoy; the one may be learned; the other, I suggest, cannot be acquired.'

Sir Robert has a distaste for 'monuments'. Consequently, the startling modern building which forms the Centre is intended as a meeting place with a restaurant and coffee bar, based on a master plan by the architect Sir Denys Lasdun. There was the deliberate aim to relate the sculpture to the landscape with fine, uninterrupted views over a forty-acre lake.

Apart from his enthusiasm for tribal art, Sir Robert concentrated on acquiring works of the nineteenth and twentieth centuries, sculpture as well as paintings, the one to enhance the other in the case of Henry Moore, Giacometti and Epstein.

There are works by Picasso, Modigliani, Mark Gertler, Balthus, and Soutine, as well as nine paintings by Francis Bacon, who took me many years ago to the Sainsburys' home in London where I saw the bronze figure by Degas of the young ballerina *Petit danseuse de quatorze ans* (1880), now in the Centre.

As I was shown the pictures, I tried to make the right noises – and failed. When we stood in front of a Bacon portrait I remarked, brightly: 'I say, it's an awfully good likeness of your father.'

'Yes,' he agreed coldly, 'except it's my mother.'

The English Impressionists?

Surprisingly, yet significantly, our foremost Impressionists were American – Whistler and Sargent. They were followed by Sickert, who was Whistler's pupil and delivered his famous *Artist's Mother* to the Paris Salon in 1883, armed with introductions to Monet and Degas; and Wilson Steer who studied in Paris that same year.

Admirable as they are, with the blurred figures in Sickert's smoky music hall, and Steer's portrayal of naked women on the beach in *A Summer's Evening* (1888), they came afterwards.

Noctes Ambrosianae, Middlesex Music Hall, Drury Lane 1906
Walter Sickert   Nottingham Castle Museum

The dates for Sickert and Steer are identical: 1860–1942, while those for Whistler, 1834–1903, and Sargent, 1856–1925, are closer to those of Monet, 1840–1926.

Whistler stands alone, inimitable in spite of the endeavours of Walter Greaves, and if the label of our 'First Impressionist' has to be attached it could be Whistler though some might argue that Turner preceded him a hundred years earlier.

John Singer Sargent has been eclipsed by his versatility and is out of fashion today, yet he is one of the most interesting artists to lay claim to the title of Impressionist. In 1887 he accompanied Claude Monet through the wood near the artist's home at Giverny, followed by Monet's daughter wheeling a barrow with six canvases – 'three for grey and three for sunny effects'. This pin-points the difference between the English and the French Impressionists – *light*. The French are brilliant compared to Whistler's fog and Sickert's gloom. Monet said that he offered Sargent his colours 'and he wanted black'.

'But I haven't any black.'

'Then I can't paint. How do you do it?'

Yet Sargent's oil of *Claude Monet Painting at the Edge of the Wood*, which he painted that day, is as impressionistic as the work of Monet himself, and the freshness lingers in *On His Holidays, Norway* (1902), a study of the fourteen-year-old sons of Sargent's friend on a fishing holiday, and one of the most popular paintings in the Lady Lever Gallery.

When I selected this for the fourth series of *Gallery* (1990) we followed with an example of the society portraits which made Sargent so successful in his day (Lady Agnew of Lochnaw, National Gallery of Scotland) though he never yielded to the vanity of his sitters, one of whom complained, 'It's positively dangerous to sit for Sargent; it's taking your face in your hands.'

John Julius Norwich said he regarded Sargent as one of our finest portrait painters, and we ended our tribute to Sargent – for this is what it had become – with his famous scene of the First World War, *Gassed*, the long line of walking wounded, blinded by mustard gas, while their comrades play football in the far background.

The panels were unanimous in their agreement that Sargent is grossly underrated today and deserves a reappraisal.

Is *popularity a fault?*

On my journey north I made a point of asking which was the most popular painting in every gallery I visited. Invariably it was sentimental, frequently a dog or cat or pretty child with a dog or cat.

In the Bowes Museum the Curator, Elizabeth Conran, favoured the painting of a poodle beside a grand, green kennel – 'Obviously an idiotic little dog but much loved' – apparently a man's dog with her master's slippers on the floor next to her ball. Dated 1768, it was skilfully executed though some might wish the mawkish dog had been executed too. Liking dogs myself, with a marked aversion to poodles as the exception, I felt a slight revulsion in contrast to my admiration for the paintings of Oudry, also represented at Bowes. My reaction made me wonder if I was suffering from a form of inverted snobbery. Did I dislike it so much because it *was* so popular?

In the Laing Gallery in Newcastle, the most popular painting is probably *Cat in a Cottage Window* by Ralph Hedley (1881), an ill-tempered animal with its eyes tight shut, while Salford sported the touching shipwreck scene *A Volunteer for the Lifeboat*, painted by a Mrs Robinson, exhibited at the Royal Academy 1892, of a comely youth welcomed by some oilskinned salts as he steps forward to man the lifeboat offshore. There is nothing wrong with such a scene except for the contrivance.

The apotheosis of the 'popular pic' can be found in Hull – *The First Born* – a carefully posed composition of a woman in bed with her newborn child, her husband, wearing a hat, adoringly beside her. The artist used models and cheated on the light supposedly streaming through the window, as a bed manufacturer discovered when he tried to re-create the scene for a special display. The popular Pre-Raphaelites were guilty of such stage-setting, too, in the cause of sentiment, and it is interesting to note that the subjects in a scene by Millais rarely look at each other even in their intimacy.

The First Born could be dismissed as cloyingly sentimental, yet it strikes such a chord with the public that it is not only the favourite in the Ferens but one of the most popular of reproductions, with strangers sending it to the Royal Family on the occasion of their own first born heir to the throne. I am told that Princess Diana was inundated. After leaving Hull, I saw a reproduction of *The First Born* in a shop window in York, outrageously overpriced at £65 because it was framed, and I am sure there were plenty of buyers.

When a picture is that popular, does it mean it is rubbish? Does it mean that all those people who treasure a reproduction of the *Lady from the Orient,* better known as the *Green Lady*, by Tretchikoff, or the wise old elephant by Shepherd, or a

A dog of the Havannah Breed   Jean-Jacques Bachelier
Bowes Museum, Bardard Castle, Durham

pretty baby with a kitten, are *wrong*? Or is this the vilest snobbery of all? (And few professions are more riddled with snobbery than art.) Surely it is simply the other end of the market, the equivalent of Mills and Boon or Coronation Street, giving no offence yet considerable and harmless pleasure to millions of people.

The information that the landscapes in the illustrated calendar sent by your local garage at Christmas are the work of the disabled, frequently using a paintbrush in their mouths, is admirable in such circumstances, for merit is hardly relevant. Conversely, because it is popular it does not mean that the painting is any good. If art is a meal, this is the ice cream or pudding part of it.

Yet, in trying to be fair, I dissemble, for a popular picture offers shallow satisfaction compared to that of a masterpiece. If only the popular pics encouraged people to look on a higher level, galleries might reserve a room for them at the furthest point so that visitors would have to pass a major work like the Hals *Portrait of a Girl* at the Ferens in order to reach *The First Born*. Would they pause in front of the greater work? I wonder.

The bridge lies in education, encouraging the young to understand art as they do at the Dulwich College Art Gallery, where knowledge leads to a greater appreciation. Once the first step is taken, the appreciation of fine art becomes a possibility and in this I dare to hope that *Gallery*, with all the power of television, might have played a minor role, judging by the letters I have received.

If not, at least the reproduction of a popular picture on the wall is better than an unloved masterpiece.

Laughter in the Gallery

Can there be humour in act? Francis Bacon is adamant that there cannot. I persist, tactlessly, in pointing out that there is abundant humour in Dickens and Shakespeare, so why not in painting?

Admittedly, such humour is just a part of a grand literary stucture, yet a gallery without light relief would be a sombre experience, reinforcing the public's suspicion that art is an awesome affair and not for them.

I am not thinking in terms of comic relief, but humour which manifests itself in various forms, sometimes affectionate – Rembrandt's woman paddling in a stream or Fragonard's *Swing*; sometimes ironic – Frans Hals' debauched cavalier who is suffering from the 'morning after'; and occasionally inadvertent, as in one of Martin's colossal biblical epics or the deadly sincere sensuality of the naked flesh beloved by the late Victorians.

My mind usually goes blank when, on protesting that many artists introduce humour deliberately, I am asked to 'name them', so I have compiled a selection of candidates – my own gallery of humorous art. Certain names spring to mind, Rowlandson and Hogarth, though the latter conveys such stern morality in *The Rake's Progress* that I prefer the joyful simplicity of *The Shrimp Girl* in the National Gallery, the embodiment of cockney cheerfulness.

It is more rewarding to find wit where least expected, in a work by the unfortunate artist Benjamin Robert Haydon (see p. 156), who grew so disillusioned that he cut his throat and when he botched the attempt, shot himself. In happier days he painted *Waiting for the Times*, which hangs in the editor's office and shows Haydon in a lighter vein, preferable to his colossal epics where his figures are struck by rigor mortis.

Sir Henry Raeburn was venerated as a portrait painter, knighted by George IV on his state visit to Edinburgh, yet few portraits have such wry good humour as that of the Reverend Robert Walker venturing forth, arms akimbo, on the frozen Duddington Loch (1784), with the confidence of a new recruit to the local skating club.

Sir Stanley Spencer is not an artist one associated with levity, yet he qualifies with the chaos of *Dinner on the Hotel Lawn* described by Marina Vaizey as 'wickedly witty'.

And though it seems doubtful that Sir Edwin Landseer possessed a shred of humour, judging by the carnage in his hunting scenes, *A Naughty Child* in the V & A makes one think again. Portrait painters lose their pretentiousness when painting children: two of my favourites are Lady Caroline Scott, a girl with blackberry eyes painted by Sir Joshua Reynolds, part of the Bowhill collection of the Duke of

Buccleuch; and his portrait of Miss Bowles with her dog (Wallace Collection) in which the girl stares at the artist, as children do at the camera today, bemused and slightly alarmed by this moment of immortality, clutching her displeased dog in a grip worthy of a wrestler.

Of all the surrealists, Magritte is the wittiest and all the more so for reversing a situation as if it were entirely *natural*. The humour of Max Ernst's *The Elephant Celebes* in the Tate may escape the majority of passers-by, but George Melly thinks it is a 'master-piece. I find it funny. A very humorous painting,' to which Patricia Hodge replied on Gallery: 'I'd loath it if I thought it was serious.'

Dali revelled in absurdity, stretching the images as far as they could go, too intense to be genuinely jolly, while the primitives who might seem the likeliest 'humorists' of all, Douanier Rousseau and our own Alfred Wallis, were deadly serious, which is why they were so successful. Contrived humour is the worst of all.

Lady Jane Bowles and Her Dog Joshua Reynolds The Wallace Collection

As I have mentioned in my section on Gilbert & George (p. 184), they are constantly misinterpreted, yet if a painting like *Coming*, with underpants raining down from the sky is not meant to be humorous, I have misinterpreted them myself.

Two British artists this century indulged in light relief as an antidote to their more disturbing work. L.S. Lowry was funnier than his dour façade implied. Though he is most famous for the large industrial scenes they seem static compared to his closer observation of life inside the streets, which most artists would have overlooked. Atkinson Grimshaw depicted northern life as well, yet his street scenes are deserted by comparison to those of Lowry, which are thronged by curious characters in ill-fitting clothes, cripples and those who are plainly desperate.

Lowry's view is not dispassionate, it is both compassionate and humorous, finding fun in everyday foibles and such details as a man lying prone on top of a wall, cigarette in mouth, his umbrella and briefcase (with the initials L.S.L.) below him.

The Funeral Party (1953, Salford Art Gallery) mocks the solemnity of such an occasion, with the man on the far right turning in the opposite direction. I am told that this fascinates children who explain that he is doing so because he is wearing a bright red tie and has just realised how unsuitable this is. When life is hard there is a certain defiance, and Lowry catches the black humour of life for the poor in a northern town.

Edward Burra could hardly have been more different: languid, sophisticated, camp, while also finding the absurd in the Silver Dollar Bar in Boston 'with a clientele of human debris interspersed with dwarfs, gangsters, marines and hostesses fresh from the morgue. It was quite a surrealist effect, especially a roller-skating act on a floor 1ft 2in, which insisted on seizing hold of a member of the audience and swinging them round upside down. I got nervous I should be chosen for one of the lucky ones.' (*The Silver Dollar Bar* can be seen in the York City Art Gallery.)

BERYL COOK

Some people might say that Beryl Cook should not be included here – and she would be the first to say it – but if there is humour in art she is the embodiment, with her breezy observations of contemporary life and her penchant for drag shows, male strippers and sleazy Plymouth pubs.

She is one of the few women I know who can be described as 'jolly' without offence. She respects her work and takes it seriously though she has no pretensions, but it is her own innate gusto that makes it memorable. Her conversation rings with laughter and her expression is one of constant wonderment, as if she can

Beryl Cook, 1988

hardly believe her good luck, not daring to find out how much her pictures fetch (around £8,000) in case the game should end.

Admittedly her success is measured by the popularity of her reproductions rather than the number of her pictures in public galleries, for these are virtually nonexistent at the moment. One of them, however, swings on a wooden sign outside the Art Centre in her home town of Plymouth due to the enthusiasm of the Director, Bernard Samuels, who gave Beryl Cook her first exhibition after he saw the famous picture of the goosing ladies on the bowling green.

Yet her cards sell in millions and the limited editions of the large reproductions sell out on both sides of the Atlantic. Her style is inimitable; if you say that a woman looks 'like a Beryl Cook' you know exactly what is meant: a large lady who has made an effort in getting herself ready and has not wholly succeeded. To say that she is in the tradition of the saucy, seaside postcards of Donald McGill is not a denigration for these are classics of their kind, and she is the more considerable.

Beryl (the perfect name) was born in 1926, and had no training in art, which explains why her work is true to herself alone. Instead, her experience as a showgirl, touring with *The Gypsy Princess* when she was seventeen, as a pub manager and seaside landlady, provided the material which she turned to good account after she borrowed her son's painting kit which she gave him one Christmas. She is slightly shocked by the suggestion that she is 'naive': 'I wouldn't have thought that. I'd hate to paint in a childlike manner *knowing* that I was doing it. I always try to do my absolute *best*. To be truly naive you've got to be totally unselfconscious and *not* see the absurd.' Certainly she sees the absurd, but though there is nothing naive in her painting, Beryl, and her husband, retain a delightful innocence.

Lunching with them at Langan's Brasserie on one of their rare visits to London, I introduced them to George Melly, who recommended a transvestite nightclub called Madam Jo Jo's – 'Where drag artists are the size of carthorses and it starts at midnight.'

'Oh, it sounds wonderful,' Beryl gasped with excitement. 'We'll have a little rest later and go tonight.'

When I met them the next morning she described the entertainment with glee: 'It was such fun. I loved the man in the dress who lay on the bar twirling his legs in time to the music, and no one took a blind bit of notice except me! One man described as Ruby Venezuela joined us after his act, complete with his wig, false breasts and heavy make-up. "Good God!" John exclaimed, "it's Brian!" And do you know' – Beryl Cook leant forward confidingly, wide-eyed with surprise, 'it was our former neighbour in Plymouth. It was so lovely to see that he has done so well.'

'Surely that's a bit naive?' I asked of John Cook. 'Not at all,' he replied indignantly, 'we both like Brian very much and are so pleased he has found his niche.' In due course two portraits of Brian were included in *Beryl Cook's London*, one dressed up as a bumblebee, the other as Miss Venezuela.

Beryl Cook's New York includes the picture of a large, lugubrious woman with wrinkled stockings on a bench in Bryant Park, puffing away at a huge cigarette. 'I didn't know whether she had spent the night there or was simply taking her ease in the morning sunlight,' Beryl explained. 'With the green trees in the background and groups of men chatting, everything looked so *nice*.'

Ruby Venezuela   Beryl Cook   Kind permission of John and Beryl Cook

'Oh no,' cried her publisher when she told him where they'd been. 'That's a notorious park for drug pushers.' Obviously the woman was smoking a 'joint', though to Beryl she was 'just a lovely vision'. Such is her innocence.

One of the advantages of her success is the chance to travel in style. They flew to New York by Concorde and came back on the *Queen Elizabeth*, where they spent every evening applauding the cabaret of a couple of genteel singers who were plainly past their prime, greeted in silence by everyone else. Beryl and John have a tenderness for people who are slightly 'off'.

John Cook is the vital encouragement and support, in view of his wife's own, innate shyness. In these days when people crave publicity, her reticence is refreshing, refusing to appear on *Wogan*, declining a dinner for Women of Distinction with the explanation that she feels more at home in a public house. He protects her devotedly, handling the business side of her work which is now formidable. She prefers to know nothing about it: 'I'm frightened in case it's too much,' and fears talking about her work in case she loses the knack: 'I don't know how my pictures happen, they just do. They exist, but for the life of me I can't explain them.' Because she is funny it is easy to underrate her skill; conversely, outrageous claims are made by her admirers which she would never dare to make herself, comparing her to Hogarth and Rowlandson. She admits that her first 'stirrings' came about when she read a book on Stanley Spencer, but is quick to describe him as 'a great artist' unlike herself: 'I'd willingly have painted like him and did my best to copy his style, until, to my distress, I realised I could not do so. I have no doubt I've borrowed from everyone, including James Thurber and the Flintstones,' she adds with hoots of laughter.

It is significant that she owns eight of McGill's original illustrations, for, at the very least, Donald McGill and Beryl Cook are jaunty footnotes to contemporary British art, recording the gallantry of the British at play, the innocent fun of seaside resorts and the sauciness of large ladies and small men. Both have reached a vast public due to their reproductions, and the closest she comes to crediting her own work is the admission: 'I seem to be able to cross barriers. My paintings are enjoyed by people who wouldn't normally go to art galleries.' She laughed as she remembered the comment from the director of the Portal Gallery, which handles her work in London: 'You've just missed the road sweeper. He came in especially to see your pictures. Now that's *real* fame for you!'

I had taken the train to Plymouth and arrived at their house near the Hoe in the early evening. It is comfortable and cluttered with bric-à-brac, two exuberant dogs, a Jack Russell called Minnie and a long-haired dachsund, Lottie, and two tortoises, Ted and Tina, in the garden. 'I decided they needed a new image,' she confided as she introduced them, 'so now they're re-christened Hercule and Desirée though anything less like Desirée could hardly be imagined, a really foul-mouthed, dirty tortoise.' There's also a cat, Felix, with six claws on each paw. Her son and two granddaughters live next door.

The walls are hung with her own pictures which she holds on to for as long as she can, hating to part with them.

Originally she ran the home as a boarding house, until her lodgers brought her paintings to the attention of the Plymouth Art Centre. 'It didn't occur to me to sell them. I had no need to for John has always earned good money.' But after her first successful show and the discovery that she was not 'a ten day wonder' she abandoned the boarding house to work for eight hours every day, drawing the picture first and then taking a further two weeks to paint it. 'What a joy it was to go upstairs and not feel guilt about the lodgers,' she said, as she described this passion. 'There is a moment of magic when you realise it's going to work. But if something goes wrong, I can't sleep because I'm so anxious to get back to it.' She showed me one picture which she is keeping, a self-portrait with the tortoises which is characteristically unflattering: 'My daughter-in-law told me "You look like someone we're caring for but are keeping very quiet about!"'

In fact her looks are striking, the severity of the iron-grey fringe belied by the humorous eyes and alert expression. Intensely interested in other people, she insists that she is ordinary: 'The only difference between myself and the women I chat to is that I paint and they don't. I haven't got an exciting life. If I had three husbands and you found me injecting my arm with drugs or lying senseless on the floor, I'd be far more interesting.' She gave a wistful sigh. Changing direction, she cried, 'The bank, we must go to the bank.'

'Of course,' John Cook agreed, 'the bank. We'll go there right away.' An odd sort of bank to be open in the evening, I thought, but it proved to be a former bank now converted to a pub. It was the first of many pubs, ending in Union Street, once an infamous sailor's 'run ashore' and still boisterous. Miraculously, Beryl was absorbed into the atmosphere without the fear of recognition – 'The last thing I need in a pub is a lengthy discussion on Art!' I watched her observe the scene with the glee of a child taken out for a treat, with a special admiration for ladies with heavy blue eye shadow and elaborate lacquered hairstyles, who teetered into the bars on high stiletto heels, and tottered out. Beryl has declared, with a twinge of envy: 'I would really like to be the one who gets up to sing in a bar, races through the streets on roller skates, juggles with beer bottles in the park or tap dances on a street corner with an admiring circle around me.' She is unaware that she is an essential part of the pub scene herself, however discreetly she scribbles her sketches on a corner table. Both the observer and the participant, and, of course, the catalyst.

'Are you the strippers?' she was asked on one happy occasion when she entered an East End pub with her friend Barbara Ker-Seymer. 'As she is in her eighties,' Beryl related with delight, 'and I am a great grandmother, this sent us into fits of giggles.' Denying the compliment with some regret, they settled down to beer and doorstep sandwiches in this 'nice, old-fashioned pub, when, to our surprise a lovely girl suddenly appeared and, dancing to the music, peeled off most of her clothes. This was only a tease, and a round of drinks later we had the full performance. What a bonus – and we'd only gone in to rest our feet.'

Since that first evening we have become friends and my post is brightened with the arrival of her cards. Her latest *Birds in St James's Park*, reveals her skill with subjects more serious than the male stripper, Ivor Dickie. Her Christmas card for 1989 reproduced one of her illustrations for the folio edition of *Mr Norris Changes Trains*. I am glad to end on this cheerful note, but in spite of the laughter she can be serious, as I realised when she discussed her husband, the only person allowed to offer her advice: 'If anything happened to John,' she confided, 'I'd still paint but I'd never show my pictures again.'

A Postscript

After leaving the Whitworth at closing time (and it closes on the second of 5.00 p.m.), I paused in a pub where I met a charming Glaswegian girl who lived nearby yet had never gone to the gallery. Nor had the Mancunian boyfriend with her. The idea appalled them.

'I don't have the right feeling,' she explained. 'I wouldn't understand.'

'But if you never go, how can you know?'

'I shouldn't like to insult the pictures,' she continued disarmingly.

'They'll withstand it,' I assured her. 'There may be something you really like, but even if a painting shocks you that will be a reaction, and if you go a second time you might see things differently.'

'I don't know,' she said undecidedly, though accepting this conversation with a stranger as perfectly natural. The rewards to be gained from gallery going has become such a cause that I persisted while trying not to be condescending in doing so, suggesting that the experience would prove so surprising and enjoyable that she might leave the gallery happier than when she entered it.

'That sounds all right,' she said, probably anxious to be rid of this intruder though she did not give that impression. 'I'll have a go.'

Leaving them on their own again, I gave her my address and she promised to let me know what she thought of the paintings if she went to the Whitworth. I have not heard from her – there is still time. How gratifying that would be.

Gallery and Museum Addresses

Aberdeen
Art Gallery
Schoolhill
Aberdeen AB9 1FQ
Tel: 0224 646333
Mon–Wed, Fri, Sat 10–5; Thurs 10–8,
Sun 2–5

Accrington
Haworth Art Gallery
Haworth Park
Manchester Road
Accrington
Lancs BB5 2JS
Tel: 0254 33782
Daily 2–5 ex Fri
Closed Jan 1, Good Fri, Dec 25, 26

Alnwick
Alnwick Castle Museum
Alnwick
Northumberland NE66 1NQ
Tel: 0665 602207
May–Sept, daily 1–5 ex Sat

Bakewell
Chatsworth
nr Bakewell
Derbyshire DE4 1PN
Tel: 024688 2204
Mar 23–Oct 26, daily 11.30–4.30
   (grounds 11.30–5)

Banbury
Upton House
nr Banbury
Oxon OX15 6HT
Tel: 029587 266
Apr–Sept, Mon–Thurs 2–6
Open Bank Holiday Mon, closed Good
   Fri

Barnard Castle
The Bowes Museum
Barnard Castle
Co. Durham DL12 8NP
Tel: 0833 37139
Mar, Apr, Oct, Mon–Sat 10–5; Sun
   2–5
May–Sept, Mon–Sat 10–5.30; Sun 2–5
Nov–Feb, Mon–Sat 10–4; Sun 2–4
Closed Christmas week and Jan 1

Bedford
Cecil Higgins Museum and Art Gallery
Castle Close
Bedford MK40 3NY
Tel: 0234 211222
Tues–Fri 12.30–5; Sat 11–5; Sun 2–5
Closed Good Fri, Dec 25, 26, Mon (ex
   Bank Holidays)

Birmingham
The Barber Institute of Fine Arts
Edgbaston Park Road
Birmingham B15 2TS
Tel: 021 472 0962
Mon–Fri 10–5; Sat 10–1
Closed public holidays, Christmas and
   Easter

City Museum and Art Gallery
Chamberlain Square
Birmingham B3 3DH
Tel: 021 235 3890
Mon–Sat 9.30–5; Sun 2–5

Bradford
Cartwright Hall Art Gallery
Lister Park
Bradford
West Yorks BD9 4NS
Tel: 0274 493313
Apr–Sept, Tues–Sun and Bank Holiday
    Mon 10–6
Oct–Mar, Tues–Sun 10–5
Closed Good Fri, Dec 25, 26

Brighton
Art Gallery and Museum
Church Street
Brighton
E. Sussex BN1 1UE
Tel: 0273 603005
Tues–Sat 10–5.45; Sun 2–5
Closed Good Fri, Dec 25, 26, Jan 1

Bristol
City of Bristol Museum and Art
    Gallery
Queen's Road
Bristol
Avon BS8 1RL
Tel: 0272 299771
Mon–Sat 10–5
Closed Good Fri, May Day, Late
    Spring Bank Holiday Mon, Tues
    Dec 25–7, Jan 1

Burghclere
Sandham Memorial Chapel
The Oratory of All Souls
nr Newbury
Berks
Mon–Sat 10.30–1.00, 2–6, or dusk if
    earlier

Calne
Bowood House
Calne
Wilts SN11 0LZ
Tel: 0249 812102
Apr–Sept, daily 11–6

Cambridge
Fitzwilliam Museum
Trumpington Street
Cambridge CB2 1RB
Tel: 0223 337733
Tues–Sat 10–5; Sun 2.15–5
Closed Mon, Dec 24–Jan 1, Good Fri,
    May Day

Kettle's Yard
Castle Street
Cambridge CB3 0AQ
Tel: 0223 352124
House, daily 2–4; Gallery, Tues, Wed,
    Fri, Sat 12.30–5.30;
    Thurs 12.30–7; Sun 2–5.30

Cardiff
National Museum of Wales
Cathays Park
Cardiff
South Glamorgan CF1 3NP
Tel: 0222 397951
Tues–Sat 10–5; Sun 2.30–5
Closed Good Fri, May Day, Dec 24–6,
    Jan 1

Carlisle
Museum and Art Gallery
Tullie House
Castle Street
Carlisle
Cumbria CA3 8TP
Tel: 0228 34781
Apr–Sept, Mon–Fri 9–6.45; Sat 9–5;
    Sun (June–Aug only) 2.30–5
Oct–Mar, Mon–Sat 9–5

Cookham on Thames
Stanley Spencer Gallery
Kings Hall
Cookham on Thames
nr Maidenhead
Berks
Tel: 06285 26557
Easter–Oct, daily 10.30–6
Nov–Easter, Sat, Sun, public holidays, 11–5

Coventry
Herbert Art Gallery and Museum
Jordan Well
Coventry
West Midlands CV1 5RW
Tel: 0203 25555
Mon–Sat 10–5.30; Sun 2–5.30
Closed Good Fri, Dec 25, 26, Jan 1

Derby
Museum and Art Gallery
The Strand
Derby DE1 1BS
Tel: 0332 31111
Tues–Sat 10–5
Closed Bank Holidays

Dundee
McManus Galleries
Albert Square
Dundee
Angus DD1 1DA
Tel: 0382 23141
Mon–Sat 10–5
Closed Christmas and New Year

Edinburgh
National Gallery of Scotland
The Mound
Edinburgh EH2 2EL
Tel: 031 556 8921
Mon–Sat 10–5; Sun 2–5. Extended opening hours during Festival
Closed May Day, Dec 25, 26, Jan 1, 2

Scottish National Gallery of Modern Art
Belford Road
Edinburgh EH4 3DR
Tel: 031 556 8921
Mon–Sat 10–5; Sun 2–5. Extended opening hours during Festival
Closed Dec 25, 26, 31, Jan 1, 2, May Day

Exeter
Royal Albert Memorial Museum
Queen Street
Exeter
Devon EX4 3RX
Tel: 0392 265858
Tues–Sat 10–5.30
Closed Bank Holidays

Falmouth
Art Gallery
Municipal Buildings
The Moor
Falmouth
Cornwall TR11 2RT
Tel: 0326 313863
Mon–Fri 10–1, 2–4.30
Closed Dec 24–Jan 1

Glasgow
Art Gallery and Museum
Kelvingrove
Glasgow G3 8AG
Tel: 041 357 3929
Mon–Sat 10–5; Sun 2–5
Closed Dec 25, Jan 1

The Burrell Collection
Pollok Country Park
2060 Pollokshaws Road
Glasgow G43 1AT
Tel: 041 649 7151
Mon–Sat 10–5; Sun 2–5
Closed Dec 25, Jan 1

Hunterian Art Gallery
University of Glasgow
82 Hillhead Street
Glasgow
Tel: 041 330 5431
Mon–Fri 9.30–5; Sat 9.30–1
Closed public holidays

People's Palace Museum
Glasgow Green
Glasgow G40 1AT
Tel: 041 554 0223
Mon–Sat 10–5; Sun 2–5
Closed Dec 25, Jan 1

Pollok House
2060 Pollokshaws Road
Glasgow G43 1AT
Tel: 041 632 0274
Mon–Sat 10–5; Sun 2–5
Closed Dec 25, Jan 1

Grantham
Belvoir House
nr Grantham
Lincs NG32 1PD
Tel: 0476 870262
Mid March–Sept, Tues–Thurs, Sat 12–6; Sun 12–7
Oct, Sun 2–6; Good Fri 12–6; Bank Holiday Mon 11–7

Hatfield
Hatfield House
Hatfield Park
Hatfield
Herts AL9 5NQ
Tel: 07072 62823
Mar 25–2nd Sun Oct, Tues–Sat 12–5; Sun 2–5.30
Open Bank Holiday Mon 11–5

Haverfordwest
Graham Sutherland Gallery

Picton Castle
The Rhos
Haverfordwest
Dyfed SA62 4AS
Tel: 043786 296
Apr–Sept, Tues–Sun 10.30–12.30, 1.30–5
Open Bank Holiday Apr–Sept, other times by appt

Horringer
Ickworth
The Rotunda
Horringer
Bury St Edmunds
Suffolk IP29 5QE
Tel: 028488 270
Apr, Oct, Sat, Sun 1.30–5.30
May–Sept, Tues, Wed, Fri, Sat, Sun 1.30–5.30
Open Bank Holiday Mon

Huddersfield
Art Gallery
Princess Alexandra Walk
Huddersfield
W. Yorks HD1 2SU
Tel: 0484 513808
Mon–Fri 10–6; Sat 10–4
Closed Bank Holiday

Ipswich
Christchurch Mansion
Christchurch Park
Soane Street
Ipswich
Suffolk IP4 2BE
Tel: 0473 213761
Mon–Sat 10–5; Sun 2.30–4.30
Closes at dusk in winter; closed Good Fri, Dec 25, Jan 1

Ipswich Museum
High Street

Ipswich
Suffolk IP1 3QH
Tel: 0473 213761
Mon–Sat 10–5
Closed Bank Holiday

Kettering
Boughton House
nr Kettering
Northants NN14 1BJ
Tel: 0536 82248
Aug, daily 2–5

Kingston-upon-Hull
Ferens Art Gallery
Queen Victoria Square
Kingston-upon-Hull
North Humberside HU1 3RA
Mon–Sat 10–5; Sun 1.30–4.30
Closed Good Fri, Dec 25, 26

Leeds
City Art Gallery
Calverley Street
Leeds
W. Yorks LS1 3AA
Tel: 0532 462495
Mon, Tues, Thurs, Fri 10–6; Wed
    10–9; Sat 10–4; Sun 2–5

Harewood House
Leeds
W. Yorks
Tel: 0532 886225

Temple Newsam House
Leeds
W. Yorks LS15 0AE
Tel: 0532 647321
Tues–Sun, Bank Holiday Mon 10.30–
    6.15 or dusk in winter

Leicester
Leicestershire Museum and Art Gallery

New Walk
Leicester LE1 6TD
Tel: 0533 554100
Mon–Thurs, Sat 10–5; Sun 2–5.30
Closed Dec 25, 26

Liverpool
Sudley Art Gallery
Mossley Hill Road
Liverpool L18 8BX
Tel: 051 724 3245
Mon–Sat 10–5; Sun 2–5
Closed Good Fri, Dec 24–6, Jan 1

The Tate Gallery
Albert Dock
Liverpool L8 4BB
Tel: 051 709 3223
Tues–Sun and Bank Holidays 11–7

Walker Art Gallery
William Brown Street
Liverpool L3 8EL
Tel: 051 227 5234
Mon–Sat 10–5; Sun 2–5
Closed Good Fri, Dec 24–6, Jan 1

Llanfairpwll
Plas Newydd
Anglesey
Gwynedd LL61 6EQ
Tel: 0248 714
Mar 28–Sept, Sun–Fri 12–5; Oct, Fri
    and Sun only

London
The British Museum
Great Russell Street
London WC1B 3DG
Tel: 01 636 1555
Mon–Sat 10–5; Sun 2–6.30
Closed Good Fri, 1st Mon in May, Dec
    24–6, Jan 1

Courtauld Institute Galleries
Woburn Square
London WC1H 0AA
Tel: 01 580 1015
Mon–Sat 10–5; Sun 2–5
Closed public holidays

Dulwich College Picture Gallery
College Road
London SE21 7AD
Tel: 01 693 5254
Tues–Sat 10–1, 2–5; Sun 2–5
Closed Good Fri, Dec 25, 26, Jan 1 and
    Bank Holidays

Guildhall Art Gallery
Aldermanbury
London EC2P 2EJ
Tel: 01 606 3030
Permanent Collection: by appt
Temporary Exhibitions: Mon–Sat 10–5

Imperial War Museum
Lambeth Road
London SE1 6HZ
Tel: 01 735 8922
Mon–Sat 10–5.50; Sun 2–5.30
Closed Good Fri, May Day Bank
    Holiday, Dec 24–6, Jan 1

The Iveagh Bequest, Kenwood
Hampstead Lane
London NW3 7JR
Tel: 01 348 1286
Feb, Mar, Oct, daily 10–5; Apr–Sept,
    daily 10–7; Nov-Jan, daily 10–4.
    Closed Good Fri, Dec 24, 25

Leighton House Museum
12 Holland Park Road
London W14 8LZ
Tel: 01 602 3316
Mon–Sat 11–5
Closed Bank Holidays

William Morris Gallery
Water House
Lloyd Park
Forest Road
Walthamstow
London E17 4PP
Tel: 01 527 5544
Tues–Sat 10–1, 2–5
Closed public holidays

National Gallery
Trafalgar Square
London WC2N 5DN
Tel: 01 839 3321
Mon–Sat 10–6; Sun 2–6
Closed Good Fri, May Day Bank
    Holiday, Dec 24, 25, Jan 1

National Maritime Museum
Romney Road
Greenwich
London SE10 9NF
Tel: 01 858 4422
Mar 30–Oct 26, Mon–Sat 10–6; Sun
    2–6
Oct 27–Mar 29, Mon–Sat 10–5; Sun
    2–5

National Portrait Gallery
St Martin's Place
London WC2H 0HE
Tel: 01 930 1552
Mon–Fri 10–5; Sat 10–6; Sun 2–6
Closed Good Fri, May Day Bank
    Holiday, Dec 24–6, Jan 1

Sir John Soane's Museum
13 Lincoln's Inn Fields
London WC2A 3BP
Tel: 01 405 2107
Tues–Sat 10–5
Closed Bank Holidays and Dec 24

Tate Gallery
Millbank
London SW1P 4RG
Tel: 01 821 1313
Mon–Sat 10–5.50; Sun 2–5.50
Closed Good Fri, May Day Bank
    Holiday, Dec 24–6, Jan 1

The Thomas Coram Foundation for
    Children
40 Brunswick Square
London WC1N 1AZ
Tel: 01 278 2424
Mon–Fri 10–4
Closed public holidays

The Wallace Collection
Hertford House
Manchester Square
London W1M 6BN
Tel: 01 935 0687
Mon–Sat 10–5; Sun 2–5
Closed Good Fri, May Day Bank
    Holiday, Dec 24–6, Jan 1

Luton
The Wernher Collection
Luton Hoo
Luton
Beds LU1 3TQ
Tel: 0582 22955
Mar 22–Oct 12, Mon, Wed, Thurs, Sat
    11–5.45; Sun 2–5.45

Maidstone
Leeds Castle
Maidstone
Kent
Tel: 0622 65400

Malton
Castle Howard
Malton
York YO6 7DA

Tel: 065384 333
Mar 25–Oct, daily 11–5

Manchester
City Art Gallery
Mosley Street
Manchester M2 3JL
Tel: 061 236 9422
Mon–Sat 10–6; Sun 2–6
Closed Good Fri, Dec 25, 26, Jan 1

Whitworth Art Gallery
The University
Oxford Road
Manchester M15 6ER
Tel: 061 273 4865
Mon–Wed, Fri, Sat 10–5; Thurs 10–9
Closed Dec 24–6

Melrose
Abbotsford House
Melrose
Roxburghshire TD6 9BQ
Tel: 0896 2043
Apr–Oct, Mon–Sat 10–5; Sun 2–5

Newcastle upon Tyne
Hatton Gallery
The University
Newcastle upon Tyne NE1 7RU
Tel: 0632 328511
Mon–Fri 10.30–5.30; Sat 10.30–4.30

Laing Art Gallery
Higham Place
Newcastle upon Tyne NE1 8AG
Tel: 0632 327734
Mon–Fri 10–5.30; Sat 10–4.30; Sun
    2.30–5.30
Closed Good Fri, Dec 25, 26, Jan 1

Northampton
Althorp
nr Northampton NN7 4HG
Daily 1.30–5.30, Bank Holidays 11–6

Norwich
Sainsbury Centre for Visual Arts
University of East Anglia
Norwich NR4 7TJ
Tel: 0603 56060
Daily 12–5, ex Mon

Nottingham
Castle Museum
NG1 6EL
Tel: 0602 483504
Apr–Sept, daily 10–5.45; Oct–Mar,
  daily 10–4.45
Closed Dec 25

Oxford
Ashmolean Museum of Art and
  Archaeology
Beaumont Street
Oxford OX1 2PH
Tel: 0865 512651
Tues–Sat 10–4; Sun 2–4
Closed Easter, Christmas and New
  Year

Christ Church Picture Gallery
Christ Church
Oxford OX1 1DP
Tel: 0865 276172
Easter–Sept, Mon–Sat 10.30–1, 2–5.30;
  Sun 2–5.30
Oct–Easter, Mon–Sat 10.30–1, 2–4.30;
  Sun 2–4.30
Closed week after Easter and Christmas

Petworth
Petworth House
West Sussex GU28 0AE
Tel: 0798 42207
Easter–Oct, Tues–Thurs, Sat, Sun 2–6

Plymouth
City Museum and Art Gallery
Drake Circus

Plymouth
Devon PL4 8AJ
Tel: 0752 668000
Mon–Fri 10–5.30; Sat 10–5

Port Sunlight
Lady Lever Art Gallery
Port Sunlight
Wirral
Merseyside L62 5EQ
Tel: 051 645 3623
Mon–Sat 10–5; Sun 2–5
Closed Good Fri, Dec 24–6, Jan 1

Preston
Harris Museum and Art Gallery
Market Square
Preston
Lancs PR1 2PP
Tel: 0772 58248
Mon–Sat 10–5
Closed Bank Holidays

Rothbury
Cragside
Rothbury
Morpeth
Northumberland NE65 7PX
Tel: 0669 20333
Apr, Oct, Wed, Sat, Sun 2–5; May–
  Sept, Tues–Sun 2–6

St Asaph
National Portrait Gallery at
  Bodelwyddan Castle
nr St Asaph
Clwyd LL18 5YA
Tel: 0745 584060
Seasonal opening times, phone for
  details

Salford
Museum and Art Gallery
Peel Park

The Crescent
Salford
Gtr Manchester M5 4WU
Tel: 061 736 2649
Mon–Fri 10–5; Sun 2–5
Closed Good Fri, Dec 25, 26, Jan 1

Selkirk
Bowhill
TD7 5ET
Tel: 0750 20732
Mon–Sat 11.30–5; Sun 2–6

Sheffield
Graves Art Gallery
Surrey Street
Sheffield S1 1XZ
Tel: 0742 734781
Mon–Sat 10–8; Sun 2–5
Closed Dec 24–6

Mappin Art Gallery
Weston Park
Sheffield S10 2TP
Tel: 0742 26281
Jan–May, Sept–Dec, Mon–Sat 10–5
June–Aug, Mon–Sat 10–8; Sun 2–5
Closed Dec 25, 26

Southampton
Art Gallery
Civic Centre
Southampton SO9 4XF
Tel: 0703 223855
Tues–Fri 10–5; Sat 10–4; Sun 2–5
Closed Dec 25, Jan 1

South Queensferry
Hopetoun House
West Lothian EH30 9SL
Tel: 031 331 2451
Easter, May–mid Sept, daily 11–5.30

Sudbury
Gainsborough's House
46 Gainsborough Street
Sudbury
Suffolk CO10 6EU
Tel: 0787 72958
Easter Sat–Sept, Tues–Sat 10–5; Sun
and Bank Holiday Mon 2–5
Oct–Maundy Thursday, Tues–Sat 10–
4; Sun 2–4
Closed Good Fri, Dec 24–Jan 1

Thetford
Euston Hall
Norfolk IP24 2QP
Tel: 0842 66366
Jun 4–Sept 24, Thurs 2.30–5.30

Thornhill
Drumlanrig Castle
Dumfriesshire DG3 4AQ
Tel: 0848 30248
Easter–late Aug. Times vary, so check
locally

Walsall
Museum and Art Gallery
Lichfield Street
Walsall
W. Midlands WS1 1TR
Tel: 0922 21244
Mon–Fri 10–6; Sat 10–4.45
Closed Bank Holidays

Wells-next-the-Sea
Holkham Hall
Norfolk NR23 1AB
Tel: 0328 710227
May 29–Sept, Sun, Mon, Thurs, 1.30–
5
July–Aug, also Wed 1.30–5

Westerham
Chartwell
Kent TN16 1PS
Tel: 0732 866368
Mar 29–Oct, Tues–Thurs 12–5; Sat,
    Sun, Bank Holiday Mon 11–5
Closed Good Fri and Tues after Bank
    Holidays

Wilton
Wilton House
Salisbury
Wilts SP2 0BJ
Tel: 0722 743115
Easter–Oct 12, Tues–Sat and Bank
    Holiday 11–6; Sun 1–6

Woburn
Woburn Abbey
Bedfordshire MK43 0TP
Tel: 052 525666
Jan–Mar, Sat, Sun 11–4.45; Mar–Nov,
    daily 11–5.45
Closed Nov 2–Dec

Wolverhampton
Art Gallery and Museum
Lichfield Street
Wolverhampton WV1 1DU
Tel: 0902 24549
Mon–Sat 10–6
Closed Bank Holidays

Wightwick Manor
Wightwick
Wolverhampton
W. Midlands WV6 8EE
Tel: 0902 761108
Mar–Jan, Thurs, Sat, Bank Holiday
    Mondays and preceding Sun
    2.30–5.30

York
City Art Gallery
Exhibition Square
York YO1 2EW
Tel: 0904 23839
Mon–Sat 10–5; Sun 2.30–5
Closed Dec 25, 26, Jan 1